This early Jumeau has red stroke marks on her head as well as the incised mark: "DEPOSE//JUMEAU." (See page 15.)

FOCUSING ON DOLLS
by Jan Foulke

A compilation of articles on antique and collectible dolls reprinted from the **Doll Reader**®, 1974 to 1986.

Photographs by Howard Foulke

Published by

Hobby House Press, Inc.
Cumberland, Maryland 21502

Additional copies of this book may be purchased at $19.95
from
Hobby House Press, Inc.
900 Frederick Street
Cumberland, Maryland 21502
or from your favorite bookstore or dealer.
Please add $2.25 per copy for postage.

Articles herein contained copyrighted © by Hobby House Press, 1975, 1976, 1977, 1978, 1979 and 1980. Beginning in 1980 articles were copyrighted © by Hobby House Press, Inc., 1980, 1981, 1982, 1984 and 1986.

© 1988 by Hobby House Press, Inc.

All rights reserved. No part of this book may be reproduced or utilized in any form or by any means, electronic or mechanical, including photocopying, recording, or by any information storage and retrieval system, without permission in writing from the publisher. Inquiries should be addressed to: Hobby House Press, Inc., 900 Frederick Street, Cumberland, Maryland 21502.

Printed in the United States of America

ISBN: 0-87588-319-2

TABLE OF CONTENTS
(according to type)

FRENCH
Focusing On... The Dolls of Jules Steiner — A Comparative Study 6
Jumeaus 10
A Jumeau Family Album 13
French Bébés 18

GERMAN
Focusing On... Gebrüder Heubach 24
Early Unmarked Dolls Attributed to J. D. Kestner, Circa 1880 to 1892 87
Many Faces of Simon & Halbig 90
German Characters 92
German Character Children 95
Hertel, Schwab & Co.: A New Name for a Familiar Face 99
Simon & Halbig Faces 107
A. M. Lady Dolls 112
German Dolly Faces 114

MISCELLANEOUS BISQUE
Focusing On... Young Baby Dolls 116
Bathing Beauties 119
All-bisque Dolls 120
Those Adorable Snow Babies 122

CLOTH
Focusing On... Izannah Walker Dolls 125
Babyland Rag Dolls 127
Steiff Dolls 130
A Photographic Essay of the Lenci 142
Lenci Children 146
Lenci Dolls, Part II 148
A Collection of Norah Wellings' Creations 151
Alexander Cloth Dolls 153

COMPOSITION/MODERN
Focusing On... Selected Effanbee Composition Dolls 155
Incomparable Compos 157
"Hi! I'm Ginny" 162
Romantic Dolls from *Gone With The Wind* 169

MISCELLANEOUS
Focusing On... 100 Years of Christmas Wishes 166

INDEX 175

Focusing On...

The Dolls of Jules Steiner

A Comparative Study

My love affair with the French Steiner dolls began in 1974, for that was the year I met "Mamselle." Standing as she was on the counter of my favorite doll shop, all 28in (71cm) of her in red velvet, she was certainly stunning, but her appeal, to me, went further: it was the special something which develops between a collector and a doll that kept drawing me back to her over the other hundred dolls on display. As I circled the shop, always coming back to sigh over her, I told myself that this feeling was ridiculous. I didn't collect bisque dolls. Not only that, I couldn't buy one with such an enormous price tag! Subsequently, I left the shop with a box of assorted smaller dolls, "Mamselle" still standing on the counter.

Sometimes the old adage "out of sight, out of mind" absolutely refuses to work — and visions of that doll spun round my head. Finally after several days I could stand the torment no longer: I must own that doll. My husband was tired of hearing about her. "Go ahead and buy her," he said. I called the shop owner in a state of euphoria, only to come crashing down to reality when she told me the doll had already been sold! I was devastated, but at least the torment was over.

However, that is not the end of my story about "Mamselle" because four months later on Christmas morning, there was "Mamselle" standing next to my tree. I hugged and hugged her, laughing and crying both at the same time that such a marvelous treasure was really mine. My husband was the one who had bought the doll, and I never suspected.

Société Steiner was founded by Jules Nicholas Steiner in 1855 in Paris, France. After 1891, he was no longer in charge and the direction of the company passed to a succession of other heads until 1908. Apparently Société Steiner did not join the S.F.B.J. conglomerate of doll makers formed in 1888 which included Jumeau, Bru and others.

Illustration 1. *Jan Foulke Collection.*

Judging from the number of patents registered to them, the Steiner firm apparently worked hard to improve their dolls and to try new innovations. They had patents for eye movement, walking, talking and other mechanisms for dolls as well as for improved processes for making heads and limbs. Several times the firm won medals for their dolls at the Paris Exhibition, the most exciting in 1889 when they were awarded the gold medal (Medaille D'or).

Steiner dolls usually have beautiful smooth bisque, almost creamy, with delicately tinted cheeks. Their eyes are alert, but not oversized like those of the Jumeaus; their lips are full, but tinting is pale so they do not show up as well in photographs as those of other French dolls. Dolls from the early 1880s often have round faces; those of the 1890s are more rectangular. Société Steiner created a wide range of dolls — too many styles and types for one small article, so we are choosing a sampling to include here and will discuss their characteristics.

The doll in **Ilustrations 1-3** is a "Bourgoin" Steiner. The head is marked (incised):

S^{TE} A O

Red writing:

J. Steiner B^{te} S.G.D.G J. Bourgoin S^{r}

Marks on body: Partial black stamped mark with a decipherable J.

This type of Steiner is usually dated about 1880. Her wide forehead and full cheeks give her face a round appearance. Her chin is not well defined, but does have a faint dimple. Her eyebrows are a delicate blonde with minute brush strokes. Her blown glass eyes each have a vivid blue iris with a black rim and many tiny dark spokes in them. Often this type of doll has wire eyes (explained later in detail), but although her head is cut for the lever, she never had moving eyes and was apparently a less expensive model. Painted lashes are a series of lightly-made black strokes and eye sockets are outlined in black. Her pierced ears are rather plain and simply modeled. Her mouth is typically Steiner with light tinting: two pronounced peaks on the upper lip and a turned up corner. The original pate is of dark brown cardboard. Her curly kidskin wig is a replacement of the proper style as her original hair had been eaten off its skin wig cap.

Her original body is in excellent condition. At the knee and elbow joints, the typical purple undercoating which Steiner used can be seen. Fingertips and toes still retain traces of the red-lined nails. As is typical of French doll bodies in general, there is little anatomical detail: upper limbs are straight, as are the knee joints; toes are only faintly modeled. There are no separate ball joints; wrists are straight and fingers are stubby; stomach is flat; derrière protrudes only slightly, gently rounded. She is 14in (36cm) tall.

The doll in **Illustrations 4** and **5** is a Baby Steiner. Her head is marked (incised):

S^{TE} C 4/0

Red stamp located at sides of crown opening at left:
J. STEINER B.S.G.D.G.
At right: illegible, but could be a repetition of the left side as on the doll in **Illustration 7**.
Marks on body: None.

This Steiner baby is a scant 7in (18cm) long with size 4/0 head. Her face is of the type associated with the "Bourgoin" mark. She has the same pate, slight nose, upper lip, ear and eye shape as the doll shown in **Illustrations 1-3**. Her brows are light and feathered also, but her gray lashes are longer and heavier in proportion to her size, and the eye sockets are not black-lined. Her eyelids have a rose tint. She has the 1880s patented wire-eye mechanism. The lever protruding behind her ear opens and closes her dark blue gray eyes. Notice how the head is cut to accommodate the lever. She probably had a lamb's wool curly wig which has been lost.

Her papier-mâché body, which shows some detail in molding of arms and legs, appears to be a forerunner of the bent-limb babies so popular after

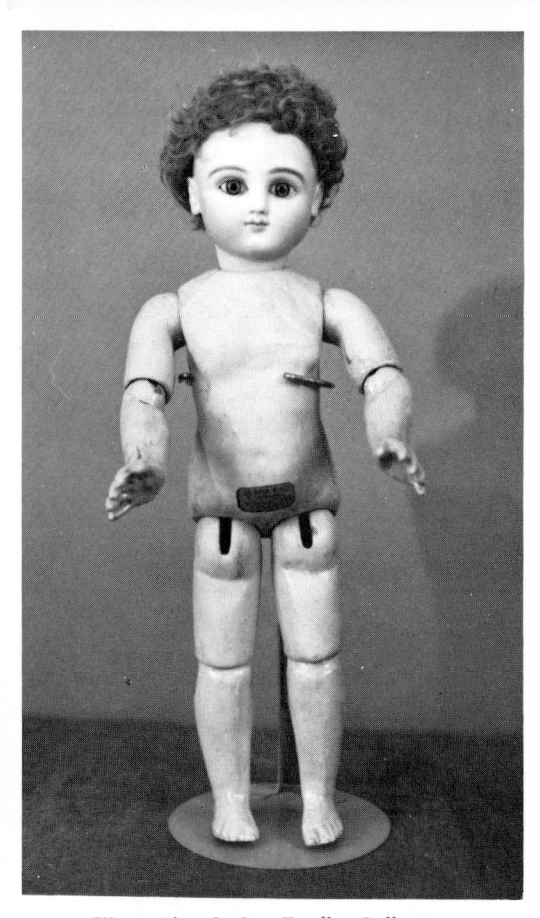

Illustration 2. *Jan Foulke Collection.*

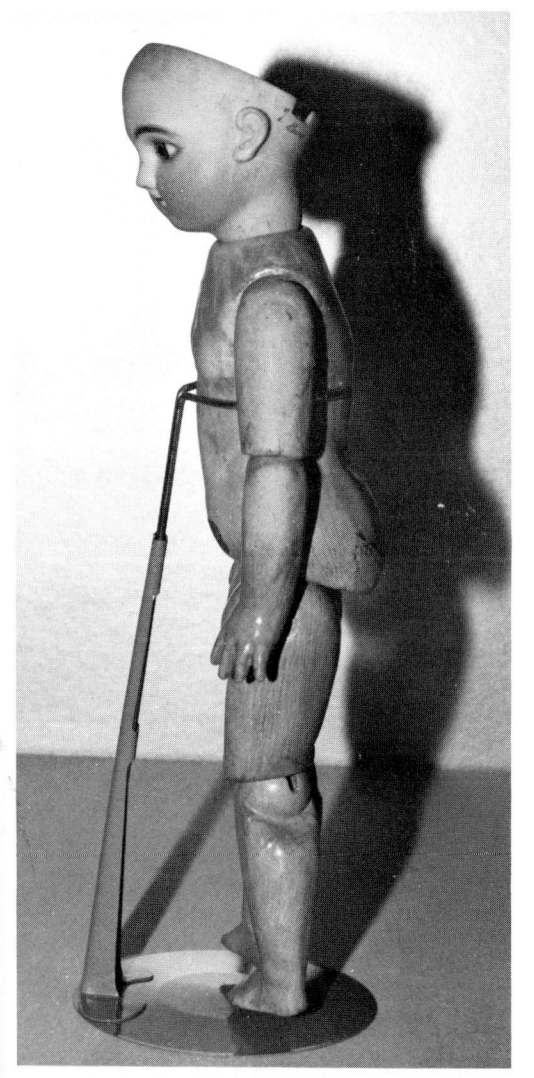

Illustration 3. *Jan Foulke Collection.*

Illustration 4. *Jan Foulke Collection.*

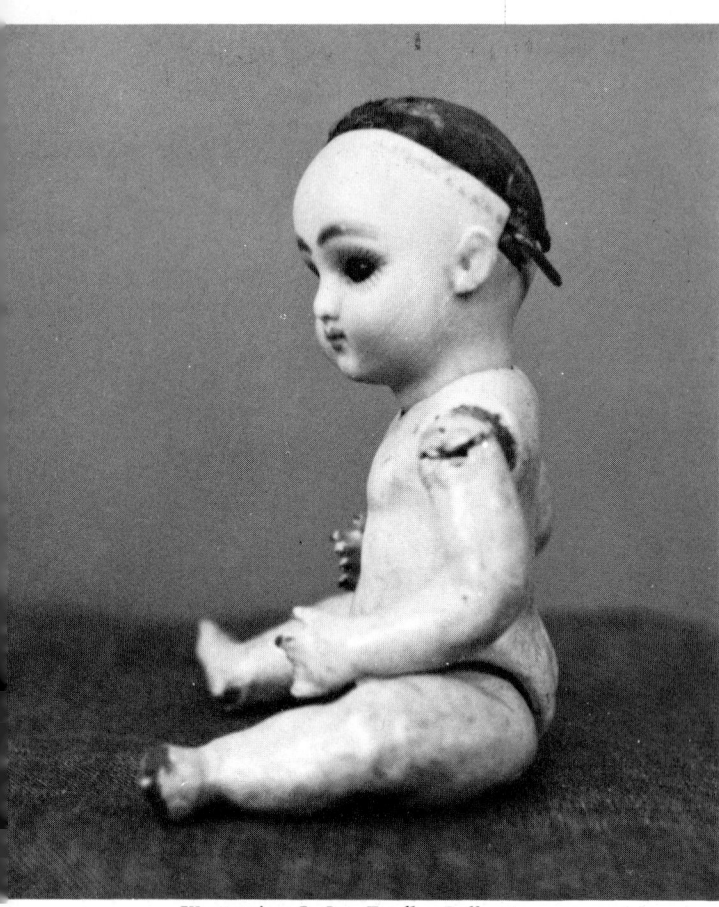

Illustration 5. *Jan Foulke Collection.*

Illustration 7. *Mike White Collection.*

1909, and certainly indicates her to be a rare Steiner type. Not shown in the illustrations is what appears to be her original clothes — a child's guimpe and dress of the late 1880s.

Hardly the prettiest of Steiners in her stripped down condition (**Illustration 6**), yet very interesting is this mechanical doll. In her torso is a mechanism which moves her legs, arms and head while she cries "Mama." This is operated by the key which protrudes from her side. Her head of a pale, almost parian finish with rosy cheeks is round with a wide short neck, completely closed dome and open mouth with two rows of tiny teeth. Her small eyes are pale blue, a paperweight type with blue lining at the eye sockets. Her eyebrows are long and tiny, arching slightly. Her pierced ears have little detail.

Her torso is cloth-covered cardboard; arms and lower legs are composition. There is no mark on the heads of these dolls, but the mechanism carries the Steiner mark. This doll is 16in (41cm) tall, but this type was also available in other sizes. She is hard to date precisely and could possibly be as early as the 1870s as she has characteristics associated with the early Steiners. Also some of these types of bodies have been found with wax-over-papier-mâché heads.

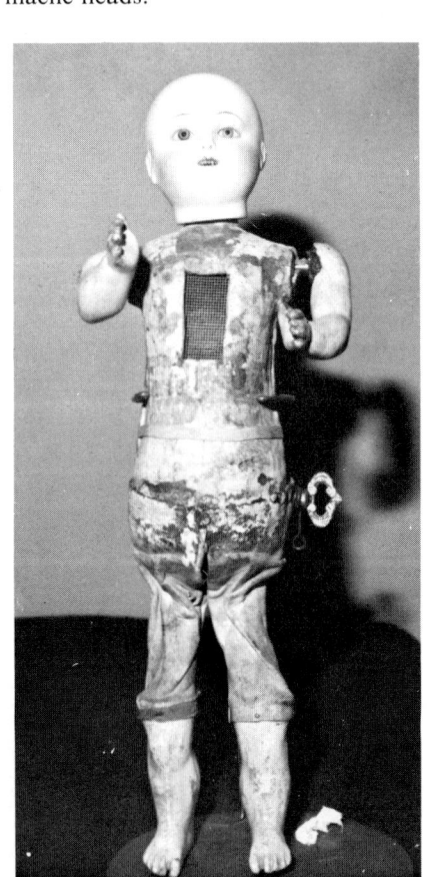

Illustration 6. *Crandall Collection.*

The doll in **Illustration 7** has her head marked (incised):

S^{TE} C 4

Red stamp at each side of crown opening:

J. STEINER B.S.G.D.G.

Eyes (incised on back of eyeball):

STEINER
4
S.G.D.G.

Marks on body: None

This 22½in (57cm) Steiner has a longer, lower face than that of the "Bourgoin" or the baby, as well as a higher forehead. She has the interesting wire mechanism to operate her blue eyes which do not have the depth of permanent paperweight eyes because they are set into what appears to be a bisque eyeball which is not as fragile as the glass eyeball of the German weighted eyes. Also the eyes must be flatter to allow room for opening and closing which is not possible with bulging eyes. She has her original purple cardboard pate, typical of many Steiner dolls. Also there is a little more detail in her ears, which are also pierced. Her eyebrows are soft. Her mouth is typical with two peaks on upper lip and turned up corners.

Her body is unmarked but has Steiner characteristics including the short, fat fingers. She is later than the "Bourgoin" since she has jointed wrists, probably dating from the late 1880s. Her long, blonde, human hair wig appears to be original.

Illustration 8. *Jan Foulke Collection.*

The doll in **Illustrations 8-13** has her head marked (incised):

A-19
PARIS

"LE PARISIEN"

Marks on body (purple stamp on hip):

BÉBÉ "LE PARISIEN"
MEDAILLE D'OR
PARIS

Finally, here is "Mamselle," easier than the others to date because her trademark, "Le Parisien" was registered in 1892. She is typical of the Steiners with the rectangular face, with just a hint of a chin. Her eyes are dark blue paperweight with good depth as she does not have the wire type. Her eyebrows are darker brown and more pronounced than those on earlier Steiners; eye sockets are wider, not as almond-shaped as earlier ones. Her neck is longer. Her mouth has the same soft color and shape. Her nose is longer with a more defined shape. One of the most interesting changes is in the intricate modeling of her ears which contain a large, deep canal as well as more intricate folds. Another unusual aspect is her original cork pate as most Steiners have cardboard ones.

Her body is similar to that of the "Bourgoin" and a comparison shows three major differences: fingers are longer and thinner; wrists are jointed; and the big toe is separated.

She is wearing her original clothes, a deep red velvet dress in Kate Greenaway style. Her shoes are marked Steiner. Her hair and hat are replacements.

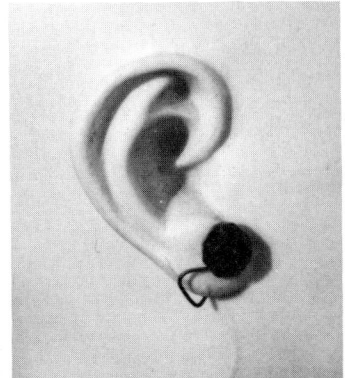

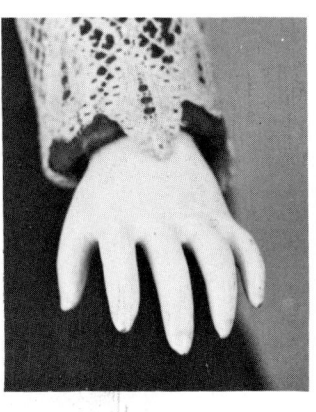

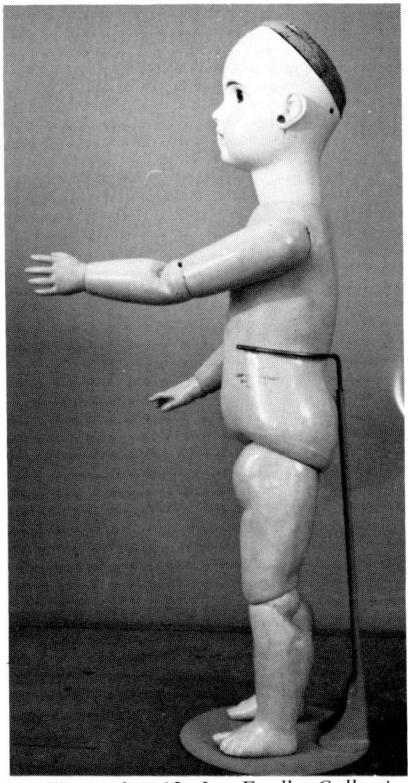

Illustration 9. Illustration 10. *Jan Foulke Collection.*

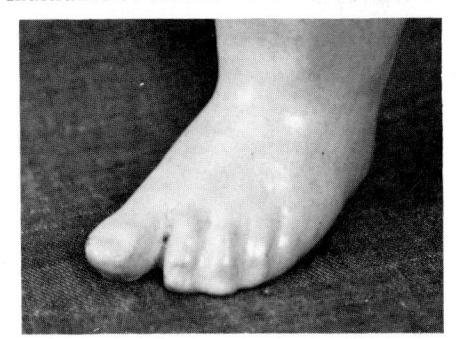

Illustration 11. *Jan Foulke Collection.*

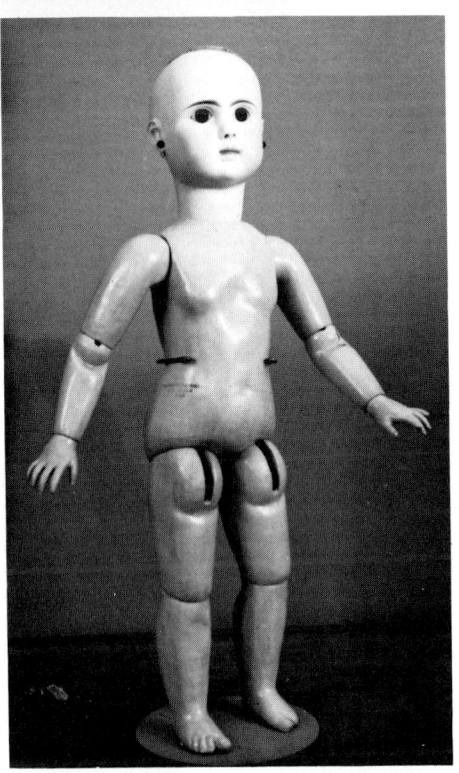

Illustration 12. *Jan Foulke Collection.*

Illustration 13. *Jan Foulke Collection.*

EXPLANATION OF SOME TERMS USED IN STEINER MARKS

S^{TE} —probably society or company
B^{TÉ} —patent registered
S.g.D.g.—without guarantee of the government

J. Bourgoin—unknown but perhaps an associate as here it is preceded by a J. Elsewhere it isn't.

J. Steiner—head of Société Steiner, 1855-1891.

Focusing On...

Jumeaus

One day long before my involvement with dolls, I was visiting an antique show looking for pattern glass for my collection and general antiques for my shop. In one booth a lovely display of dolls caught my eye. Although I always thought they were pretty, I had always given just a quick glance to dolls as they were not in my line and I knew nothing about them, but this day one doll in particular caught my eye, and I could not pass without looking at her more closely. Her eyes sparkled up at me and her face was so joyful and shining that she just seemed to say to me: "Don't you think I'm a sweet little girl?" I could not believe how real she seemed. And even though I did not buy her, I will never forget her. The dealer volunteered the information that the doll was French — a Jumeau...JUMEAU, the magic word in dolls; the creator of the most beautiful and lifelike Bébés (child dolls) in the world. Since my initial experience with Jumeaus, I have tried my own personal experiment by asking casual sightseers, not seasoned doll collectors, who come into my shop, "If you could pick any of these child dolls to take home, which one would you choose?" Invariably the choice is a Jumeau. "Why?" I ask. "Because she looks so pretty and so real." And that I think is the secret of the success of the Jumeau Bébé.

Jumeau obtained his reality by a combination of many factors in the manufacturing. First of all, he started with an unblemished, smooth, polished bisque to which was applied two coats of pale pink to give the head a natural flesh color. The decoration of the heads was skillfully executed by artists who applied the delicate pink cheeks; the red gracefully curved lips often with the hint of a smile at the corners; the heavy multi-stroked, arched eyebrows, almost meeting, a distinctive Jumeau feature; and the thick eyelashes. One of the most striking features of the Jumeau Bébé is the large, luminous glass eyes, handblown with a

Illustration 1. 24in (61cm) Parisienne; closed mouth; head unmarked except for size number; kid body stamped in blue: "Jumeau//Medaille D'or//Paris." *Helen Teske Collection.*

Illustration 2. 24in (61cm) Long Face; composition body with straight wrists; closed mouth; applied ears; head unmarked except for size number; body stamped in blue: "Jumeau //Medaille D'or//Paris." *Helen Teske Collection.*

threaded iris covered with a drop of clear glass which gives to them the brilliance of the natural eye. These are now referred to as paperweight eyes because of the illusion of depth. Last were added the cork pate and wig of curly soft mohair or flowing human hair. This delicacy of artist's touch transformed the head into a delightful and smiling Bébé.

Now for a bit of history. Pierre Jumeau opened his house in 1842, but the dolls of the early years had china heads imported from Germany on sawdust-stuffed kid bodies. Probably by the early 1860s Jumeau was making the "Parisiennes," lady dolls commonly referred to today as French Fashions. The first ones had all-kid bodies and stiff necks, but soon the necks swiveled, and by 1865 Jumeau was advertising carved dolls, probably the wood-bodied ones. In 1873, Jumeau announced that he specialized in porcelain doll heads made in his own factory. These were recognized at Vienna for their loveliness — the first citation for doll heads produced in France surpassing in beauty the German products. Though it could have been as early as 1873, 1878 seems to be the date that the Bébés (child dolls) were introduced. That year Jumeau won the important recognition of the Gold Medal at the Paris Exposition. It seems that only after this Exposition did Jumeau start marking his dolls, at first only on the bodies with the now-familiar blue stamp "Jumeau//Medaille D'or//Paris." The so-called portrait and long-face Jumeaus appear to be among the early Bébés.

In 1877 Emile Jumeau, son of Pierre, took over the firm. By 1879 the *Bébé Jumeau* was taking the industry by storm. In 1881 there were 85,000 Bébés produced; 115,000 in 1883; 220,000 in 1884. The open mouth came in about 1890, and it increased the cost of production, but was very popular with customers.

In 1892 Jumeau announced that it produced all articles for the dolls it sold from heads, eyes, wigs and bodies to clothing, boxes and packing crates. During the 1890s Jumeau went into quantity production and in order to be competitive with other manufacturers, created several models which were lower in price, but did not carry the Jumeau name. By 1897 Jumeau was producing three to four million Bébés a year. In 1899 Jumeau joined with other manufacturers to make the Société Française de Fabrication de Bébés & Jouets, the now-famous S.F.B.J.

Illustration 3. 26in (66cm) Emile Jumeau; composition body with straight wrists; original mohair wig; closed mouth; applied ears; original clothes; incised: "E. J." with size number; body stamped in blue: "Jumeau//Medaille D'Or//Paris." *Helen Teske Collection.*

Illustration 4. 24in (61cm) Tête Jumeau; composition body with jointed wrists; closed mouth; stamped in red: "Deposé//Tete Jumeau" with size number; body stamped in blue: "Bébé Jumeau." *Helen Teske Collection.*

Now, exactly what accounts for this tremendous success achieved by Jumeau? Again, it would seem that it must be because the dolls are so lifelike, just like happy children with joyful faces, sparkling laughing eyes, soft rosy-hued cheeks and lovely natural-looking hair with loose tendrils to frame their faces. Also chunky child bodies of posable composition and wood added to the reality of the natural look. Today the name Jumeau is again a magic word in the doll world suggesting a true work of art worthy of admiration and delightful to own — as M. Cusset observed in his 1885 pamphlet of Jumeau — all the *Bébé Jumeau* needs to be real is a soul!

Addenda

An 1892 listing from a Marshall Field catalog showed the *Bébé Jumeau* to be wholesaling for $1.50 to $4.50, depending on size. This was dressed in chemise only. The retail price was probably about double the wholesale price.

FAR LEFT: Illustration 5. 18in (46cm) Checkmark; composition body with jointed wrists; closed mouth; marked on head with red checks and incised size number; blue oval sticker on body reads: "Bébé Jumeau." *H&J Foulke, Inc.*

LEFT: Illustration 6. 13in (33cm) X mark; unmarked composition body with jointed wrists; open mouth with molded teeth; incised with "X" and size number. Sometimes this doll is found with the Jumeau stamp on the head and/or the body. *H&J Foulke, Inc.*

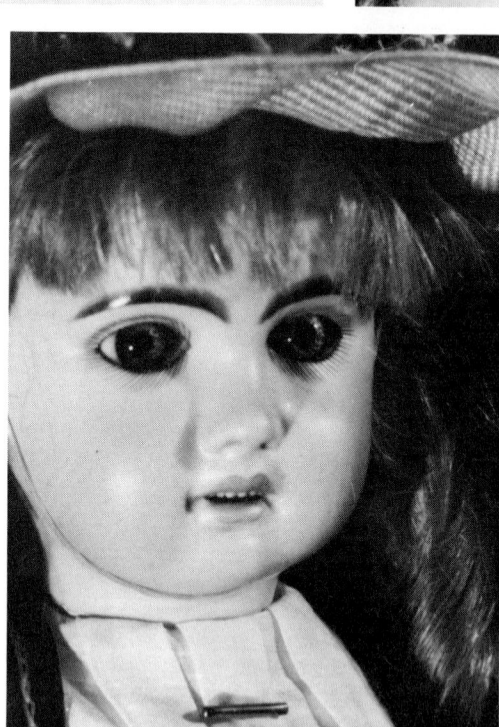

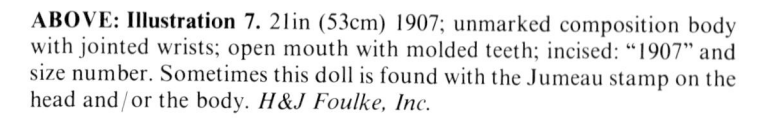

ABOVE: Illustration 7. 21in (53cm) 1907; unmarked composition body with jointed wrists; open mouth with molded teeth; incised: "1907" and size number. Sometimes this doll is found with the Jumeau stamp on the head and/or the body. *H&J Foulke, Inc.*

ABOVE RIGHT: Illustration 8. 25in (63cm) character child; composition body with jointed wrists; incised: "Jumeau//230//Paris" and size number. Body stamped: "Jumeau//Medaille D'or//Paris." This particular doll has a phonograph in the torso and was called the "Lioretgraph Bébé Jumeau." *Helen Teske Collection.*

RIGHT: Illustration 9. 20in (51cm) DEP; unmarked composition body; original human hair wig; high cut crown; flat sleep eyes with hair upper eyelashes and painted lower eyelashes; open mouth; incised: "DEP" and size number. Sometimes this doll is found with the Jumeau stamp on the head and/or body. *H&J Foulke, Inc.*

Focusing On...

A Jumeau Family Album

JUMEAU — the magic word in antique dolls, the creator of the most lovely and life-like Bébés in the world. The doll creations of Maison Jumeau look like happy children with joyful faces. Sparkling laughing eyes, soft rosy-hued cheeks, lovely natural looking hair with loose tendrils to frame their faces — all of these details contribute to the special appeal of a Jumeau doll. Chunky child bodies of posable composition and wood also add to the reality of the natural look. To doll fanciers the name Jumeau suggests a true work of art worthy of admiration and delightful to own.

The most rare and beautiful of Jumeaus, the elusive Long Face, probably one of the earliest Bébés of the family. Only the composition and wood body of the Long Face is marked with the blue stamp; her head has only a size number, but her look is unmistakable. Such softness of expression! This doll is usually found only in sizes larger than 24in (61cm). Jumeau won the gold medal at the Vienna Exhibition in 1873 and at the Paris Exhibition in 1878. Her blond mohair wig appears to be original. Her ears are separately applied. Marked: JUMEAU//MEDAILLE D'OR//PARIS. *Crandall Collection.*

June/July 1980 Doll Reader

LEFT: Since Emile Jumeau took over the firm around 1877, the dolls which carry his initials probably date just after that. This Bébé with the E.J. mark on her head has exceptionally gorgeous large deep brown eyes which provide a marvelous contrast to the pale bisque of her face. She is 21in (53cm) tall. *Richard Wright.*

ABOVE: This diminutive Tête Jumeau is an exquisite confection in her peach satin and ecru lace dress with chiffon bonnet. Her body with jointed wrists has the blue oval BÉBÉ JUMEAU sticker. She is 13in (33cm) tall. *H & J Foulke.*

LEFT: This 23in (58cm) E.J. has blond eyebrows which match her apparently original human hair wig styled in exceptionally long and narrow corkscrew curls. Her large luminous glass eyes, typical of Jumeau dolls, are handblown with a threaded iris covered with a drop of clear glass which gives them the brilliance of the natural eye. These are referred to as paperweight eyes because of the illusion of depth. Her body has the blue Jumeau stamp: her wrists are unjointed. Marked: DEPOSE E. 10 J. *H & J Foulke.*

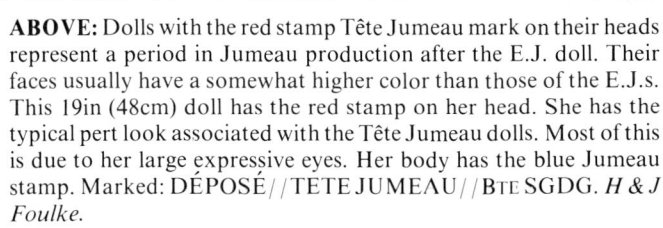

ABOVE: Dolls with the red stamp Tête Jumeau mark on their heads represent a period in Jumeau production after the E.J. doll. Their faces usually have a somewhat higher color than those of the E.J.s. This 19in (48cm) doll has the red stamp on her head. She has the typical pert look associated with the Tête Jumeau dolls. Most of this is due to her large expressive eyes. Her body has the blue Jumeau stamp. Marked: DÉPOSÉ//TETE JUMEAU//BTE SGDG. *H & J Foulke.*

ABOVE: A rarely found Tête Jumeau with the lady body. This is not the kid body of the early Parisiennes, but a jointed composition and wood body with a molded bust, tiny waist and rounded hips. Her pink lips give a hint of a smile at the turned up corners, a feature typical of Jumeau dolls. She is 20in (51cm) tall. *Richard Wright.*

LEFT: Seldom found is this Jumeau family member with the incised marking on the head, also with red stroke marks. Her eyes, smaller than those of the later Jumeaus, are a beautiful blue which matches her blue leather marked E. Jumeau shoes. This blue has been carried out in her costuming, a newly made outfit of old blue and ivory satin. Her body has the blue Jumeau stamp; her wrists are straight. She is 15in (38cm) tall. Marked: DÉPOSÉ//JUMEAU. *H & J Foulke.*

LEFT: This 26in (66cm) Tête Jumeau has the same small eyes as the incised Jumeau doll, which is unusual for a doll with the Tête marking. *Richard Wright.*

BOTTOM LEFT: Another E.J., this one is 20in (51cm) tall. She has the heavier and darker eyebrows which are characteristic of the Jumeau dolls. Her clothes are replacements of an appropriate style. *Richard Wright.*

BOTTOM RIGHT: Another of the early Bébés is the so-called Portrait Jumeau. Like the Long Face, the head of the Portrait Jumeau is marked only with a size number, and her body has the same blue stamp. These early Jumeau bodies are rather chunky and solid; the wrists are not jointed; the fingers are fat. The eyes of this doll, which are longer and narrower than those of other types of Jumeau dolls, are very distinctive in color as well as shape. The iris is composed of a series of vivid light blue rods surrounded by a black background. She is 25in (64cm) tall. *Richard Wright.*

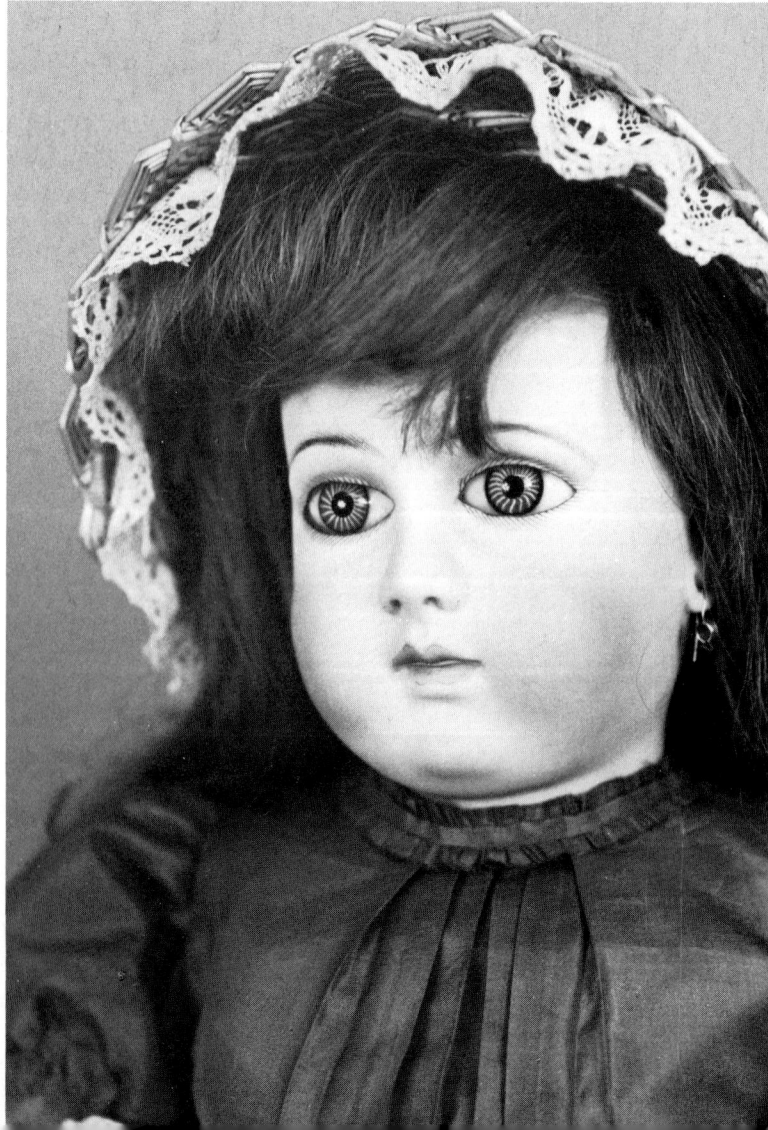

Jumeau, marked "DÉPOSÉ//E. 10 J." *Photograph by Howard Foulke.*

French Bébés

Illustration 1. Standing: 24in (61cm) Tête Jumeau. Sitting, left to right: 16in (41cm) E. J. Jumeau; 7in (18cm) Bourgoin Steiner with wired eyes; 15in (38cm) Bourgoin Steiner. *Jan and Beth Foulke Collection.*

Focusing On...

French Bébés

The last quarter of the 19th century was an age of opulence and luxury which was reflected in the doll industry by the products of the French doll makers. The increasingly wealthy upper middle class had money in unprecedented amounts to spend, and the French doll makers supplied them with a luxury product on which to spend it. A French doll today still carries the same aura of expense and elegance which it had when it was first created. This era of doll making has been referred to as "The Golden Age of Dolls," and few would dispute this appellation. It was a time when unpleasantness and ugliness were relegated to the background; beauty, sweetness and light were emphasized. This is evident in the French bébés (child dolls) of the time which were actually only one aspect of the age that mirrored an idealized and romanticized idea of childhood. The French doll has today still a certain mystique, an appeal almost beyond explanation but certainly encompassing her creamy complexion, soulful eyes and ethereal expression.

ABOVE: Illustration 2. The dolls produced by Bru Jne & Cie are among the most sought-after of the French dolls. Even the name Bru seems to have magical quality about it when one is discussing French dolls. The faces of the bébés are hauntingly beautiful; one seldom forgets the expression. This particular doll is 17in (42cm) tall. She has the Bru Jne marking on her head and her deep shoulder plate; her body is of kid with the beautifully molded bisque hands that are practically a trademark of this company. She is in a completely original outfit of turquoise and ecru satin and lace; on the bottom of her shoe is the name of the toy store which originally sold her. *Ruth Noden Collection.*

RIGHT: Illustration 3. This 22in (56cm) bébé is one of the earlier Tête Jumeau dolls. Her beautiful liquid blue eyes are so nearly lifelike that she is almost real. Her blonde mohair ringlets also contribute to her soft look. She is the reflection of her age: elegant and opulent. In spite of the fact that the Jumeau dolls are the most plentiful of the French dolls, they continue also to be the most popular with collectors. *Ruth Noden Collection.*

Illustration 4. Dolls by Jules Nicholas Steiner were generally unappreciated by American collectors until the late 1970s when they finally started to bring prices more worthy of their rarity and quality. This 18in (46cm) little girl is one of the "A" series, which usually have the "Le Petit Parisien" paper label on their composition and wood jointed bodies. The faces on these "A" series Steiners usually have larger eyes and a more alert expression than those of the Bourgoin Steiners. *Ruth Noden Collection.*

Illustration 5. "Paris Bébé" was registered as a trademark by Danel & Cie in 1889. As is typical of French dolls of this period, she has fairly heavy eyebrows, although they are not so dark as those on many Jumeau dolls made during this same period. Her eyes are smaller than usually expected for this type of doll, and her mouth is distinctive with a pronounced upturn at each end of her upper lip and quite a wide white space between her lips. Her curly blonde mohair wig is original. *Ruth Noden Collection.*

Illustration 6. "Bébé Mascotte" was a trademark registered by May Fréres Cie in 1890. The doll's lovely face is characterized by large, expressive eyes of deep dark blue; her long narrow light-colored eyebrows with soft feathering at the top contrast to those of some French dolls which have very heavy eyebrows. Other distinctions are her upper lip with two decidedly sharp peaks and her pointed chin with incised dimple. She is 20in (51cm) tall on a composition and wood jointed body, which was the most popular type for a French doll. *Ruth Noden Collection.*

Illustration 7. This 20in (51cm) bébé is unmarked and difficult to attribute to any known maker. She has a lovely peaches and cream complexion accented by deep brown paperweight eyes and eyebrows a few shades lighter. Both of these features contrast with her spectacular original blonde mohair wig. An interesting feature is the way her ears are pierced with one hole straight through her head. She is also on a composition and wood jointed body of the type found on most French dolls. *Ruth Noden Collection.*

Illustration 8. One of the most elusive of French dolls is the Bébé Schmitt. She is marked on both head and body with a shield containing the letters "SCH," the trademark of Schmitt & Fils. Her paperweight eyes have great depth and several shades of blue are combined to create a stunning effect. Her chubby cheeks and her double chin contribute to making her look like a small child with well-rounded features. The Schmitt doll bodies are characterized by a flat-bottomed torso, cupped hands with fingers together and large ball joints at the thighs. *Ruth Noden Collection.*

Illustration 9. One of the earlier dolls by the Jumeau factory is this lovely 26in (66cm) bébé with the "E.J." for Emile Jumeau marking. These dolls are thought by some collectors to be the most beautiful of all the Jumeau bébés. This one has an especially serene look. Her face is more oval in shape with a higher brow and longer cheekline than that of the Tête Jumeau. Her body is the early type of Jumeau body, very chunky and sturdy with unjointed wrists. *Ruth Noden Collection.*

ABOVE: Illustration 10. This is another doll with the Bru Jne mark, but an entirely different facial treatment. Her eyes are larger and are accented by the heavily painted luxurious eyelashes. Her lips are more slightly parted and her cheeks are much chubbier. She retains her original skin wig and is just a mere 12in (30cm) elegance. *Ruth Noden Collection.*

ABOVE RIGHT: Illustration 11. This Tête Jumeau is 20in (51cm) tall. With her open mouth and molded upper teeth, she is one of the Jumeau factory's later products. Although she has a pert attractive face, the expression is more like that of the German dolly-faced doll, rather than the earlier French bébés. Her brown human hair wig matches her heavy Jumeau eyebrows; her vivid blue eyes are almost alive. *Ruth Noden Collection.*

RIGHT: Illustration 12. Dolls incised with the mark "F.G." are usually attributed to the Gaultier firm which had a long history in making dolls. One of the favorite "F.G." bébés is the one with this particular face. She has chubby cheeks and a small pink bow-shaped mouth with a hint of a molded tongue between her lips. Her eyebrows are not so overpowering as those on some French dolls; they are actually made of a multitude of tiny individual brush strokes. Her brown human hair wig is very full and luxurious. She is on a composition and wood jointed body and measures 27in (69cm) tall. *Ruth Noden Collection.*

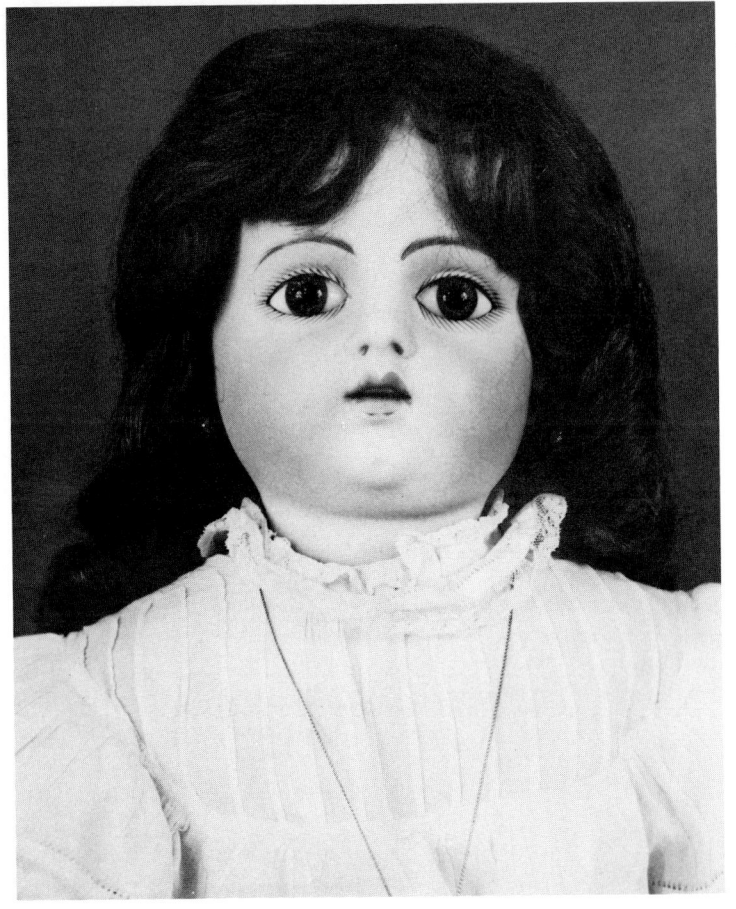

Focusing On...

Gebrüder Heubach Dolls

Left to right: 15in (38.1cm) pouty with mold number 6969 discussed in detail on page 39 (Illustration 8); 7in (17.8cm) wigged "Bonnie Babe" incised 1393 discussed on page 58 (Illustration 63); 8in (20.3cm) wigged "Bonnie Babe" impressed with the Heubach square mark and number 12386 discussed on page 58 (Illustration 64); Mechanical "Whistling Jim" discussed on page 62 (Illustration 70); 15in (38.1cm) pouty with mold number 6969 discussed on page 39 (Illustration 9).

TOP: One of the most spectacular Heubach pieces with babies in this bisque basket trinket box with a removable lid. The woven basket is tinted a natural straw color with the top edge, basket rim and clasps and hinges in a darker brown. Four blonde haired babies peek over the rim of the basket. BOTTOM: 14in (35.6cm) Heubach googlie discussed on page 63 (Illustration 71).

RIGHT: Color Illustration 2.
LEFT: This 21in (53.3cm) pouty boy is incised with a sunburst and 7622. He is described on page 46 Illustrations 26, 27 & 28. RIGHT: One of the most rare of the Heubach characters with glass eyes is this 17in (43.2cm) boy. For further information see page 53, Illustrations 46 & 47. The 9in (22.9cm) dog with molded cap and bib is also a Heubach product having the sunburst mark.

LEFT: Color Illustration 1. This 17in (43.2cm) dandy in full day dress is discussed in full detail on page 85, Illustration 140.

Color Illustration 3. FRONT ROW: 4in (10.2cm) action figure is discussed on page 76, Illustration 112. LEFT TO RIGHT: Surprised fellow with side-glancing large round eyes discussed on page 72, Illustration 102. 6in (15.2cm) unmarked doll shown on page 71, Illustration 99. Knock-kneed, pigeon-toed child with large eyes discussed on page 73, Illustration 104. Smug look doll with tiny molded pony tail discussed on page 73, Illustration 103.

Color Illustration 4. Further details about this 14" boy are given on page 54, Illustration 50.

26

LEFT: Color Illustration 5. This boy and girl pair both bearing the mark 8192 are discussed further on page 68 Illustration 90.

ABOVE: Color Illustration 6. 26in (66.0cm) boy on a bent-limb composition body is described in detail on page 42, Illustration 16.

LEFT: Color Illustration 7. 16in (40.6cm) doll has the sunburst mark and mold number 7247. For more details see Illustrations 18 & 19 on page 43.

27

Color Illustrations 8 & 9. Indian pair incised with square mark and 8457. For more details see Illustration 2, page 31.

28

Color Illustration 10. 15in (38.1cm) pouty has a companion doll shown in Illustrations 8 & 9 on page 39.

Color Illustration 11. 22in (55.9cm) boy impressed with mold number 10532. For more details see Illustration 5, page 36.

29

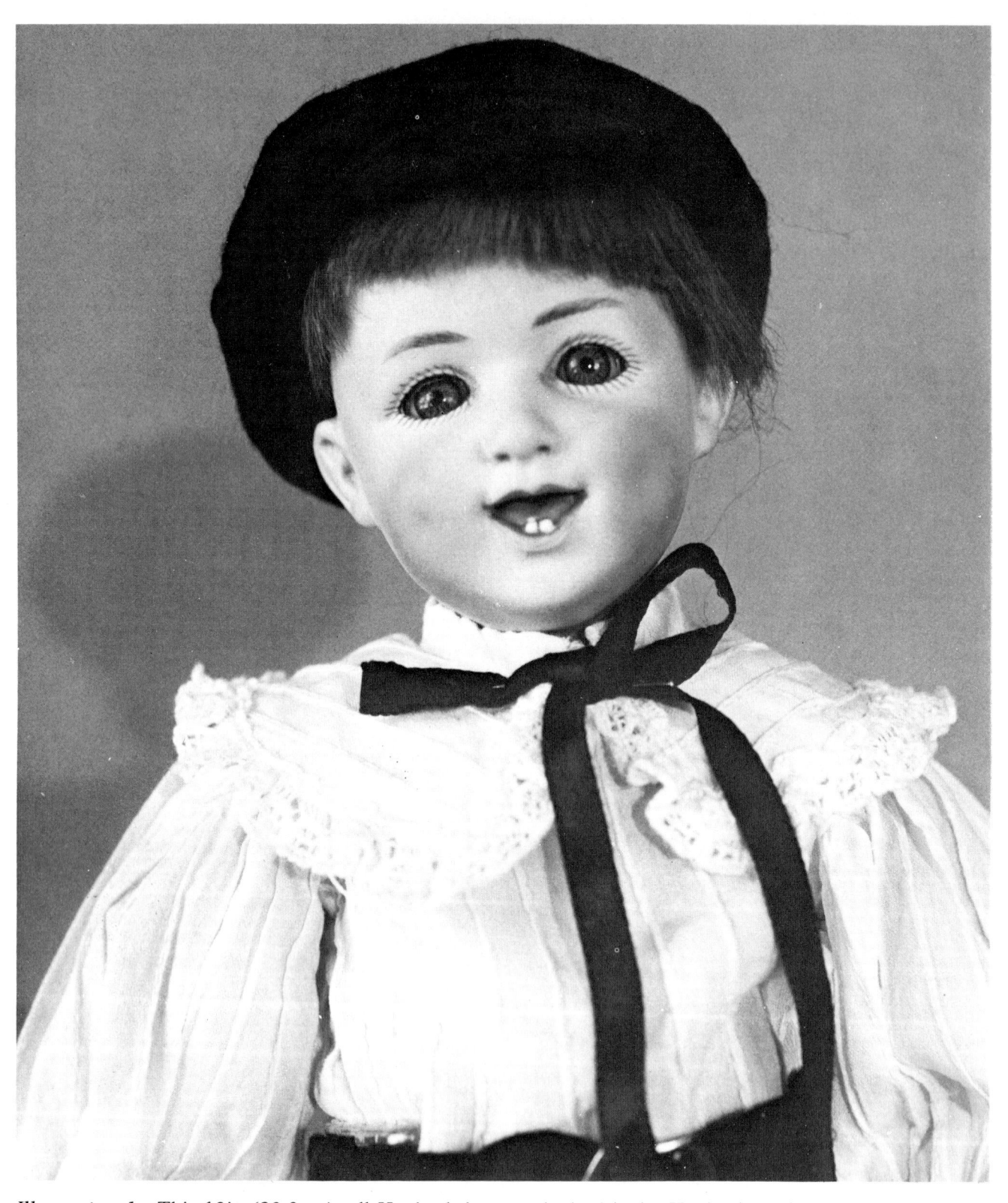

Illustration 1. This 13in (33.0cm) tall Heubach boy marked with the Heubach sunburst and 5636 is possibly one of "The Smiling 'Jubilee' Babies" advertised in the January 1909 *Playthings* by Strobel and Wilken, a company which distributed German bisque dolls. These dolls had jointed composition child bodies, not baby bodies. *Mary Lou Rubright Collection.*

Introduction

The factory of Gebrüder Heubach is on record as having been established in 1820. The Heubach family apparently was quite large, and several other branches were also involved in porcelain making. The Gebrüder Heubach factory at Lichte, Thüringia, Germany, made china tableware, novelties and figurines as well as dolls. They probably made china head dolls and later the bisque lady dolls with the molded fancy hairstyles and the beautifully decorated shoulder plates. However, this is conjecture as these types of dolls are never marked with a factory name.

It is fairly easy to trace the development of doll styles of most companies making bisque dolls, but the dolls of Gebrüder Heubach are much more difficult to classify. Most of the older factories follow logically through the stages of the closed-mouth child dolls, the open-mouth child dolls and then the character dolls. Although Gebrüder Heubach was presumably making dolls through all of these periods also, and indeed had doll agents, still it is puzzling as to what dolls he was producing before the early 1900s. It seems as though he

RIGHT: Illustration 2. Not a beautiful doll by any means, but certainly one of the outstanding character faces created by the Heubach brothers is this rare American Indian doll. The face is similar to the many paintings of Indians which were done by the frontier painters and were so popular in the United States. It is lined with worry and care, and the brows are furrowed. The eyelids are heavy with age; the nose is broad. The mouth is turned down, probably toothless. Her wig is done in gray mohair braids over a solid dome head. As the original leather clothes had rotted, this squaw was re-dressed by the Sioux Indians in 1950 in a copy of an 1891 war dress worn by that tribe. This shoulder head doll is on a body of cloth with composition arms and legs. She is incised with a square mark and 8457. An Indian chief, a companion doll to her, can be seen in the color section. Chief. *Richard Wright Collection.* Squaw. *Ruth Noden Collection.*

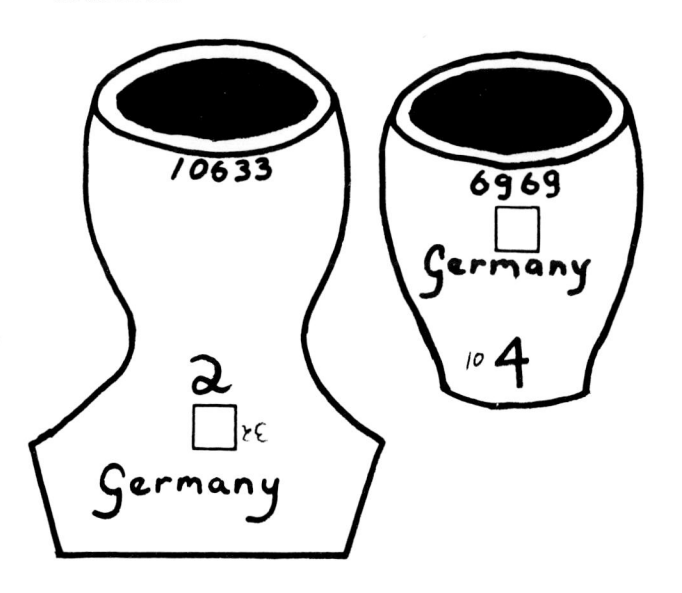

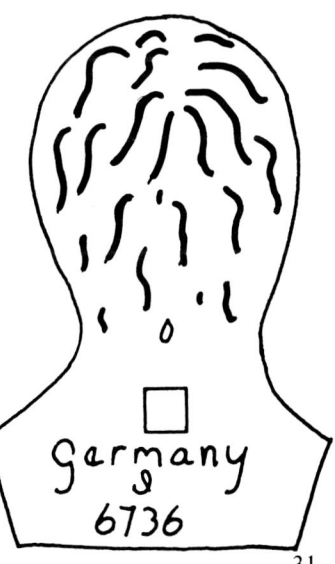

Sample Heubach markings

specialized in the production of character dolls, and they did not come on the market until about 1909. Even if he were making character dolls by the early 1900s, as he might have been, this leaves a great gap in our knowledge of what bisque dolls Heubach made from 1880 until 1900.

Even the mold numbers seem to be of little help in this problem. Some companies, for instance Simon & Halbig, used a fairly consistent numbering system. At least the mold numbers were in chronological order. But I have not yet figured out the Gebrüder Heubach system. Possibly the five-digit mold numbers are the last dolls that were made, however. The googlies, which are known to be later dolls, have high four-digit numbers. Further study of the Heubach mold numbers is definitely indicated. Working on the Heubach mold numbers has been a most frustrating task since the numbers are small and lightly impressed which often makes them very difficult to decipher. The 3s, 6s and 8s are very confusing; 0s and 9s are particularly bad. The number usually consists of four digits, sometimes five. Sometimes part of the number does not even stamp. On open crown dolls, the mold number is usually high at the crown opening, often covered by glue from the wig; on shoulder head dolls with molded hair, it is usually down at the bottom of the shoulder covered by the body. On socket dolls with molded hair, it is usually divided into two parts, with two numbers on each side of the square mark. Beside the mold numbers, there are also occasionally two other numbers sometimes upside down impressed together, some numbers stamped in green and possibly a size number as well. These mold numbers have been recorded as accurately as possible, but there is still some possibility of error. Perhaps with careful tabulation, these numbers will yet get sorted out. This is actually just the beginning of our work with Heubachs and we will continue collecting photographs and numbers of dolls not shown here.

Another problem in classification arises when some of the dolls have no mold numbers at all, simply a square mark or a sunburst. Then there are a few obviously Heubach dolls which are marked only Germany. Also some do not have the trademark, only the mold number. Evidently the factory was not thinking in terms of convenience for collectors 100 years down the road!

Gebrüder Heubach Marks

Incised

Square Mark

Sunburst

Germany

Stamped in green, red or blue

Also in addition to the mold number and trademark

Incised

D   meaning unknown

5/0   fraction or whole number probably denotes size

12   one or two numbers, sometimes upside down

Stamped

9   single or double green number, often blurred

Illustration 3. Very rare among Heubach dolls are the black characters. Only occasionally is one found. This doll could be treated as a boy or girl. The black molded hair is short and given a fuzzy look. The dark eyes are deeply incised with painted highlights, and, of course, the whites are very outstanding in the very dark black face. Her eyebrows are molded as are her upper and lower eyelids. Her pink lips are thick and slightly parted as though ready to speak to whoever is calling her name. She is 19in (48.3cm) tall on a very good black jointed composition body. She is incised with a sunburst and 6, possibly a size number. Unfortunately there is no mold number on her, but an identical doll has been recorded as mold No. 7671. *Old Curiosity Shop.*

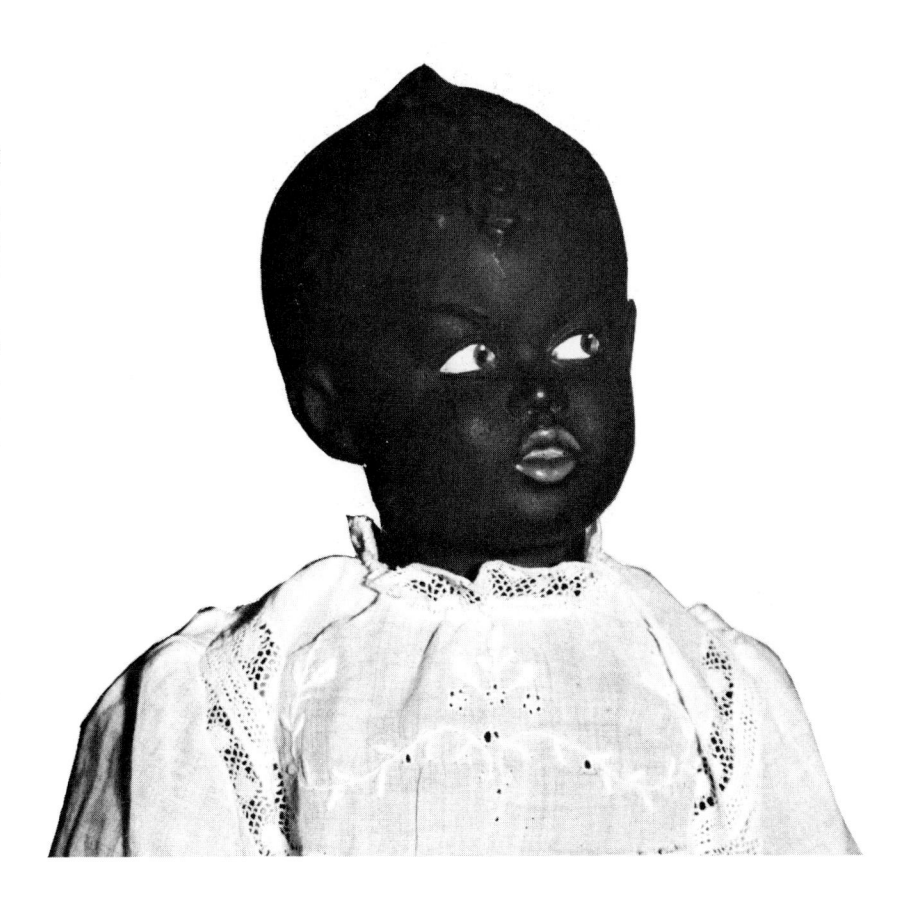

Index of Mold Numbers

Index of mold numbers on doll heads shown here, not including all-bisque dolls

5636	— Laughing with glass eyes and wig, socket head	Illustration 48
5777	— Dolly Dimple, socket head	Illustrations 41 & 42
6692	— Pouty shoulder head, intaglio eyes, molded hair	Illustration 31
6736	— Laughing shoulder head, intaglio eyes, molded hair	Illustrations 54 & 67
6897	— Laughing socket head, intaglio eyes, molded hair	Illustration 52
6969	— Pouty, glass eyes, wig, socket head	Illustrations 8, 9 & 10
6970	— Pouty, glass eyes, wig, socket head	Illustrations 11 & 12
7246	— Pouty, glass eyes, wig, socket head	Illustrations 13, 14, 16 & 17
7247	— Pouty, glass eyes, wig, socket head	Illustrations 18 & 19
7248	— Pouty, glass eyes, wig, socket head	Illustration 15
7256	— Pouty, glass eyes, wig, socket head	Illustration 20
7307	— Smiling, intaglio eyes, wig, socket head	Illustration 56
7314	— Laughing, intaglio eyes, molded hair, socket head	Illustration 68
7407	— Pouty, glass eyes, wig, socket head	Illustrations 21 & 22
7602	— Pouty, intaglio eyes, molded hair	Illustration 33
7604	— Smiling, intaglio eyes, molded hair, socket head	Illustrations 53 & 65
7622	— Pouty, intaglio eyes, molded hair, socket head	Illustrations 26, 27 & 28
7671	— Black child	Illustration 3

Index of Mold Numbers continued

7711	— Traditional, open mouth, glass eyes, wig	Illustration 83
7763	— Coquette, socket head	Illustration 62
7764	— Girl, molded hair with enameled bow	Illustration 6
7788	— Coquette, socket head	Illustrations 60 & 61
7911 or 7971	— Smiling, molded hair, intaglio eyes, socket head	Illustration 57
7977	— Baby Stuart, socket head	Illustrations 37 & 38
8017	— Pouty, glass eyes, wig, socket head	Illustration 23
8191	— Smiling, molded hair, intaglio eyes, socket head	Illustration 59
8192	— Traditional, open mouth, glass eyes, wig, socket head	Illustrations 89 & 90
8306	— Smiling, molded hair, intaglio eyes, shoulder head	Illustration 58
8316	— Grinning, glass eyes, wig, socket head	Illustrations 46 & 47
8420	— Pouty, glass eyes, wig, socket head	Illustrations 24 & 25
8457	— Indian, shoulder head	Illustration 2
8589	— Googly, intaglio eyes, molded hair, socket	Illustrations 79 & 80
8729	— Googly, molded hair, intaglio eyes, socket head	Illustration 81
8774	— Whistling Jim	Illustration 70
8878	— Pouty, molded hair, intaglio eyes, socket head	Illustration 40
9081	— Googly, painted eyes, molded hair girl, socket head	Illustration 82
9141	— Winking, socket head	Illustrations 74 & 75
9167	— Pouty, molded hair, socket head, intaglio eyes	Illustration 30
9355	— Dolly Dimple, unmarked shoulder head	Illustrations 43 & 44
9573	— Googly, glass eyes, wig, socket head	Illustrations 76 & 77
9578	— Pouty, intaglio eyes, socket head	Illustration 35
10532	— Traditional, open-mouth, wig, glass eyes, socket head	Illustrations 84, 85 & 86
10586	— Traditional, open-mouth, wig, glass eyes, socket head	Illustration 88
10633	— Dolly face	
12386	— Bonnie Babe with wig	Illustration 64

Background

Judging from the known output of the Gebrüder Heubach factory, it seems safe to assume that they specialized in the production of character dolls. Their line seems to have included very few of the "dolly-faced" girls which were the dominant production of the other German doll makers. Even after the introduction of the character doll, the "dolly-faced" doll continued to dominate the market in sales as well as production. The character dolls were considered by many people to be innovative and arty, and appealed more to liberal than conservative people who liked to stick by the familiar.

The revolution in character dolls was essentially a German movement. It began in Munich in the early years of the 20th century with a group of designers, the foremost of whom was Marion Kaulitz whose dolls were known as "Munich Art Dolls." These dolls were more real-looking and childlike than the pretty doll-faced dolls of the time which represented an idealized child instead of a real one. Social history is of necessity entwined with the history of toys, as are industrial developments and changes in artistic tastes. It seems that an awakened interest in children as real people in their own right instead of being merely tiny copies of adults had a profound effect upon the design of dolls. The time was ripe for this drastic change, but the success of the character doll was not an overnight happening.

In the February 1908 *Playthings* Samstag and Hilder Brothers advertised "Dolls with the real childlike face. The accomplishment is announced after years of careful experiments and persevering effort . . . . These dolls have been modeled from living subjects under the direction of the most famous artist of Munich, and they represent the very latest development of doll making." The dolls are not pictured, but they could have been the Munich Art Dolls.

The first ad actually picturing bisque character dolls was from the January 1909 *Playthings* where Strobel and Wilken Co. advertised "The Smiling 'Jubilee' Babies," three dolls which appear to be Heubach dolls from mold number 5636 with smiling faces, having the open/closed mouth with two lower teeth, glass eyes and wigs. These dolls, while dressed as babies, are on regular jointed composition bodies. This ad shows that Heubach was early into character dolls, and probably a leader in the field. It is always exciting to make a discovery like this in an area as elusive as the Heubach company. Later in the same issue the "Smiling Doll" is referred to as "hand-modeled to represent—not the ideal type, but the double of many a little girl in real life." And in the same issue George Borgfeldt advertised "dolls with human expressions modeled by well-known artists in Munich from living subjects; boys', girls' and women's faces in a variety of expressions." And so the era of the character doll had arrived in the United States.

In April 1909 Strobel and Wilken ran the first of their ads for the character dolls produced by

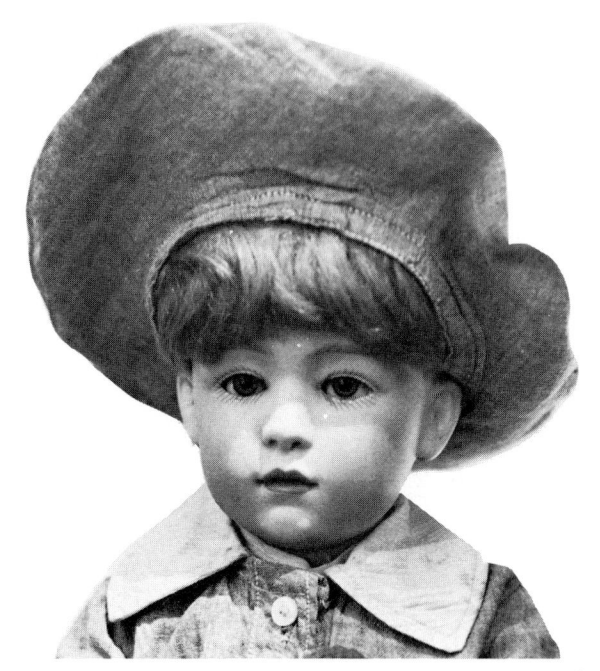

ABOVE: Illustration 4. A 16in (40.6cm) pensive-faced Heubach character boy, mold No. 6970, who appears to have been modeled from real life by an artist. *Mike White Collection.*

Kämmer & Reinhardt. The bisque heads were actually made by Simon & Halbig, a company which is never mentioned since, like Heubach, they made heads for other producers who put the whole doll together.

In January and February 1910, Strobel and Wilken also advertised "K & R character dolls modeled from living subjects by artists--babies, boys, and girls in a large variety of natural facial expressions."

In February 1910 "Boy dolls with smiling character faces in all styles and prices with hearty, carefree faces" were mentioned. Heubach dolls were doubtless included with these. A store display window of Christmas 1910 shows a case of dolls which appear to be tiny Heubach pouty babies.

In January and February 1911, Louis Lindner & Sons advertised dolls which appear to be Heubachs: two laughing girls, a pouty boy and a pouty baby. These apparently were popular models as they are the most commonly found today. In their October 1914 ad they were still showing characters with laughing faces which appear to be Heubach dolls.

In May 1911 Selchow & Righter advertised dolls from leading European factories. Two which are shown appear to be a Heubach pouty baby with intaglio eyes and molded hair, and the almost unmistakable Heubach crying baby.

In 1910 the editorial pages of *Playthings* contained quite a few discussions about the new character dolls, mostly promoting them as an addition to the doll-faced doll, not a replacement for her. Apparently the character dolls were not an instant success, and it took several years for the line to become established. But it never did replace the ever-popular doll-faced doll.

The Art of Heubach

The basis of the art of the Heubach brothers is the ability to create faces in bisque which are believably real. An astounding sidelight is the variety of characters which they produced. Without a doubt it can be said that Heubach specialized in the production of bisque character dolls, many of them quite unusual, and some of them far surpassing the attempts at characterization of other doll makers of that time. Many of the ultimate examples of character dolls are indeed products of the factory of Gebrüder Heubach.

The Heads

As will be seen throughout this book, the Heubach brothers produced heads in a wider variety than any other doll maker. Apparently, their intent was to appeal to as broad a market as possible through the wide range of dolls available. Bisque heads were produced in both the socket type, which would be mounted on a jointed composition body, and the shoulder head type with head and shoulders in one piece, which would be mounted on a cloth or kid body. Apparently, Heubach continued to produce the shoulder heads in fairly large quantity far after the time when they were considered old-fashioned by other doll makers. Obviously, there was a market for them or the line would have been dropped. In analyzing the situation, it would seem that the shoulder heads were perhaps cheaper to produce and could be sold as a less expensive line of dolls, especially those which had no need for wigs or inset glass eyes which would, of course, add extra expense. Then probably the cloth bodies were less expensive than the jointed composition bodies which would have involved many more steps to make.

The Bisque

The Heubach bisque is of the highest quality, sanded to a smooth finish. Gebrüder Heubach is the only factory known to have sometimes used the pink bisque in the manufacture of its doll heads, although many were also made of standard white bisque. Looking into that head and seeing that pink bisque can be quite shocking if one is not aware of this fact! This was a sensible move, however, as it eliminated one step in the manufacturing process; the head did not have to be given the preliminary coat of flesh color but was simply tinted and fired. Although Heubach did use the pink bisque, his use of it for doll heads is not to be confused with the use of pink bisque for the later all-bisque dolls, which do not have the fired-in tint that the doll heads have.

ABOVE: Illustration 5. This 22in (55.9cm) boy is impressed with mold No. 10532. He has a more traditional-style face with an open-mouth and four upper teeth, possibly a later doll because of the higher mold number and the jointed composition toddler body which was a development of later years of the second decade of the 20th century. *Ruth Noden Collection.*

RIGHT: Illustration 6. Two girl shoulder heads with molded hair. The one on the left is the popular "Coquette," which also was available as a socket head. The one on the right is a quite rare model. She has also been seen as a socket head with the square mark and 7764. *1914 Marshall Field & Company catalog.*

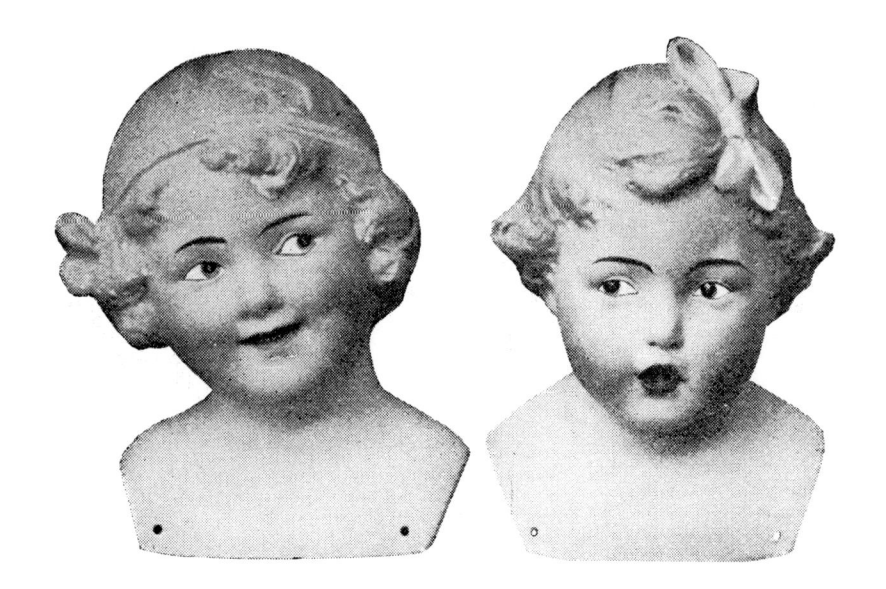

The Decoration

Although sometimes an inferior head appears, for the most part the Heubach dolls are very beautifully decorated. The sometimes inferior ones tend to be small heads which were probably produced in enormous quantities for use not only as dolls, but as novelty items, and perhaps not as great care was given to their production. The flesh tones are pink in contrast to the tones of the early German and French dolls which are white and pale. The cheeks are rosy, as befits a healthy German child. The eyebrows are usually feathered in tiny brush strokes, although sometimes in the smaller and perhaps later dolls only one stroke is used for each eyebrow. The eyelashes are often heavily painted; sometimes none at all or only the upper ones are given to the painted-eye dolls. The mouths are tinted a pleasing color, and the lips are wide or thin, often depending upon the mood of the artist. Seldom is any shading done on the lips. A large number of the Heubach dolls have open/closed mouths where the lips are parted, but there is no actual slit in the bisque. Many of these dolls have molded and/or painted teeth. Some of the Heubach dolls have closed mouths. A few have open mouths with a slit in the bisque to accommodate inset teeth and a tongue if desired.

The Eyes

The Heubach brothers followed the fashion in dolls by using the standard blown glass eyes with weights which would allow the doll to sleep. This was a popular innovation and doll catalogs widely advertised the fact that dolls could be put to sleep by laying them down. However, one eye type was almost uniquely their own, the artistic intaglio eye, of which their artists became masters. Other companies did produce dolls with painted eyes having a round molded eyeball, but Gebrüder Heubach was almost alone in making the intaglio eye which had an indented pupil and iris to give the eye more depth.

The Heubach intaglio eye is in itself a work of art. When the eyes are painted, the pupil is usually larger than the iris. Each iris is given a raised white dot highlight which adds to its look of reality. The upper and lower eyelids are molded. A dark line outlines the upper lid; two red dots usually mark the inside corner of the eye. Occasionally upper and lower or only upper eyelashes are added. It is true that perhaps the intaglio eye was cheaper to produce as it was probably easier to simply paint an eye rather than have to cut eyeholes and inset the glass eyes; even then eyelashes would have had to have been painted. But perhaps most important to doll collectors today is the fact that the intaglio eye allowed a wider range of expressions to be produced. In modeling the faces, the artists did not have to be concerned with accommodating a sleeping eye mechanism, and therefore they were allowed much more artistic freedom to create faces with modeling detail around the eyes. Some models were made which could be produced with either intaglio or glass eyes.

The Hair

Probably no other company used the molded hair styles to the extent that the Heubach factory did. This, too, was doubtless considered old-fashioned, and was certainly a throwback to the molded hair dolls of the 1870s. Here again it was a savings as it precluded the purchase of wigs for the dolls. As manufacturers of figurines, the Heubach people were apparently very capable of producing quite lovely molded hair. A look at some of the dolls illustrated here will prove that point. Very seldom, except sometimes for the babies and the later all-bisque items, were the dolls given bald heads with just painted on hair. Mostly the hair was styled

Illustration 7. Another character in real life style, the so-called "laughing child" mold No. 5636, shown this time as a girl. *Gail Hiatt Collection.*

realistically with lovely long and short curls, brush strokes around the face to add reality, comb marks throughout the hair to give texture, a crown from which the hair swirled out and sometimes a part. Little girls were often given a molded ribbon or bow.

Among the most sought after Heubachs are those with the molded bonnets. These dolls have wisps of hair sticking out from the sides or bottoms of their bonnets. This was a rare feature tried by only a few companies other than Heubach.

While molded hair was popular with the Heubach designers, they also produced dolls which could be given wigs. Some of their models were made both ways.

Another interesting way Heubach coped with hair was to flock the head. This gave texture and felt fuzzy to the touch, but was not particularly long lasting, and much has worn off by this late date. However, Heubach was not alone in flocking hair; other companies did this also.

As mentioned, some of the small babies and the all-bisque items have bald heads, or nearly bald heads with only a tiny curl or two. The hair on these dolls was achieved by painting, usually with brush marks, but sometimes on the cheaply produced dolls simply an overwash of color was used.

The Bodies

It has come to be generally accepted that Heubach probably did not make bodies at all. Certainly it is known that Heubach did sell heads to many doll producers and distributors who provided their own bodies for the dolls. This at least accounts for the tremendous range of types of bodies on which Heubach dolls appear. Apparently a great number of socket heads were sold to French producers because many Heubach heads turn up on jointed composition or wooden bodies of French manufacture. Some of the papier-mâché bodies on particularly the smaller dolls are terribly crude. In fact, some are of such a poor quality that it is a wonder that they have not just disintegrated over the years. The torsos are just a tough cardboard, and the arms and legs seem to be just stuck on. Sometimes the whole thing looks put together until one has seen enough of these to know that indeed, as terrible as they are, they are right. Some of the composition bodies are of excellent quality on both babies and children indicating that they are probably top-of-the line dolls. Price consideration would have to be the only explanation for these contrasts.

The shoulder heads also appear on many body types of varying quality. Some of them are pink or white muslin with sometimes undistinguished papier-mâché hands, sometimes nice bisque ones. Other fabric bodies were also used, as were real and imitation kid bodies, again in varying degrees of quality. It is sometimes nearly impossible to determine whether or not a Heubach head is on its original body, as there are so many possibilities. It is a great temptation to transfer some of the lovely heads on very poor bodies to a body which is better in quality! This probably boils down to a question of preserving originality whenever one is sure.

Some of the companies for which Heubach supplied heads are Cuno and Otto Dressel, whose wing mark is found on the backs of excellent quality pink composition bodies carrying Heubach heads with the 6969 mold number. Others known are Gebrüder Ohlhaver for whom Heubach made a coquette with his Revalo trademark, Eisenmann & Company for whom they made a googly and Wagner and Zetzsche for whom they made a character baby. Johannes Dietrich who used the Igodi trademark also purchased Heubach heads. There must be others which will someday come to light as more bits and pieces of this puzzle are fit together. However, most companies probably just ordered stock Heubach heads which would carry only the Heubach mark. Several companies could be buying the same head, which again would account for the fact of the same head turning up on several different types of bodies.

The Pouties
Pouties with Glass eyes

Beloved by most collectors of character dolls are the pouties. These somber-faced little people seem such a drastic departure from the standard German dolly that it is a wonder people did not run out and buy them right away. Apparently these dolls were such a change from the accepted standard doll look, that they took some getting use to. Yet the time was apparently now right for these dolls which were actually real children captured in miniature form. As with real children, the Heubach children are not always smiling and laughing; sometimes their emotions tend in the other direction: somber, thoughtful, pensive or sad. They have real expressions copied from real children.

Illustrations 8 & 9. One of the favorite Heubach pouties is mold number 6969. This face has such a sweet sensitive look that collectors just want to pick up the doll and take it home. The eyes and the mouth are the outstanding features which make this mold a character doll. The sleep eyes are set into tiny eye sockets surrounded by lightly painted lashes. The mouth with full lips is turned down. The eyebrows are feathered in a natural style. These particular dolls have blue sleep eyes and blonde mohair wigs. They were family dolls, and are entirely original. The lady from whom they were purchased referred to them as a boy and girl; however, the boy is outfitted in a dress when most boys of this period would have worn a romper-type suit. Both of the dolls are 15in (38.1cm) tall and have excellent quality jointed composition bodies stamped with the winged trademark of Cuno and Otto Dressel on the back shoulders, showing that this producer did indeed buy heads from the Heubach Brothers. The girl has her hair styled in braids coiled around her ears which is a typical style for little German girls of the period. She is wearing a blue and white checked cotton dress with lace trim, underclothes, white crocheted stockings and white leather shoes with pom-poms. The boy has short blonde hair and a plaid blue and white dress with simple trim. It has a pleat on each side of the front and loops for a belt which is missing. He has plain white cotton stockings and black high-button shoes. These dolls came with a wardrobe of extra clothes: four white dresses, a pair of matching black velvet and white wool coats, two chemises, three pairs of stockings, three Dutch-style hats for the girl and an extra pair of shoes for each doll. *Jan Foulke Collection.*

LEFT: Illustration 10. Here is a tiny 10in (25.4cm) version of the 6969 mold. She has blue glass eyes and an auburn mohair wig. Her jointed composition body is of good quality, and she has been redressed in old fabric. Although this mold is particularly desirable, it is only moderately difficult to find. *Gail Hiatt Collection.*

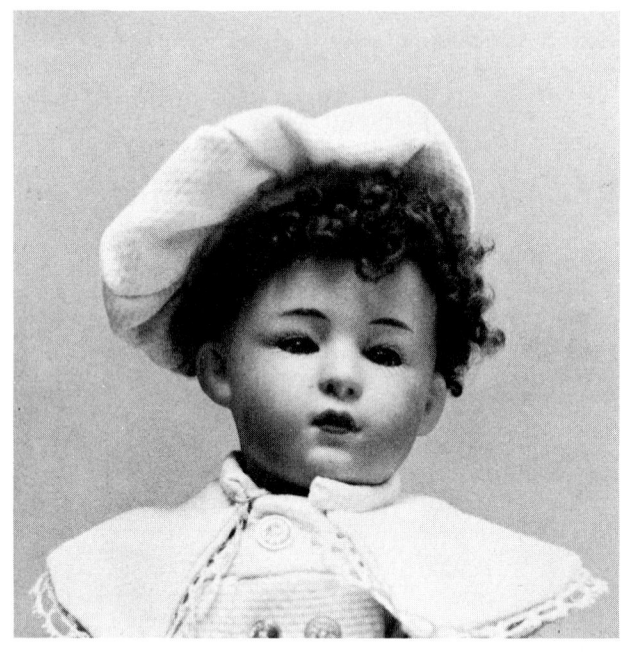

Illustration 11. In the 11½in (29.2cm) size, this doll with mold number 6970 is dressed like the bigger brother of the girl in Illustration 10. He has blue sleep eyes and a caracul wig. This mold is very similar to the 6969 except that the ears appear to be more prominent and the treatment of the mouth and lower face is different. His lips are much more pronounced and slightly parted as though he just might break into a smile; whereas there seems to be little possibility that the 6969 will smile at all! He is also on a jointed composition body of good quality. This mold seems harder to find than the 6969. *Gail Hiatt Collection.*

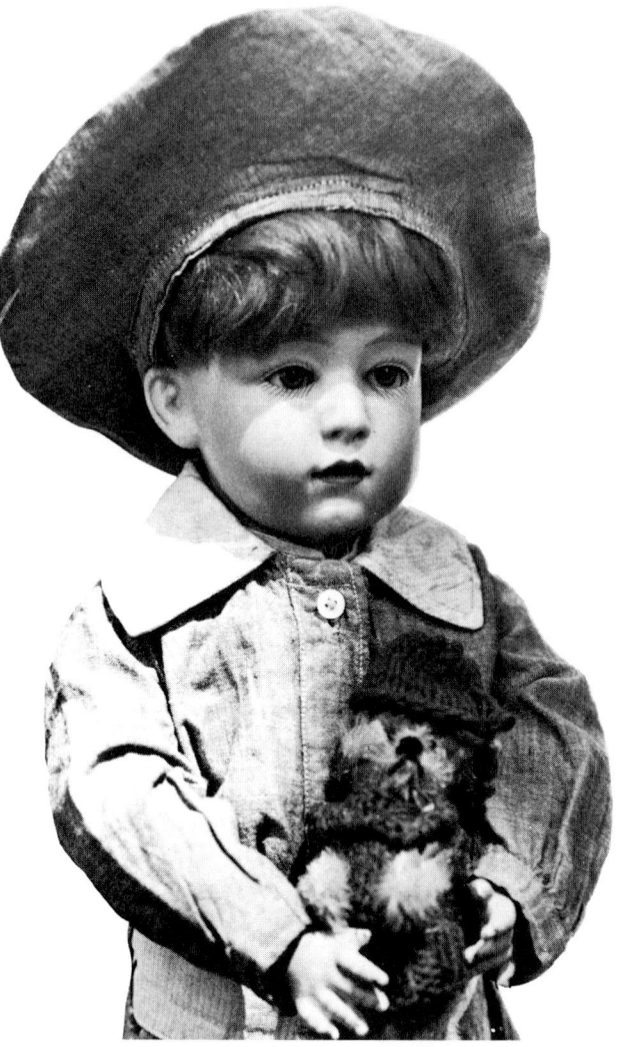

Illustration 12. Here is another boy with the 6970 mold number. He is a large 16in (40.6cm) tall, and as is true with most Heubach dolls and figures, the features of the larger sizes are much sharper and have much more detail than can be included in the smaller sizes. Speak of realism in dolls! This boy is so real looking that he could be easily mistaken for a photograph of a boy of 1911. He has blue sleep eyes, a brown mohair wig and clothes which are possibly original. *Mike White Collection.*

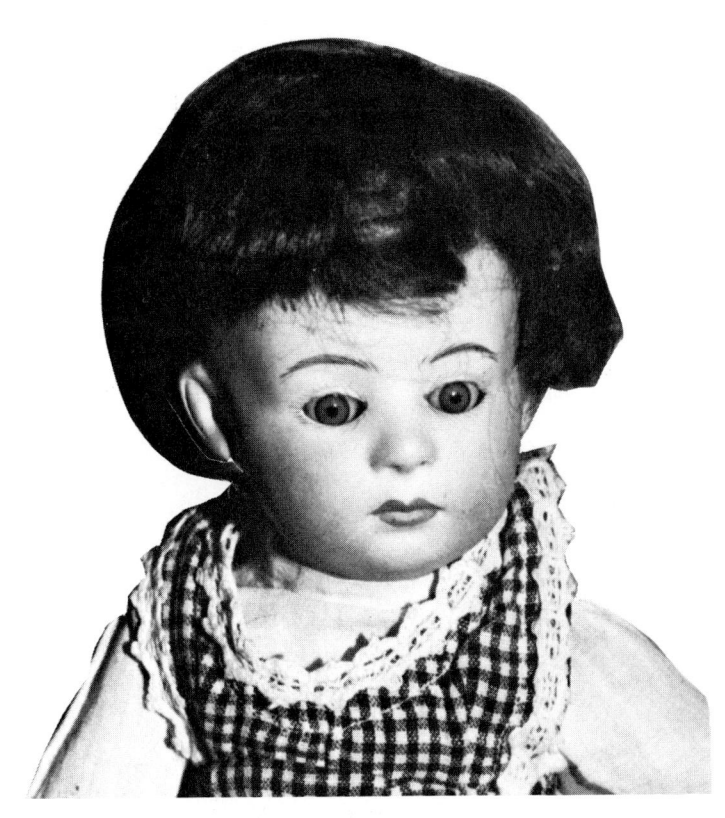

Illustration 13. This 12in (30.5cm) girl could probably be taken for a 6969, if you did not look at the number on the back of her head which is 7246. Comparing her to the 6969 shows that while her mouth treatment is very similar, her eyes are larger. She is on a jointed composition body. Her clothes and wig are replacements. *Old Curiosity Shop.*

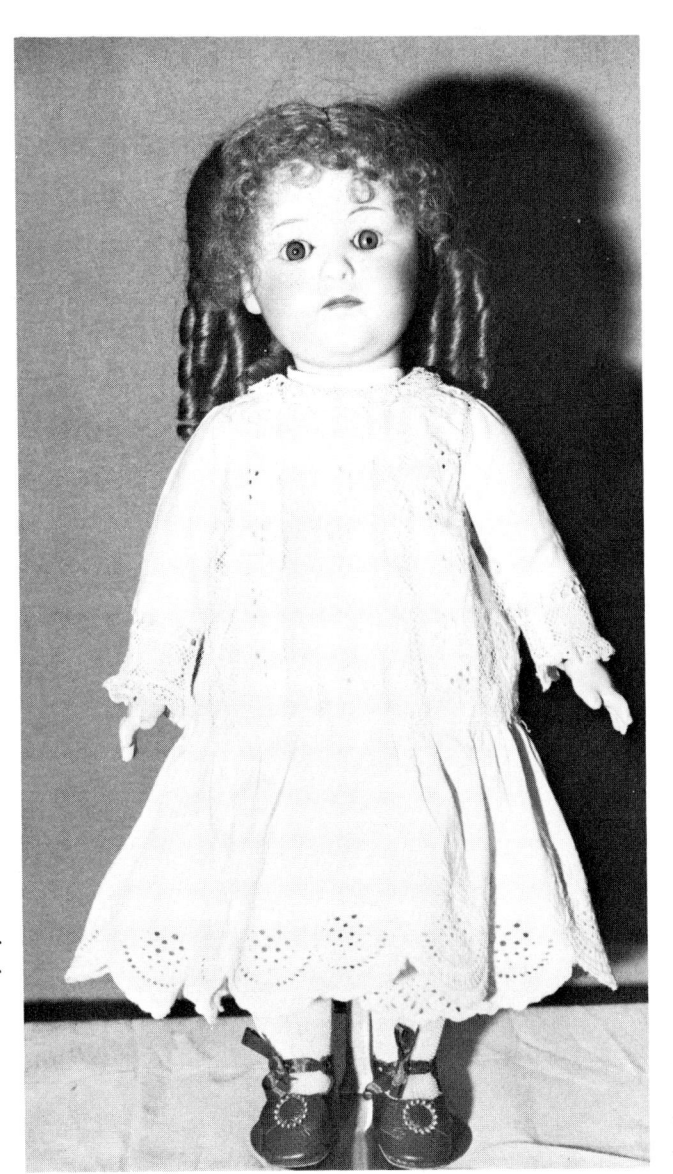

Illustration 14. This doll has the same mold number as Illustration 13, but looks dissimilar because the artist has given a different treatment to the face. The eyebrows are softer, thinner and at a different angle. The mouth is painted wider and thinner also. The eye sockets have been cut larger. She is 13in (33.0cm) tall on a very nice ball-jointed composition body. Her wig is replaced, but her clothes appear original. *Mackemull Collection.*

Illustration 15. Although this is not a very good photograph, it needs to be included since it is another face in this series, this time mold number 7248. She is very similar to the 7246 doll, except that her eyes are tinier and her lips are thinner. She is 9in (22.9cm) tall, with blue sleep eyes and a blonde mohair wig. She is on a five-piece papier-mâché body of fair quality and has on her original clothes. *Ruby K. Arnold.*

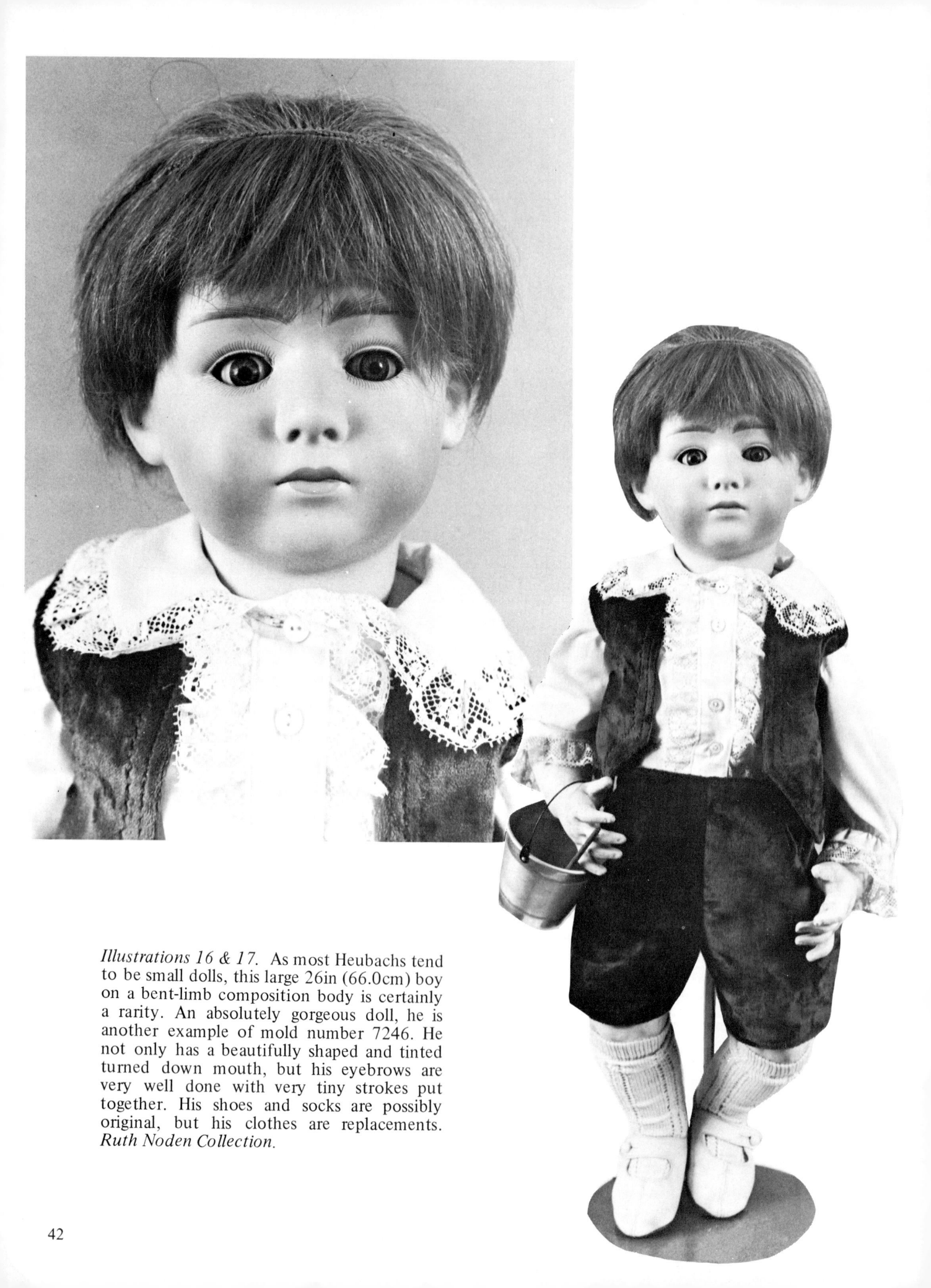

Illustrations 16 & 17. As most Heubachs tend to be small dolls, this large 26in (66.0cm) boy on a bent-limb composition body is certainly a rarity. An absolutely gorgeous doll, he is another example of mold number 7246. He not only has a beautifully shaped and tinted turned down mouth, but his eyebrows are very well done with very tiny strokes put together. His shoes and socks are possibly original, but his clothes are replacements. *Ruth Noden Collection.*

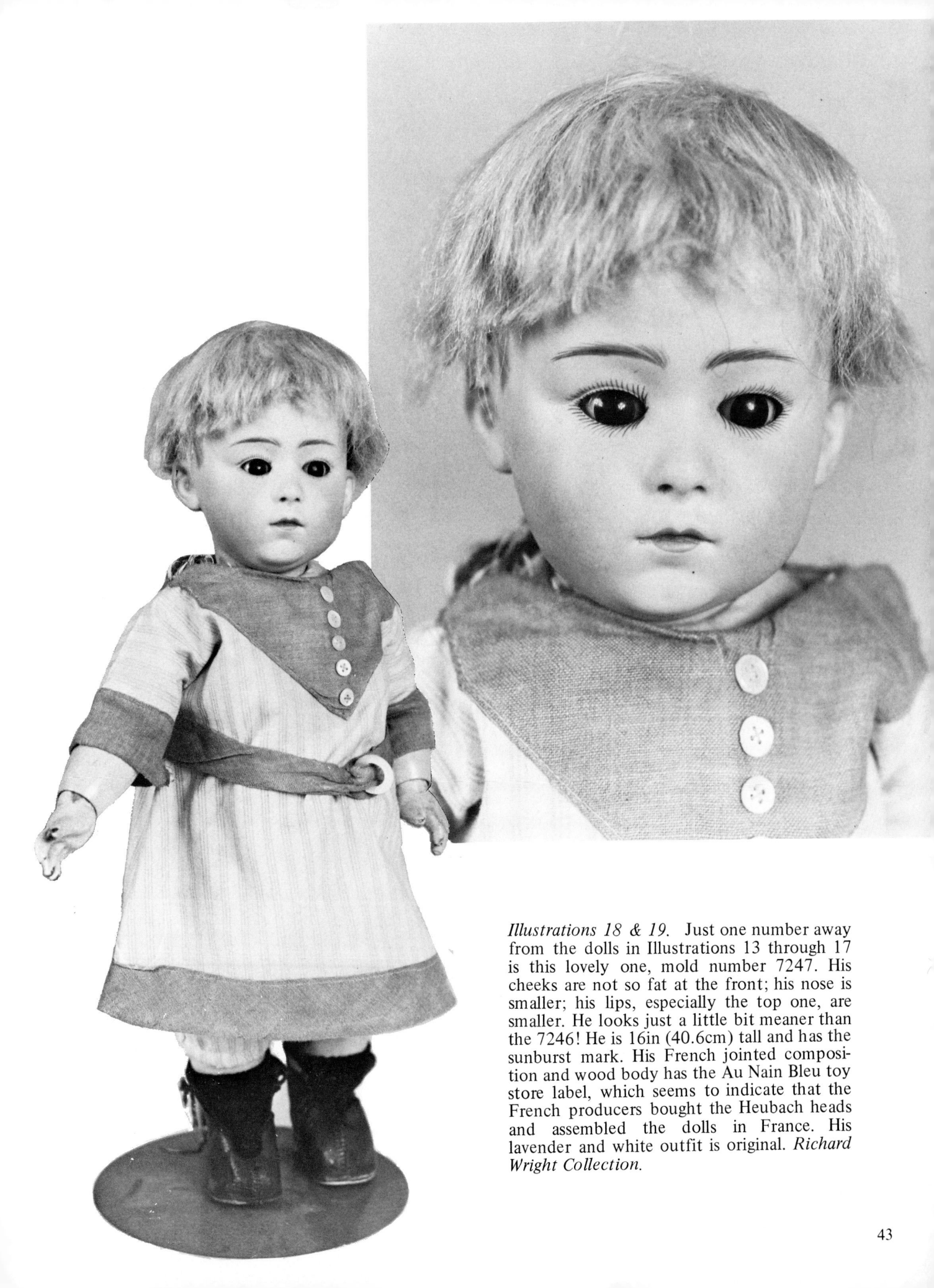

Illustrations 18 & 19. Just one number away from the dolls in Illustrations 13 through 17 is this lovely one, mold number 7247. His cheeks are not so fat at the front; his nose is smaller; his lips, especially the top one, are smaller. He looks just a little bit meaner than the 7246! He is 16in (40.6cm) tall and has the sunburst mark. His French jointed composition and wood body has the Au Nain Bleu toy store label, which seems to indicate that the French producers bought the Heubach heads and assembled the dolls in France. His lavender and white outfit is original. *Richard Wright Collection.*

43

Illustration 20. One of the dearest little babies is this 8in (20.3cm) one with mold number 7256. She has tiny glass eyes, a blonde baby mohair wig and the cutest pouty mouth. Her jointed baby body is of a very poor quality; however, her clothes are all original and quite fancy. Often when companies were presenting beautifully dressed babies, they were careless of the bodies, figuring that they did not show anyway underneath all of the clothes. *Richard Wright Collection.*

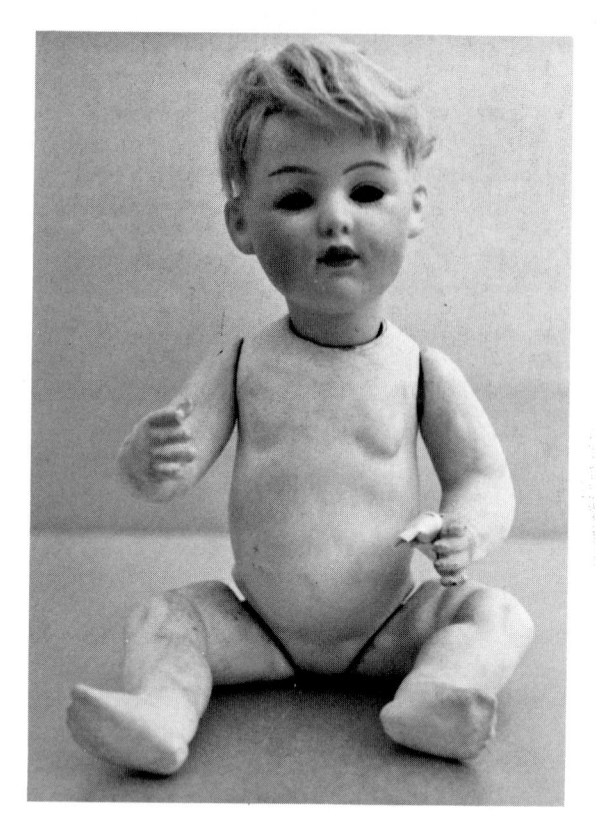

Illustration 21. One of the most charming Heubach babies is this 12in (30.5cm) pouty incised 7407 only, no Heubach mark. His eyes are very expressive, but his most outstanding features are his deep cheek dimples and his lips, which are thick and almost puffy, but they are pulled to the front to make his mouth narrow. His wig is original, as is his very nice quality composition bent-limb baby body. *Dorothea and Ronald Baer Collection.*

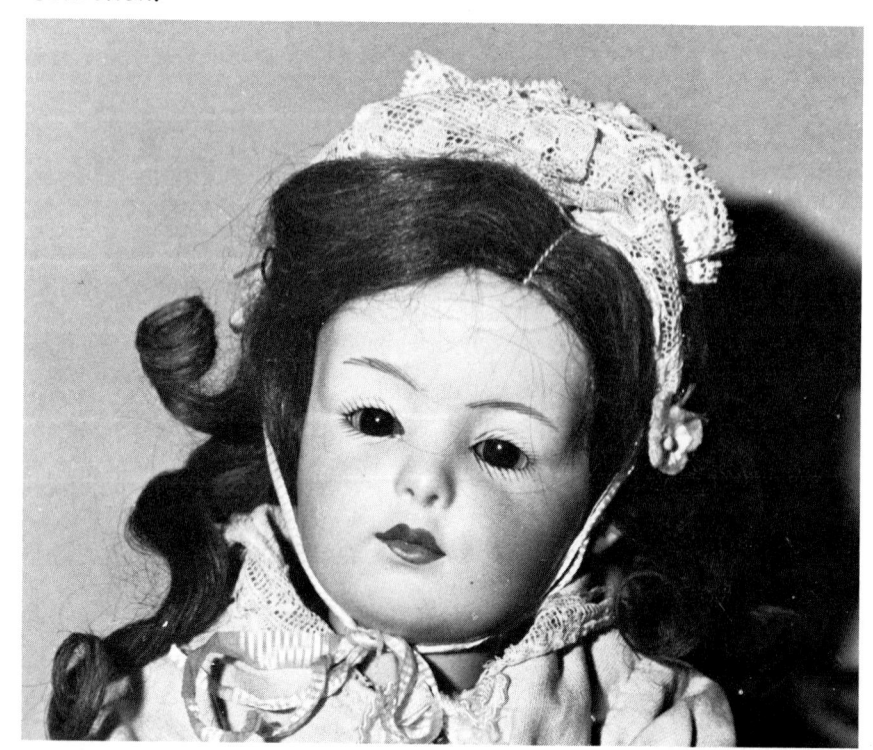

Illustration 22. The mold number of this girl is recorded as 7497, but her features appear to be identical to the doll in Illustration 21, and as difficult as Heubach numbers are to make out sometimes, the 0 and 9 may have been mistaken. Her quality and decoration are lovely, and she is on a jointed composition body. She is incised with a sunburst. *Old Curiosity Shop.*

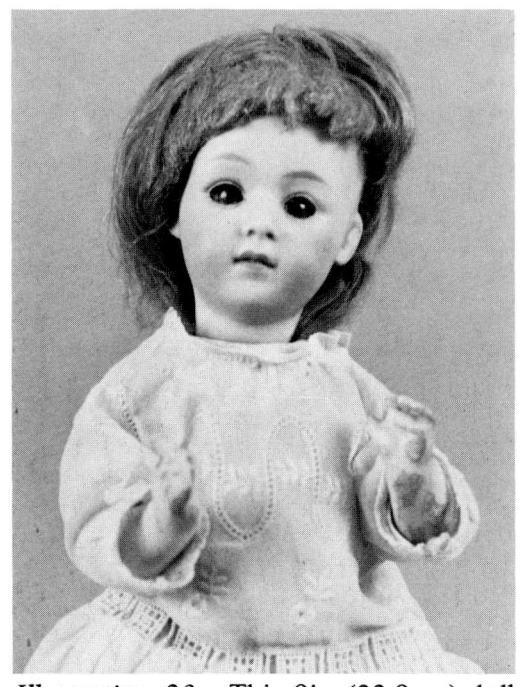

Illustration 23. This 9in (22.9cm) doll is marked with a sunburst and 8017. She has lovely coloring and lightly stroked eyebrows. Her sleep eyes are a gray blue color. She appears to be just about like several dolls already shown and illustrates the fact that there is often very little if any difference between Heubach faces which have different mold numbers. And, of course, this does present a problem in trying to classify the work of this company. It makes one wonder if sometimes the same face was given several numbers, maybe to indicate that it was made for several different producers. This doll is on a baby body, but the face is thinner like an older child would have and could also have been used on a jointed composition body. *Ruth Noden Collection.*

Illustration 24. Another doll which is very similar to the face on the doll in Illustration 23, yet a trifle different in the mouth and just a little chubbier in the lower cheeks to represent a younger child, is this toddler marked with mold number 8420. This style body is unusual for a Heubach head, but appears to be original for him. He still has the remains of his original wig. *H&J Foulke.*

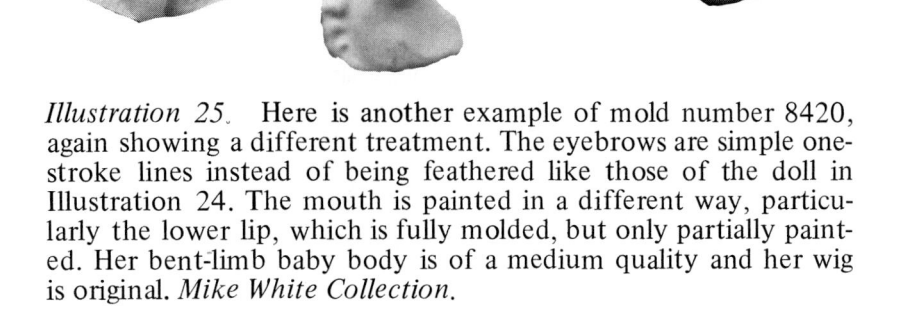

Illustration 25. Here is another example of mold number 8420, again showing a different treatment. The eyebrows are simple one-stroke lines instead of being feathered like those of the doll in Illustration 24. The mouth is painted in a different way, particularly the lower lip, which is fully molded, but only partially painted. Her bent-limb baby body is of a medium quality and her wig is original. *Mike White Collection.*

Pouties with Intaglio eyes

Although for some strange reason most collectors prefer dolls with glass eyes, the ones with the lovely molded and painted or intaglio eyes are much more artistic. The intaglio eyes are an important Heubach feature. Kestner, Kämmer & Reinhardt, and others simply painted, albeit very artistically, the eye on a molded eyeball, whereas Heubach eyes have a sunken pupil and iris to give the illusion of depth. These are called *intaglio* eyes. When the eyes are painted, the pupil is usually larger than the iris. Each iris is given a raised white dot highlight to indicate a light reflection in the eye, as is natural. Upper and lower lids are molded; a dark line outlines the upper lid. Two red dots usually mark the inside corner of the eye. Occasionally upper and lower eyelashes are painted on.

Illustration 26. This pouty boy is considered by many to be one of the most desirable of the Heubach boy dolls. He certainly looks real enough to take by the hand to the ice cream store. Also, he is one which can be found in the larger sizes. The boy pictured is 21in (53.3cm) tall, with a sunburst and 7622, but often this doll appears with no mold number. He has deeply molded blonde curly hair and is a good example to use for studying the intaglio eyes described above. It seems that no detail was overlooked when he was designed. Even his ears are very intricate with molded natural curves. His lips are puffishly childlike. His cheeks have dimples. The French ball-jointed composition and wood body serves again to show that the French distributors purchased heads from the German makers. *Richard Wright Collection.*

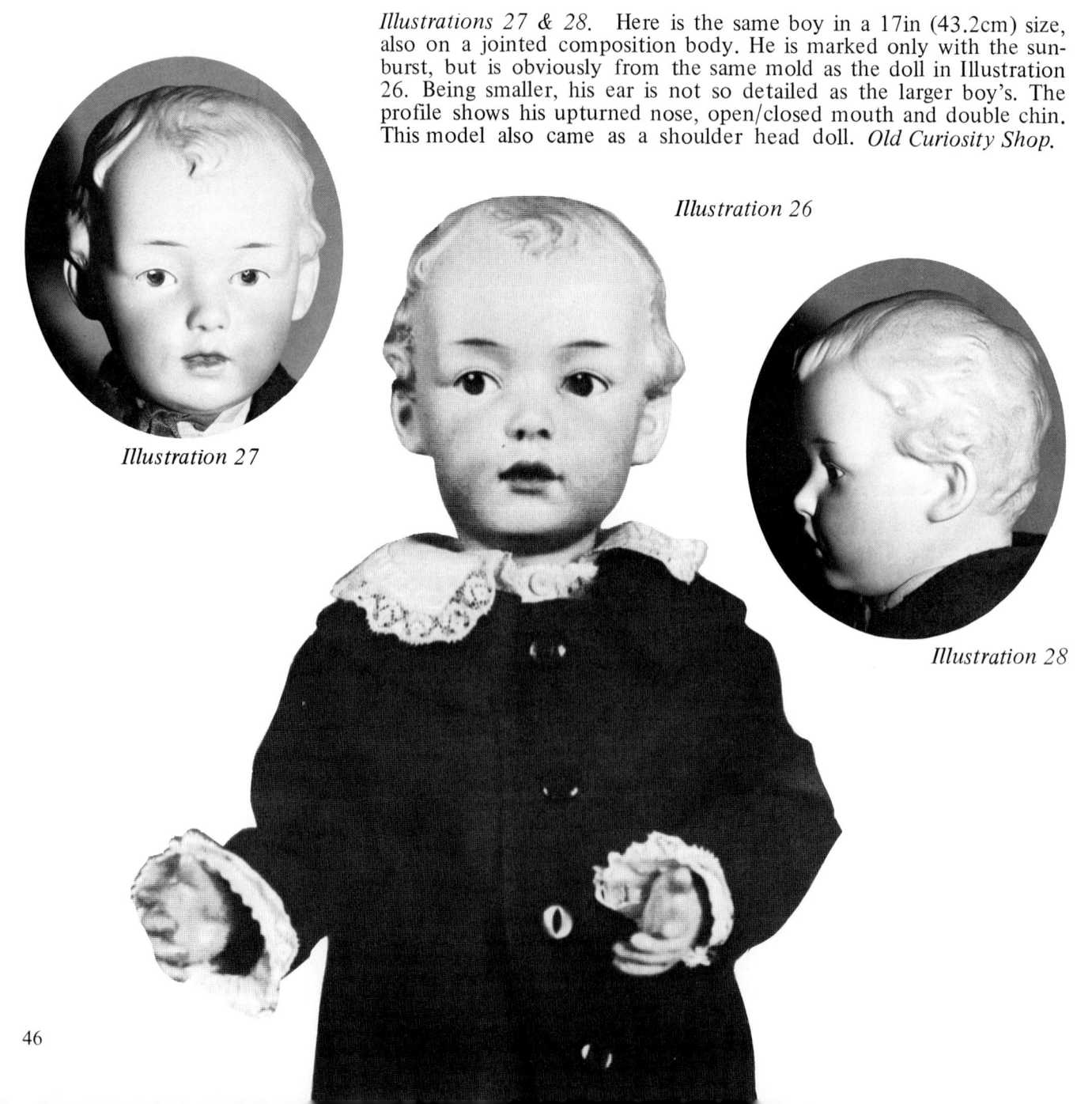

Illustrations 27 & 28. Here is the same boy in a 17in (43.2cm) size, also on a jointed composition body. He is marked only with the sunburst, but is obviously from the same mold as the doll in Illustration 26. Being smaller, his ear is not so detailed as the larger boy's. The profile shows his upturned nose, open/closed mouth and double chin. This model also came as a shoulder head doll. *Old Curiosity Shop.*

Illustration 26

Illustration 27

Illustration 28

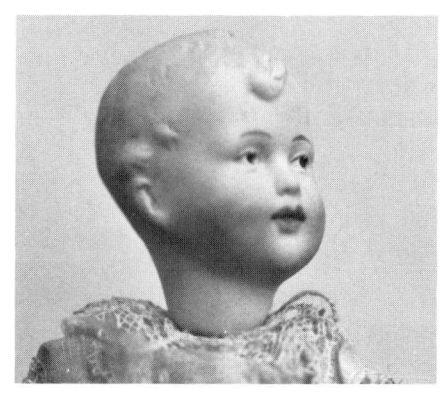

Illustration 29. This fellow is just 7½in (19.1cm) tall, but for such a small doll he has a lot of molding detail in his features. His eyes are done the typical Heubach way. The eyebrows are just one brush stroke. The lips are puffy, and he has deep cheek dimples. He is a miniature version of the two larger dolls in Illustrations 26 through 28! Even his hair is molded in exactly the same way. Unfortunately, he has a terrible body, a powdery papier-mâché torso and arms and legs which are not much better. He is, however, wearing his original shift. He is marked with the square mark only. As is the case with many of the small dolls, he does not have a mold number included. Obviously there would have been no place to put it, as this is what he actually has. *H&J Foulke.*

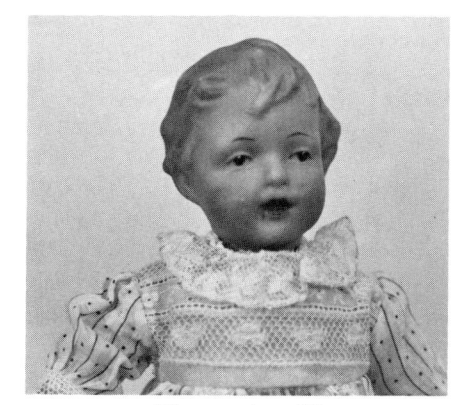

$$\frac{5}{0} \, D$$
• ☐ 1Z

Germany

Illustration 29

Illustration 30

Illustration 30. Little girls with molded hair, with the exception of the "Coquette" dolls, are much more rare than the little boys. It seems that most of the dolls used as girls had wigs. But here is a sweet, pensive little 10in (25.4cm) girl. She is marked with the square mark and 9167. She has the curly, yet wispy hair of a toddler, and fairly small eyes. Sometimes it is difficult to decide whether these short-haired dolls are boys or girls, but I think she is a girl. She is on a papier-mâché body of not very good quality. *H&J Foulke.*

The next group of pictures presents the pensive-faced Heubach babies. These are quite easily found and must have been made by the millions! Most of them are in the smaller sizes, and probably only sold for 10 or 15 cents when they were new. These have no mold numbers, simply a square mark, but a baby with this same face has been recorded as mold number 7602.

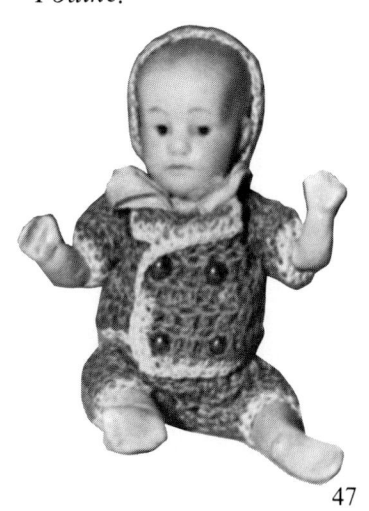

Illustration 32. Certainly the tiniest Heubach baby we have seen is this little 4½in (11.5cm) one. He just fits in the palm of my hand. It is easy to imagine a little girl's delight in such a doll. On the tiny babies, the heads are bald with hair brush-stroked on. The eyebrows are a simple one-stroke, but the eyes and mouth are nicely done. He is on a five-piece bent-limb baby body. His clothes appear to be original. *Mackemull Collection.*

Illustration 31. This somber-faced fellow is a frequently-found Heubach boy, sometimes as a socket head, but this one is a shoulder head on a very nice cloth body with composition hands. These bodies are generally not as popular with collectors as they are harder to pose and display than the composition ball-jointed bodies. This fellow is marked with the sunburst and 6692. He provides a good link to the next section as this face was also used for the baby dolls. *H&J Foulke.*

Illustration 33. This Heubach baby is 6in (15.2cm) and is the same mold as the doll in Illustration 32, but this one has been given the flocked hair, fuzzy to the touch. He is on a five-piece baby body of poor quality, but he does have his original chemise. *Ruby K. Arnold.*

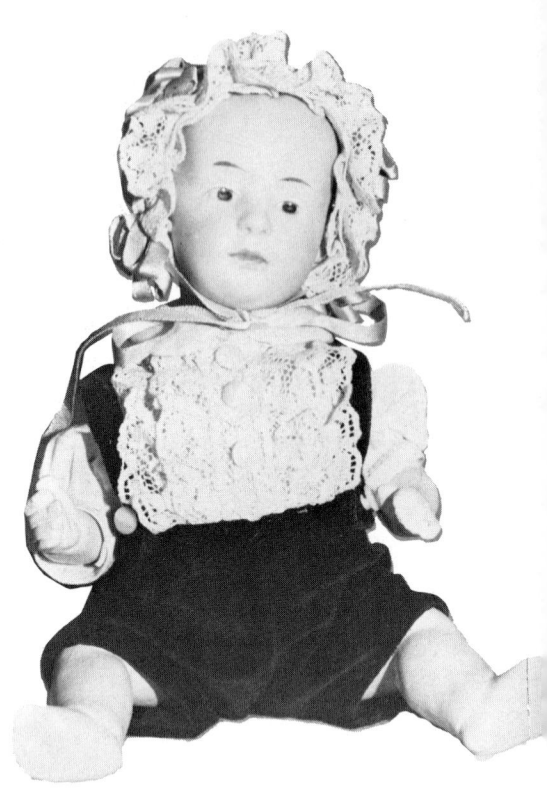

Illustration 35. This 8in (20.3cm) baby is fatter of face than the previous babies. He is on an excellent bent-limb baby body, and was probably a more expensive doll. This head also came on a jointed composition body and could be dressed as a little boy. He has no mold number but a similar baby is recorded as number 9578. *Mackemull Collection.*

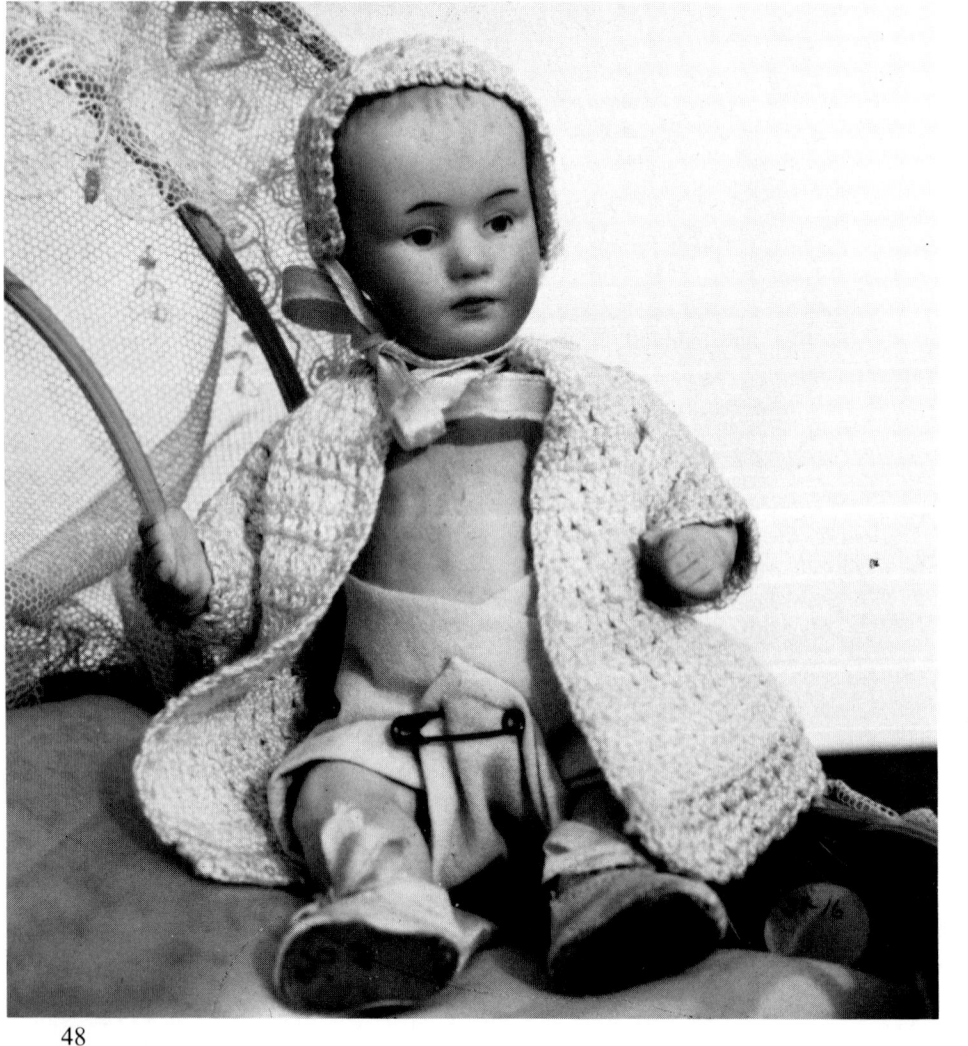

Illustration 34. This 6½in (16.5cm) Heubach baby has a very good quality body and is in his original clothes: a pink and white crocheted coat and hat, diaper and tiny leather shoes. He also has an additional coat and hat. This doll is one of a pair of identical twins from the same family who owned the pair of 6969 pouties. *H&J Foulke.*

48

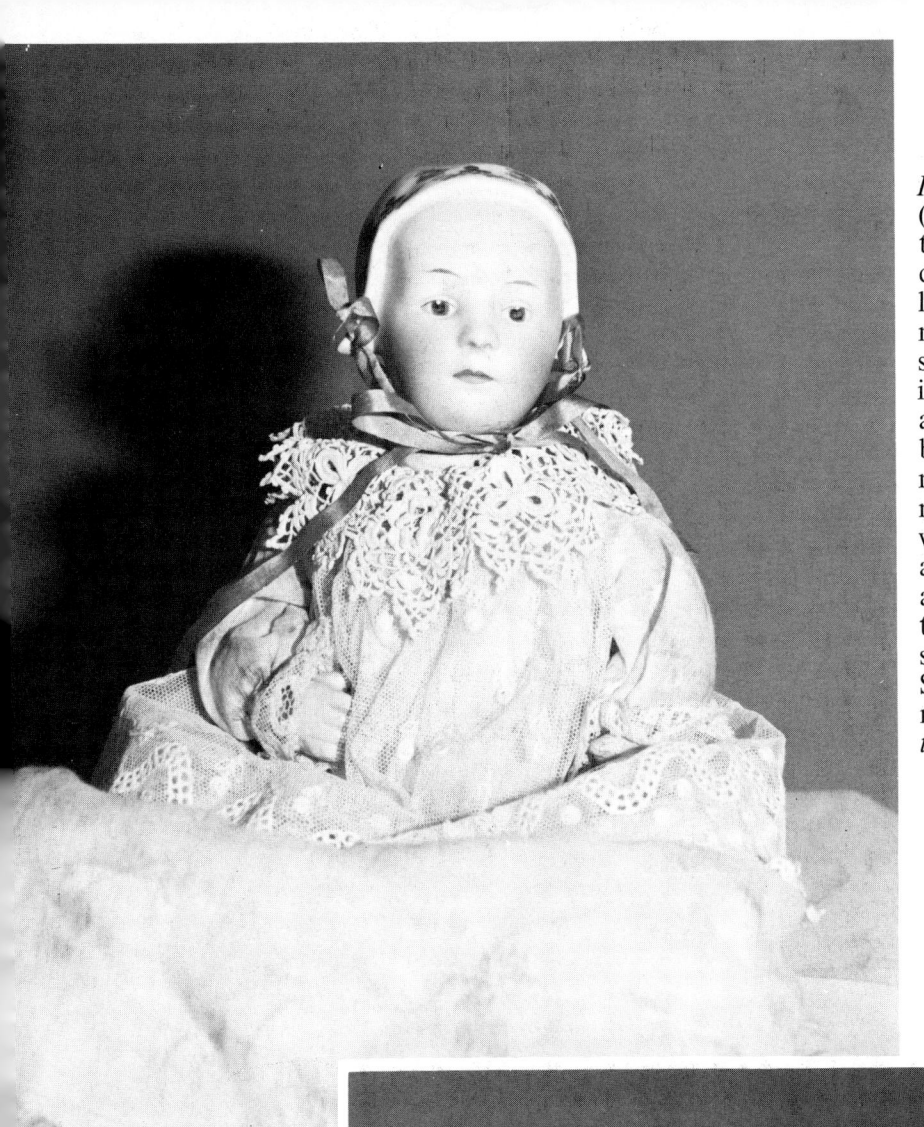

Illustration 36. This lovely 9in (22.9cm) baby, referred to by collectors as the "Stuart Baby," is a very desirable Heubach doll. It is also a link between the figurines with the molded hats and the dolls. It must surely have been the figurines which inspired this concept in doll making, although beginning around 1890 the bisque shoulder head ladies with molded hats were very popular. The molded bonnet of this baby is white with a trim of painted pink flowers and green leaves. Holes are pierced at the sides of the cap for the insertion of ribbon ties. Her face is the standard Heubach pouty baby one. She is marked with a sunburst, but no mold number. *Mackemull Collection.*

Illustration 37. Another 9in (22.9cm) Stuart Baby is positioned so that the flowers on her hat can be more clearly seen. She is also on a bent-limb baby body and is impressed with a sunburst and 7977. *Old Curiosity Shop.*

Illustration 39

Illustration 38

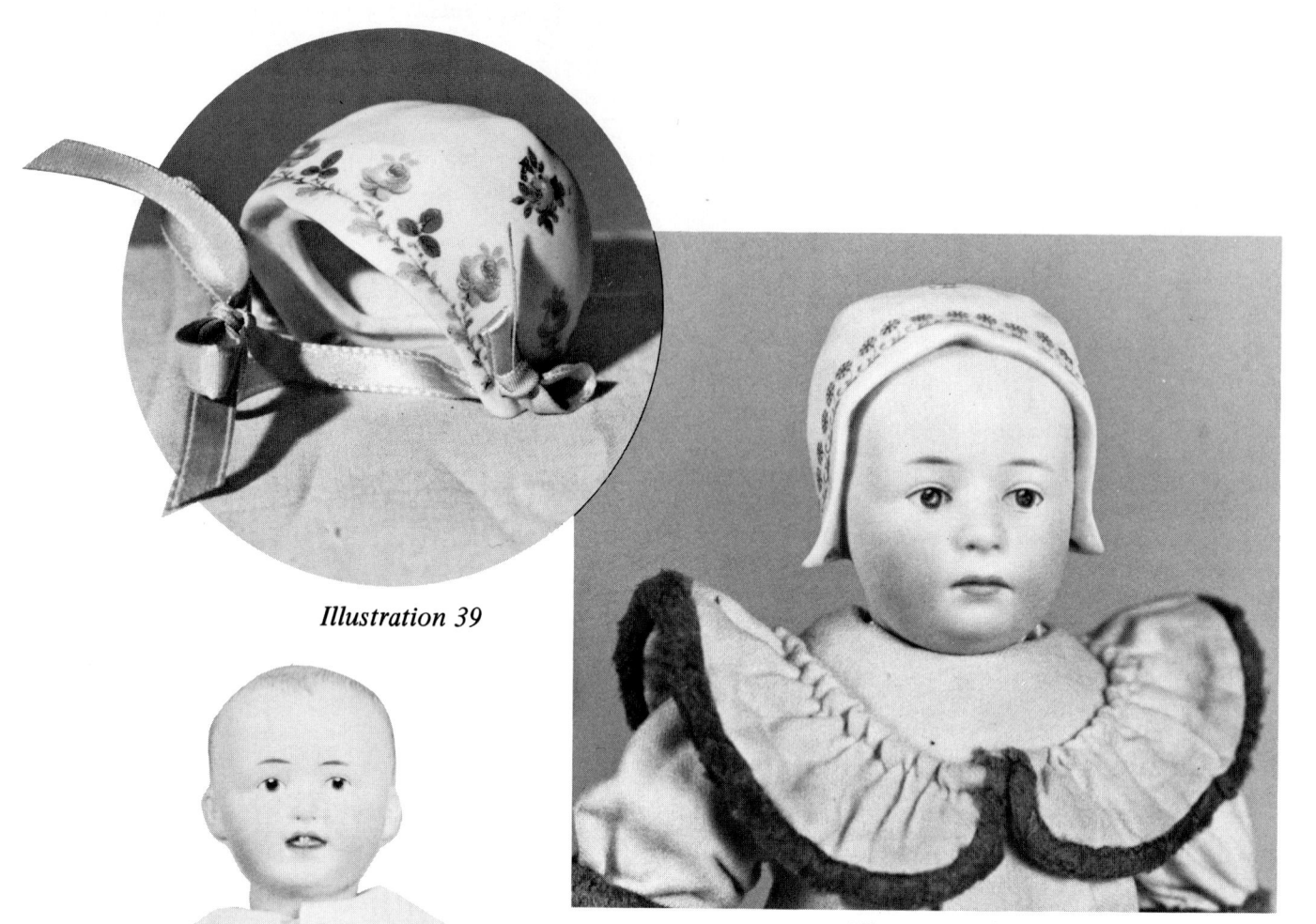

Illustration 40

Illustration 38. This 14in (35.6cm) Stuart Baby also has the mold number 7977, and is the same as the others except that the flower trim on her hat is different; it is a border of tiny blue flowers with green leaves. *Richard Wright Collection.*

Illustration 39. A rare glass-eyed version of the Stuart Baby has a removable bisque cap like this one to allow for the setting of the glass eyes. Maybe someday the doll which goes with this cap will turn up! *Mackemull Collection.*

Illustration 40. I was not quite sure in which section to place this boy, since he is not smiling, and I am not sure that he is pouting either. But he certainly is being impudent with his tongue sticking out between his lips, and he surely is unusual for a Heubach doll. His head has little evidence of molded hair at all, just brush strokes to indicate that he is not really bald. He has a very high and wide forehead. His eyebrows are just one stroke. His most unusual feature is his mouth with the tongue resting on his lips and the two upper painted teeth. He is 14in (35.6cm) tall on a very good jointed composition body, and is impressed with a square mark and 8878. *Richard Wright Collection.*

Smiling Children

Many Heubach dolls are just brimming over with the happiness and laughter of life, and a good sampling of these faces is pictured. Of course the term *smiling character* brings to mind primarily the multitude of character babies created by the average German doll company. Cute, yes, but generally of a run-of-the-mill type of smiling face. However, the creations of the Heubach Brothers are distinctively different. Nearly all of them look like some little boy or girl that we once knew or saw.

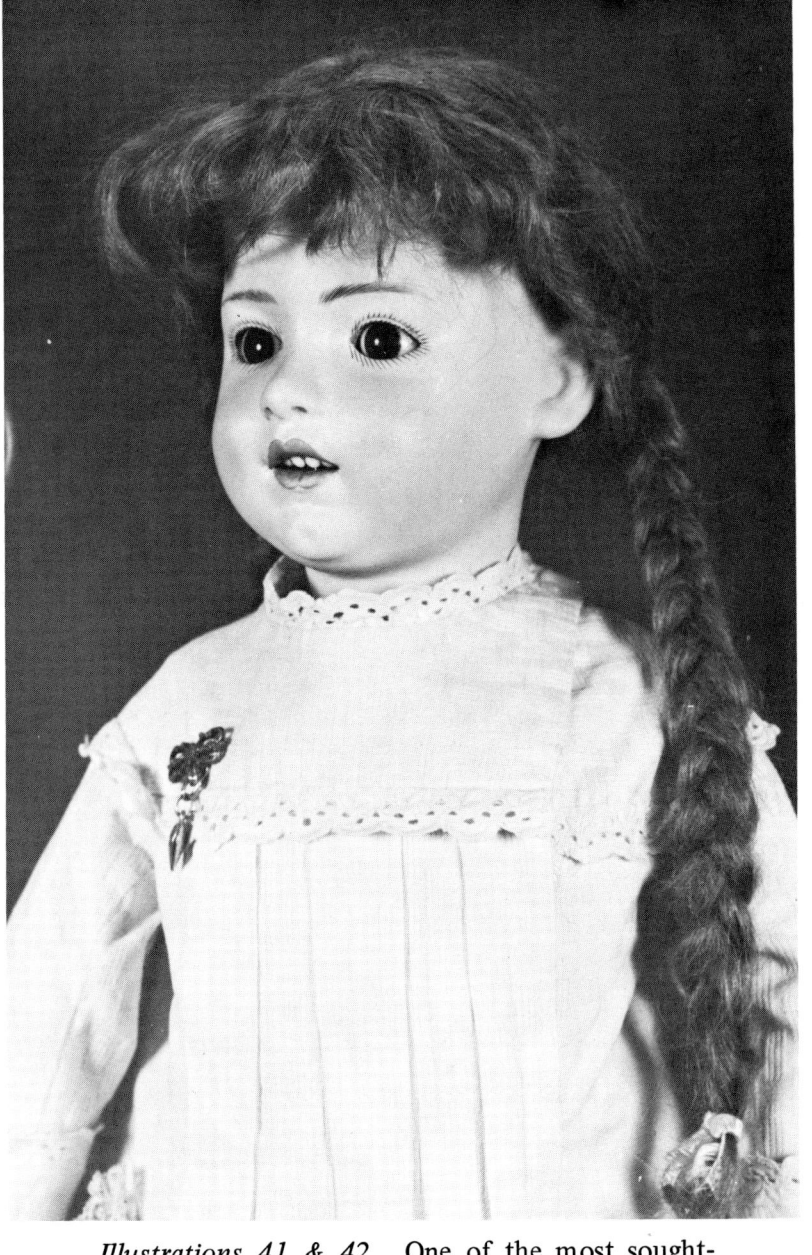

Illustrations 41 & 42. One of the most sought-after smiling Heubach girls is incised on the back of her head "Dolly Dimple." And, indeed, she is a charming dolly with three very deep dimples. Her lovely eyes radiate happiness; her lips are parted just as though she were ready to burst out telling about her latest adventure. There are very nice details in the decoration of her eyebrows and her lips which are attractively painted with shading on the lower one. Even her ears are quite pronounced. This particular "Dolly Dimple" is 21in (53.3cm) tall, on a very good ball-jointed composition body. She is impressed with the sunburst and 5777 in addition to her name. A very similar character doll is shown in the March 1908 *Playthings* in an ad by Samstag & Hilder Bros. who imported German dolls and toys. The doll in the ad is distinctive for her large eyes, a more open mouth than was usual at the time and shading on the lower lip. If she is a Heubach, this again puts this company early into the manufacture of character dolls. In *Playthings* February 1911, an article on dolls mentions a "Dolly Dimples" [sic] doll, a laughing beauty and further notes that the "youthful radiance of these faces is particularly charming." *Sheila Needle Collection. Photograph by Morton Needle.*

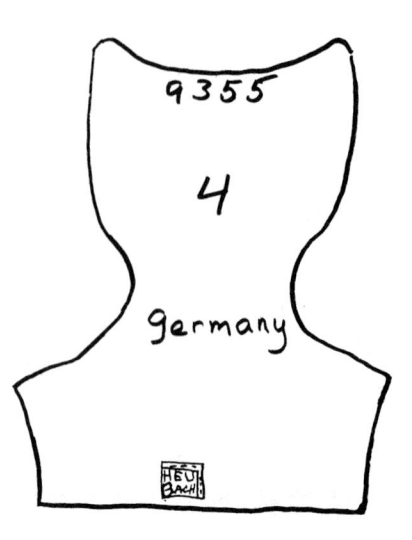

Illustrations 43 & 44. This 18in (45.7cm) girl appears to be another use of the "Dolly Dimple" face, this time as a shoulder head on a real kid body. The molding is the same as the doll in Illustrations 41 and 42, and several features can be noted in this front view which were not so easily seen on the first doll. The nose is rather wide and short, and there is a very distinctive double chin. However, the painting of the mouth is entirely different; the lips are not as full as those on the other doll, and the bottom one lacks the shading detail. This doll is marked with a square and the numbers 9355, but she is not incised "Dolly Dimple" and was perhaps made for a different company. Her present owner found her in an old toy store still tied in her original box. She is wearing her original blonde mohair wig with a bow in her hair and her original shoes and socks. Of course, many dolls were sold unclad to be dressed at home. Her brown sleep eyes are accented with beautiful blonde eyelashes. The line drawings by the owner show her markings and the label on her original box. She appears to be the doll which is advertised on page 4 of the *1914 Marshall Field & Company* catalog, except that her knee joint is different. The doll's wholesale price was $13.50 per dozen. She was listed as a doll with character face, dimpled cheeks, moving eyes and kid body. *Jilda Sallade Collection.*

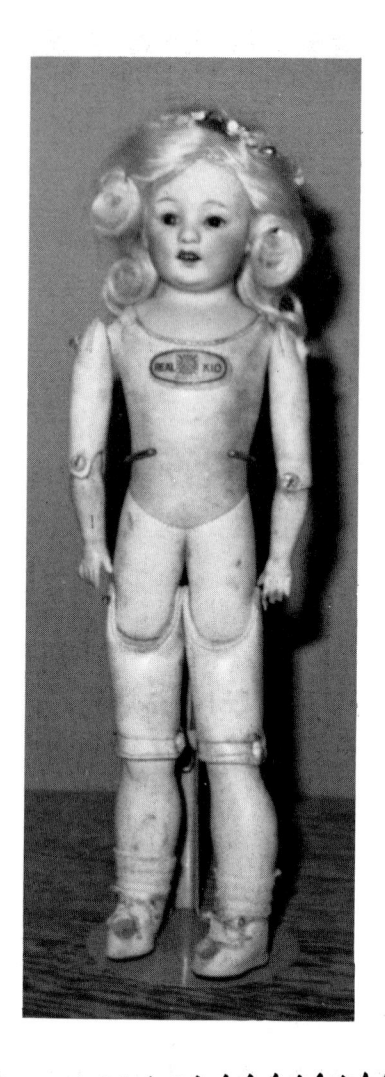

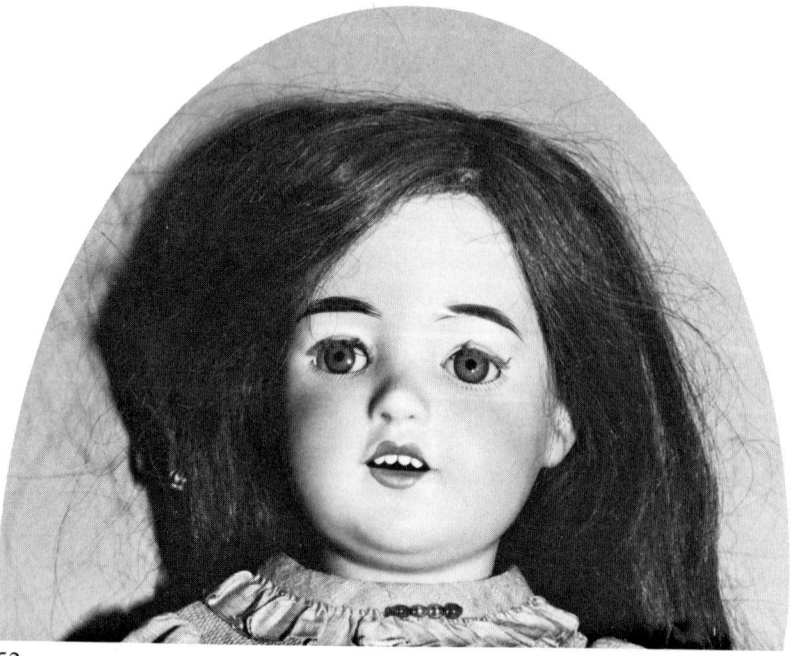

LEFT: Illustration 45. Obviously a relative of the two girls in Illustrations 41 through 44 is this 20in (50.8cm) doll incised "Santa" and the Heubach sunburst. She is indeed a rarity. A similarity can be seen in the full lips of the mouth, although the "Santa" has no shading on the lower lip, and in the smiling blue sleep eyes and eye lashes. But the dimples are conspicuously absent on "Santa," and the nose is not so wide across the bridge. Her eyebrows are thick and very glossy, a departure from the usual feathery treatment used by the Heubach artists. *Old Curiosity Shop.*

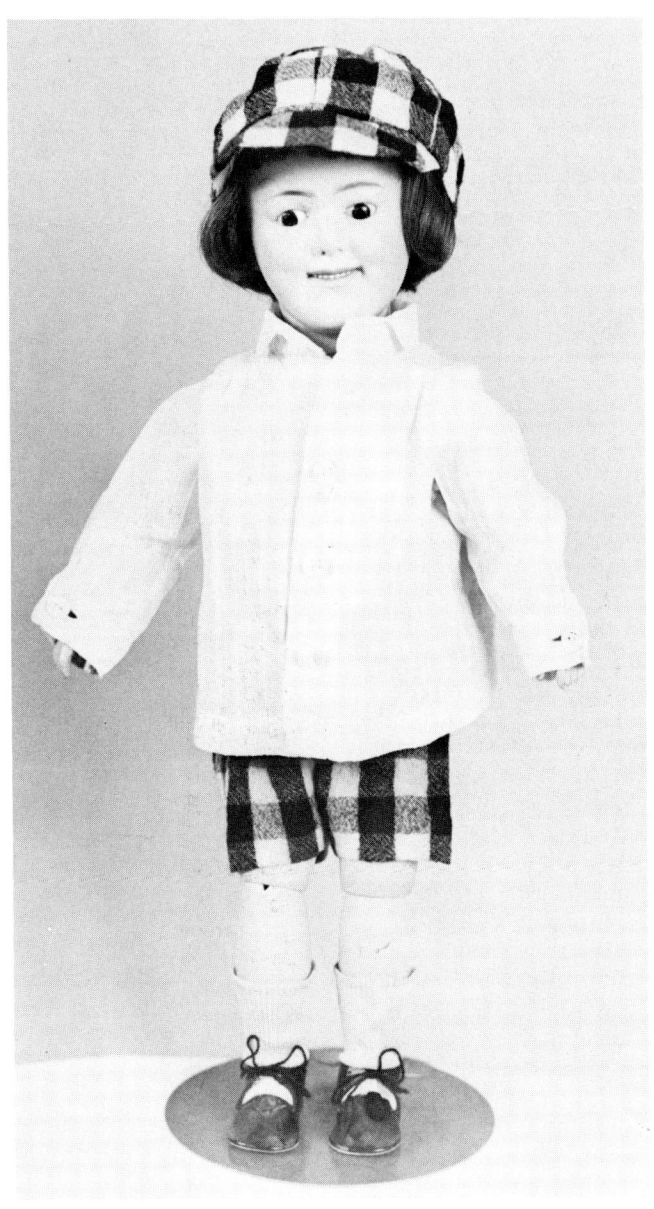

Illustration 46

Illustration 47

Illustrations 46 & 47. One of the most rare of the Heubach characters with glass eyes is this grinning boy incised with a square mark and 8316. He is 17in (43.2cm) tall on an all-wood jointed body. The fact that one of his eyes has been set in at an off-angle certainly contributes to his mischievous look. Most spectacular, however, is his broad mouth with a row of seven enameled teeth. His dark eyes and hair give good contrast to the lovely flesh coloring of his face. Obviously he is an older child than many of the Heubachs, judging by his features. His nose is sharper, he has no double chin and his lower face is thinner. *Richard Wright Collection.*

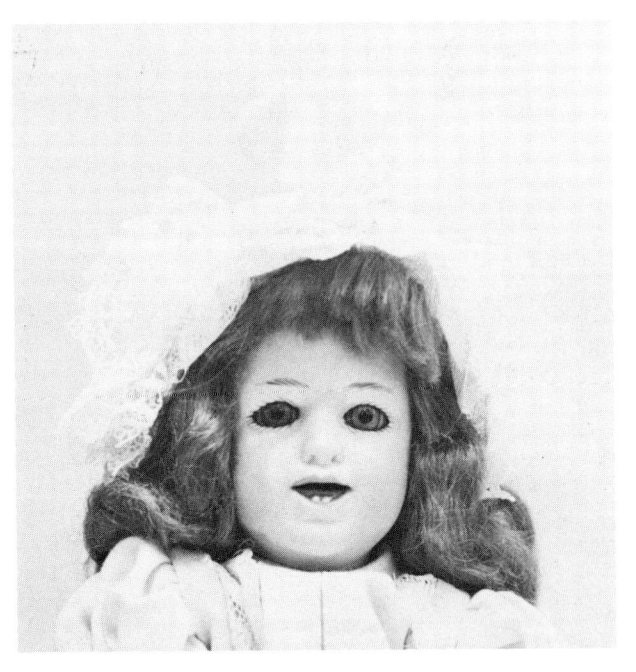

Illustration 48. There are probably more Heubach variations of this "laughing child" than any other Heubach mold. Apparently this was a very popular style for them, with the molded, fairly wide open/closed mouth and the two lower molded teeth. This particular little girl has the sunburst mark and mold number 5636. Her large blue eyes give her a very intelligent look. She has a chubby lower face with a double chin. Just 11in (27.9cm) tall, she is on a very good ball-jointed composition body. *Gail Hiatt Collection.*

53

Illustration 49. Here is a little girl with the same happy face, as the doll in Illustration 48, this time in a smaller 8½in (21.6cm) size on a chubby toddler body. She has no mold number but is impressed with the square mark. *Richard Wright Collection.*

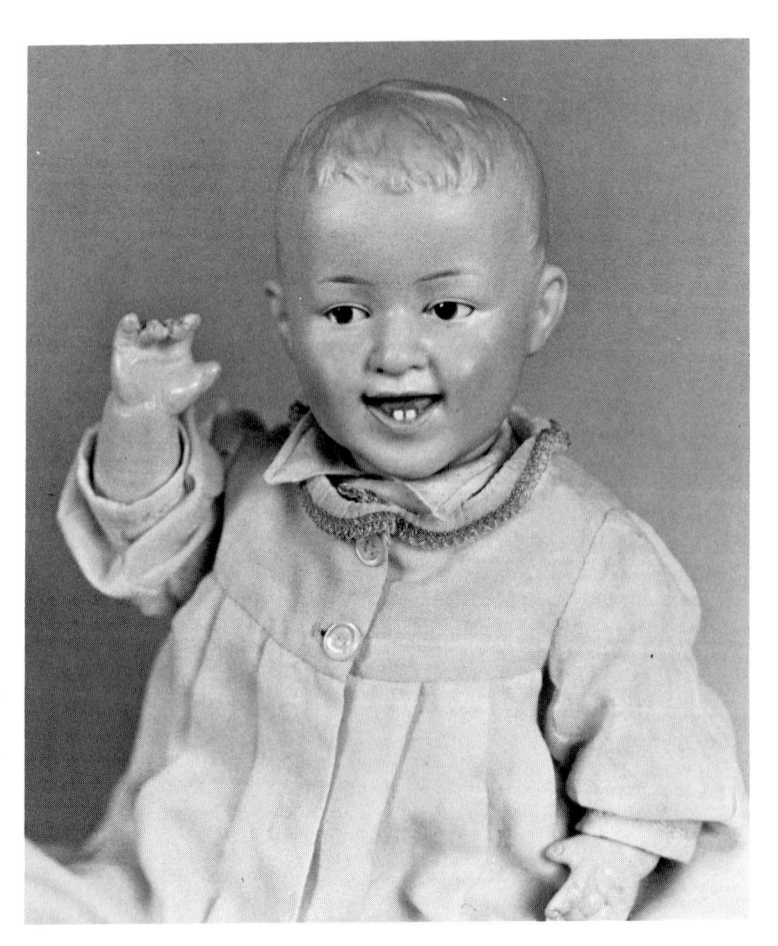

ABOVE: Illustration 50. At first glance this boy looks like the same mold as the two girls in Illustrations 48 and 49, but closer inspection shows that his mouth is not nearly so broad and that his bottom lip is lower. This, of course, makes him thinner through the lower face than the girls; his dimples are more pronounced. He is 14in (35.6cm) tall, on an excellent composition jointed body. His clothes are possibly original. Unfortunately, he has no mold number, but he does have the sunburst mark. *Richard Wright Collection.*

Smiling Dolls with Intaglio Eyes

LEFT: Illustration 51. The molding on this 16in (40.6cm) happy, smiling baby has to be recognized for its outstanding attention to detail. This is basically the same face as the preceding doll's, except that this one has deeply incised dark intaglio eyes and molded blonde hair with just enough raised portion to softly frame his face. He is on a five-piece toddler body of good quality and is marked with the round green "Made in Germany" stamp as well as a green stamped 28. *Richard Wright Collection.*

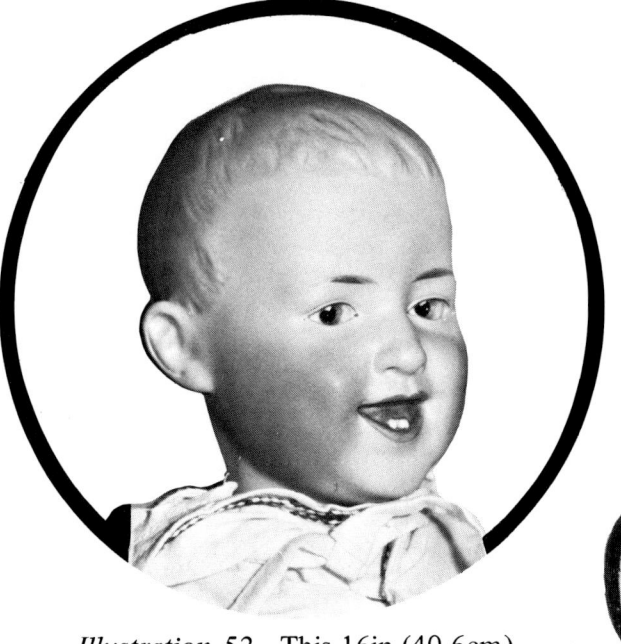

Illustration 52. This 16in (40.6cm) boy is of the same mold as the doll in Illustration 51, but this side view gives a better look at the molding of the ear and hair. It also is an interesting angle from which to look at the intaglio eyes; one can see how depth was achieved, especially in his left eye. He is on a jointed toddler body and marked with a sunburst. A doll of apparently identical mold has been reported with a 6897 number. *Old Curiosity Shop.*

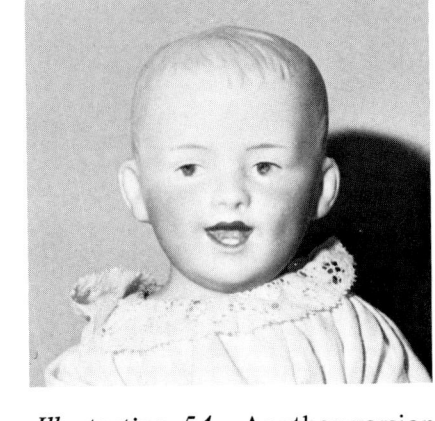

Illustration 54. Another version of these dolls occurs as a shoulder head which can be mounted on a cloth or kid body. Just 10in (25.4cm) tall, this boy is incised only with Germany, but an identical doll has a square mark and the mold number 6736. *Old Curiosity Shop.*

Illustration 53. A member of the same family, but his mouth is not so wide open, is this 9½in (24.2cm) boy with the same two lower teeth! His eyes do not show up as well because they are a light color. However, his deep dimples are very noticeable. He is incised with a sunburst and 7604. *Old Curiosity Shop.*

Illustration 55. This 6½in (16.5cm) baby appears to be a much younger version of the previous laughing dolls. Not only does he have less hair and a rounder face, he was also probably a cheaper model, as he does not have the detail of modeling for which Heubach is known. He is on a papier-mâché baby body of inferior quality, but does appear to be wearing his original clothes. These are apparently the dolls which Heubach mass produced for the cheaper market and probably retailed for 10 or 15 cents. *Richard Wright Collection.*

55

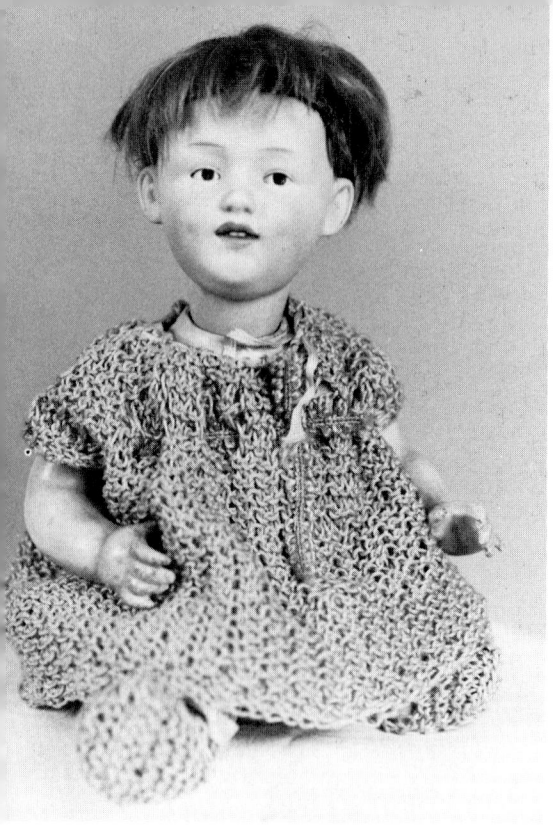

Illustration 57. This small sweet-faced baby is 10½in (26.7cm) long, on a body of papier-mâché which certainly does not match the quality of his head. His mouth is a departure from the preceding dolls since he does not have molded teeth. Instead, he has a little tongue which sticks out between his lips. He is wearing his original chemise and is impressed with a square mark and 7971 or 7911. *Ruth Noden Collection.*

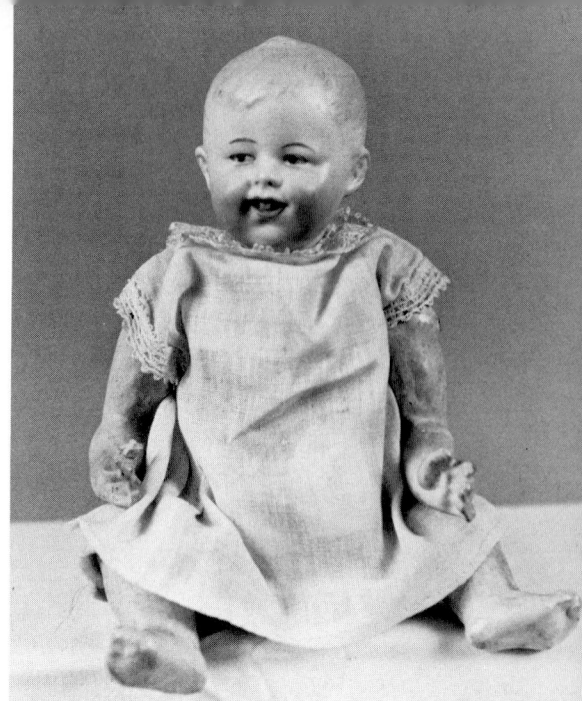

Illustration 56. This fellow has quite a few departures from the previous dolls. The most prominent is his wig. One would just expect him to have molded hair, judging from experiences with Heubach dolls. I have been calling this doll a boy, but perhaps it is a girl, as she does have on a knit blue dress which is perhaps original. I like the prominent ears on this doll, and the fact that the mouth is more closed, instead of so wide open. She has the ubiquitous two molded teeth and the deep cheek dimples. She is 10½in (26.7cm) tall, on a fairly nice composition baby body. High on her crown is her mold number 7307. *Richard Wright Collection.*

Illustration 58. Again, we are getting back to the teeth, but this time the boy has two rows in a fairly wide-open mouth. He has a pleasant look with side-glancing eyes, yet I do not think he qualifies for the googly section which must have some special quality about the face other than simply side-glancing eyes. This boy is 14in (35.6cm) tall and is a shoulder head doll, marked simply with a Heubach square. Another doll of this same mold has the number 8306. *Old Curiosity Shop.*

Illustration 59. This head appears to be a younger version of the one in Illustration 58. This doll does not have as much hair, although it is in the same style. He also has only upper teeth, although these do not show up well in the photo. He is just 9in (22.9cm) tall, on a jointed composition body and is impressed with a square mark and 8191. *Old Curiosity Shop.*

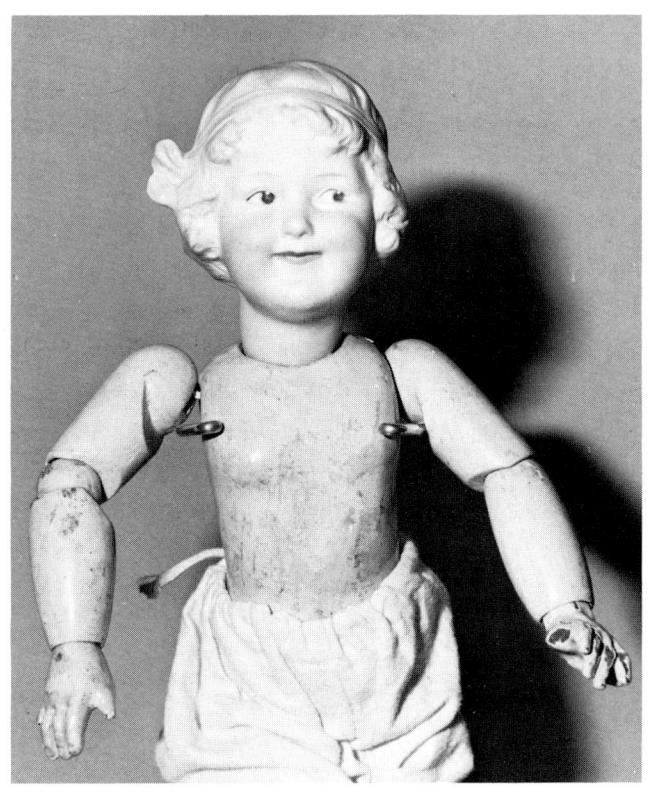

Illustration 60. The best known of the Heubach girls, perhaps because she is the most easily recognizable is the "Coquette," which is found in fair abundance. Her blonde hair has masses of lovely short curls in the latest fashion of the day, and her head is surrounded by a ribbon which is usually painted turquoise. She has an unmistakably flirtatious look with her lips pressed together in mirth as though she is trying to stifle a giggle at an inappropriate time. Her side-glancing eyes only contribute to her coquettish look. This particular doll is shown on her French ball-jointed composition and wood body. Enough Heubachs have been found on French bodies to substantiate the theory that French producers bought the German heads for their dolls. She is impressed with a square mark and 7788. *Old Curiosity Shop.*

BELOW: *Illustration 61.* Here is a 12in (30.5cm) "Coquette" shown from a different angle. She is on a German jointed composition body and is wearing clothes which are possibly original. She is also incised with a square mark and 7788. Judging from the numbers of these dolls available, it must have been a very popular model. *Old Curiosity Shop.*

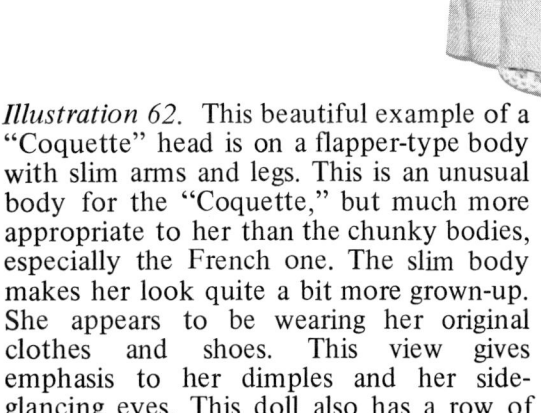

Illustration 62. This beautiful example of a "Coquette" head is on a flapper-type body with slim arms and legs. This is an unusual body for the "Coquette," but much more appropriate to her than the chunky bodies, especially the French one. The slim body makes her look quite a bit more grown-up. She appears to be wearing her original clothes and shoes. This view gives emphasis to her dimples and her side-glancing eyes. This doll also has a row of painted teeth which the other two "Coquettes" lack. Her head is marked with a sunburst and 7763. Another "Coquette" has been reported with a mold number of 7768, and at this point we are not sure whether there were three different mold numbers or whether the numbers might have been recorded incorrectly as sometimes they are very difficult to read. This doll also comes as a shoulder head which is shown in the introductory section. *Mackemull Collection.*

57

"Bonnie Babe"

Nearly everyone is familiar with "Bonnie Babe" created by Georgene Averill in 1926. The famous Averill baby, almost ugly in its reality, is a popular collector's item. Attached to a cloth body with composition arms and legs, the solid dome head has wisps of molded hair. The forehead is broad and high; the ears stick out; the open mouth is fairly large with a tongue and two teeth. "Bonnie Babe" has dimples on her chubby cheeks and, of course, two chins. The "Bonnie Babe" made all of bisque is a darling toddler doll, with swivel neck and joints at hips and shoulders. Her hair is deeply molded, and she has tiny glass eyes which open and close. Of course, she also has the unmistakable dimples and chubby cheeks, as well as an open mouth with two lower teeth. However, there is another version of "Bonnie Babe" which is very rarely found, and unless you have a sharp eye for faces, you might entirely overlook her as a "Bonnie Babe." This is the rare wigged version which was produced as a socket head on a chubby composition body with molded shoes and socks, the same type of body which is used for the googly dolls. This "Bonnie Babe" has the same little face that is on the all-bisque doll, just as cute and darling! The first of these dolls I acquired is dressed like a little girl. She is 7in (17.8cm) tall with a blonde mohair wig and brown sleep eyes. She is marked with the mold number 1393 high at the crown, and at first I thought she was a Heubach, but now I feel that she is probably not a Heubach because of the low number sequence, and because the numbers are not impressed like Heubach numbers and the Germany is written in a different manner. Possibly she is by Alt, Beck, and Gottschalk who made some of the larger "Bonnie Babe" dolls. However, the second one of these wigged little ones was a treasure because he is clearly incised with the Heubach square mark. Also up high on his crown opening are the numbers 12386. His coloring and decoration are different from that of the little girl, suggesting a different manufacturer as well as a different decorator, but the mold is identical. The bodies are identical, suggesting that perhaps the distributor, in this case, George Borgfeldt, ordered heads from two different manufacturers.

LEFT: Illustration 63. This is a 7in (17.8cm) wigged "Bonnie Babe" incised 1393. Her bisque is quite pale with very rosy cheeks; her eyebrows are very pale with a smudged look. Her eyelashes are very lightly applied. She has the typical "Bonnie Babe" mouth, although she is lacking her teeth. She also has dimples and a cute pug nose. Her lip color is muted. She has a papier-mâché toddler body with painted shoes and socks. *Jan Foulke Collection.*

RIGHT: Illustration 64. Here is an 8in (20.3cm) wigged "Bonnie Babe" impressed with the Heubach square mark and numbers 12386. He has a pinker overall complexion and rosy cheeks. His eyebrows are very light, but painted in one definitive stroke. His eyelashes are heavily applied in the Heubach manner while the lip color is bright. He has the "Bonnie Babe" mouth with two tiny lower teeth. His dimples are there, but are not so pronounced as hers. *Jan Foulke Collection.*

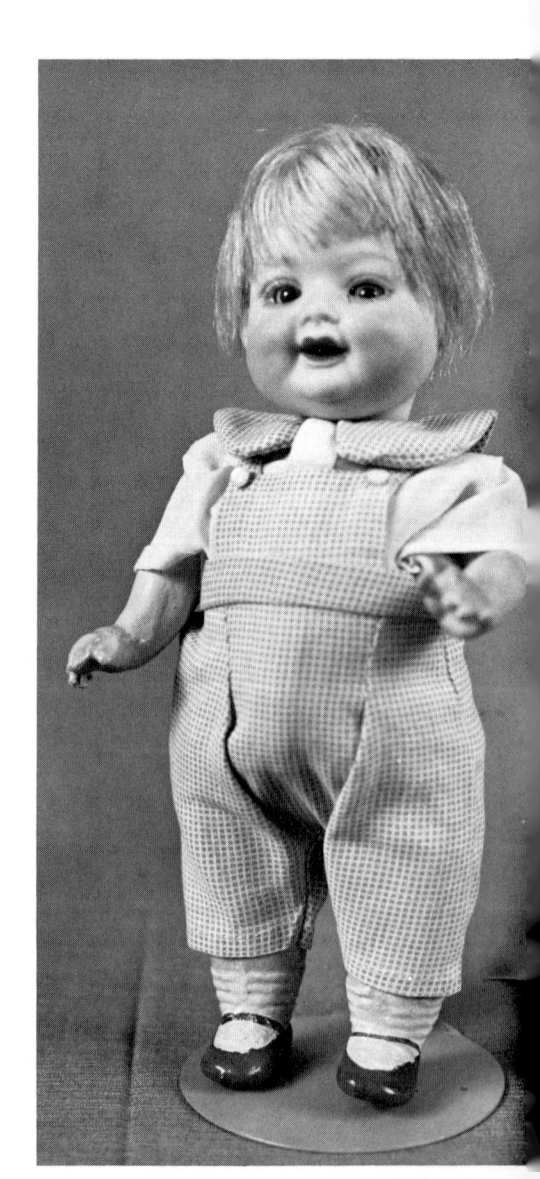

12386
$\frac{3}{0}$
□
Germany

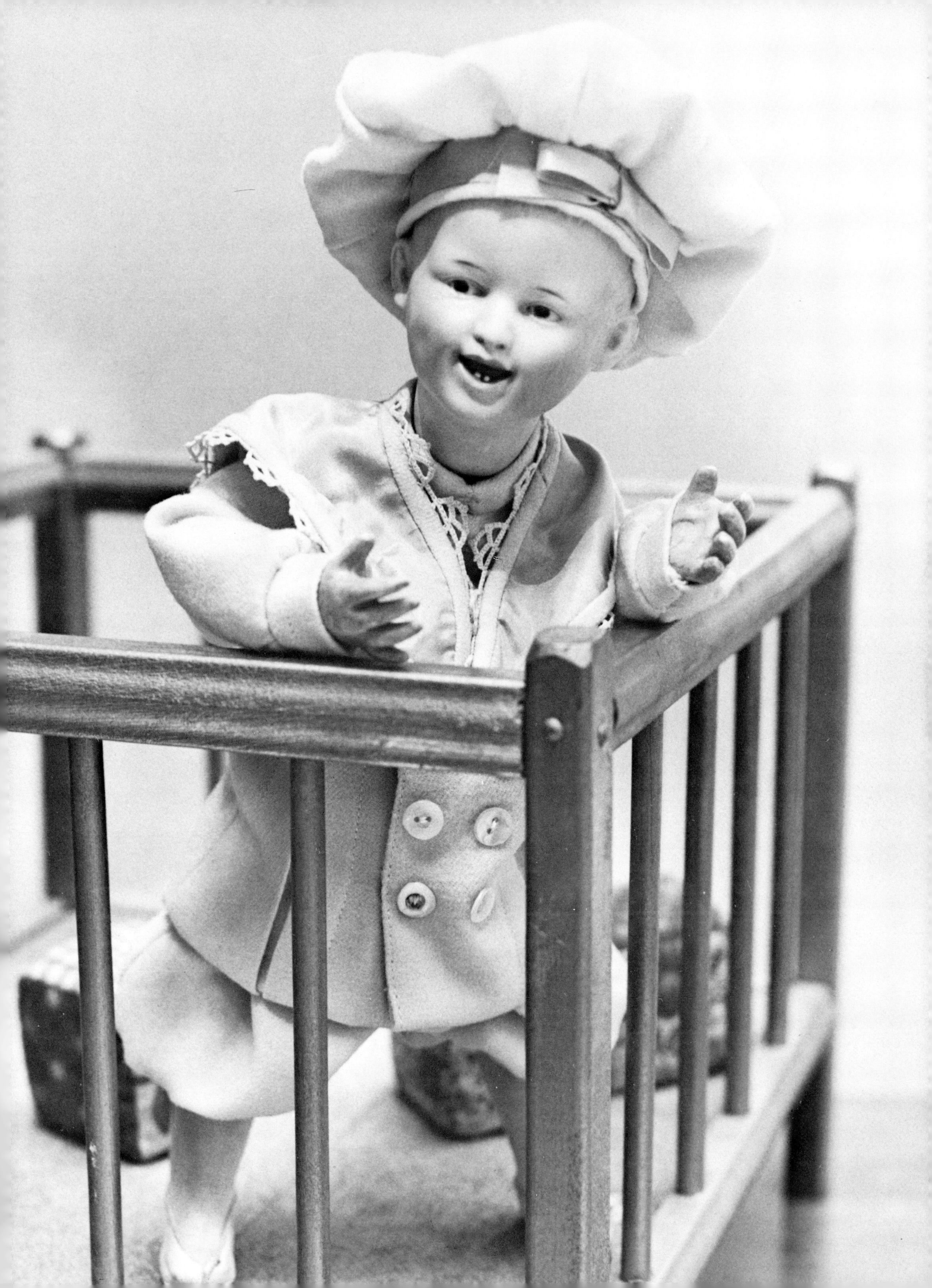

Mechanical Dolls

Dolls that do things are not at all modern inventions. Dolls have been doing things for over a hundred years. There is always a certain fascination about seeing a doll in motion or making some sort of noise, and apparently these types of dolls have always been popular novelty items. Of course, Heubach probably made only the heads for these dolls, the bodies made and the doll assembled by another company or distributor.

Illustrations 65A, 65B & 65C. Again, here is a problem in classifying Heubach heads. One would expect this doll to be of the same mold number as the one in Illustration 68, but not so. He is incised with a sunburst and 7604. A nice large 12in (30.5cm) size, large at least for these mechanical Heubachs, he has the same smiling face with intaglio eyes, pronounced dimples in his cheeks and very nice molding of mouth, lips and teeth. His socket head fits into the mechanical body. When he is wound, he walks first on one leg, then on the other; as he toddles from side to side, he also swivels from the waist. He does look a little ridiculous, but fun nonetheless. *Gail Hiatt Collection.*

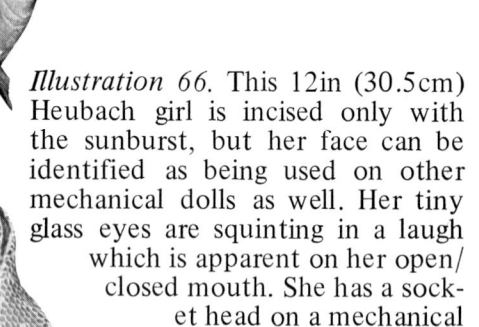

Illustration 66. This 12in (30.5cm) Heubach girl is incised only with the sunburst, but her face can be identified as being used on other mechanical dolls as well. Her tiny glass eyes are squinting in a laugh which is apparent on her open/closed mouth. She has a socket head on a mechanical body. Unfortunately all of what is going on cannot be seen in the photograph, as she is trying to ward off a dog by keeping the chair between the two of them. I am not sure she should be smiling; perhaps she should look frightened! *Old Curiosity Shop.*

Illustration 68. This little doll has a mechanism in its cardboard cone. When she is wound, she goes forward; at the same time she moves from side to side at the waist and waves her hands up and down. She is in her original clothes and altogether presents a most interesting concept of a baby, but one which would be fairly limited as far as child's play is concerned. Her socket head is incised with a square mark and 7314. She is almost like the "Pat-a-Cake Baby," but on close inspection, her mouth looks a little different in shape. She was available at the wholesale price of $9.00 per dozen in the *1914 Marshall Field & Company* catalog. *Ruth Noden Collection.*

Illustration 67. This "Pat-a-Cake, Pat-a-Cake Baby" is all original and in working order. He still has his cap with a printed band that identifies him. His action is simple, but cute. When his stomach is pressed, he pats his hands together. This was a type of action often found on old toys, especially clowns with cymbals in their hands. This doll has a stock Heubach shoulder head of the so-called laughing boy with molded hair, intaglio eyes and an open mouth with two lower molded teeth. It must have been a fairly popular head as it is found quite often. This 8in (20.3cm) baby is incised with a square mark and 6736. It is easy to see why such a laughing happy face would be attractive to buyers. Also, it was probably a fairly inexpensive face as it did not have inset eyes or teeth, needed no wig and was a shoulder head which was easier to mount than a socket head. *Mackemull Collection.*

Illustration 70. "Whistling Jim" has his original tag still on him, so we know just who he is. His lips are pursed with a hole through them. When the bellows in his chest is pressed, one hears a very realistic whistle from him! Jim has a flange neck on a pink cloth body with composition arms. He is impressed with a square mark and 8774. His coloring is very natural with nice rosy cheeks. His eyes are deeply incised with painted blue and white dot highlights. His eyebrows are put on in one stroke; his hair is dark blonde, a typical Heubach light coloring. He is wearing completely original clothing, a blue romper suit, lacy socks and imitation leather shoes. A penciled note on the back of his tag dates him for us: "Christmas 1915, From Clara." He was still being offered, or perhaps offered again would be better, since the war caused a cessation of the doll business, in the 1924 Montgomery Ward catalog. By that time he was called "Tom." The ad reads: "Can you whistle? Tom can. Just press his chest and hear him give a fine, loud, boyish whistle. Tom is a good little chap with which to amuse baby." His cost was 89 cents plus 6 cents postage! *Jan Foulke Collection.*

Illustration 69. The face of the 12in (30.5cm) boy matches that of the girl in Illustration 66. His eyelashes are more pronounced and emphasize his tiny glass eyes. Both of the dolls have beautifully painted eyebrows, done in tiny little strokes. The boy, when wound, walks along pulling his cart. *Old Curiosity Shop.*

Googlies

The imps of the doll world, the googlies are very popular with collectors and have a wide-ranging appeal. Their prices are high because of their scarcity, as they are a later doll and, therefore, were made for a much shorter period of time as their production was interrupted by World War I in Europe.

Illustration 71. The most captivating of the Heubach googlies is this 14in (35.6cm) doll which can be made up as a boy or a girl. The eye sockets are perfectly round, and the eyes themselves can be moved to look in different directions by means of a wire lever. This is certainly one of the rarest of all googlies, by Heubach or any other maker. The impertinent face is achieved not only by the prominent eyes, but also by the mouth with a large bottom lip but a tiny upper lip, almost as though she were biting her top lip to keep her mouth closed. Of course, the chubbiness of the face and the little double chin add to her appeal. Her heavy eyebrows are quite high on her forehead and are long for the size of her face, but they are covered by her bangs in the photograph. She also has an impudent nose. All of her facial characteristics put together contribute to make her an amusing character. She has a five-piece toddler body of composition. Her head is incised with a square mark and "Einco," the trademark of Eisenmann & Co. for whom Heubach made this doll. It would date around 1911 to 1913. According to Carol Ann Stanton, it was part of the "Kiddieland" series. This doll has also been found as a shoulder head incised with mold number 8164 on a cloth body. *Richard Wright Collection.*

Illustrations 72 & 73. This googly girl has beautiful eyebrows, feathered with a myriad of tiny brushstrokes which appear on some of the Heubach dolls. They certainly show that great care was taken in her decoration as opposed to drawing just one line above each eye. Her eye sockets are large, but not as perfectly round as on the "Einco" googly, and her eyes are set to look to the side in a roguish manner. She has pronounced dimples on her chubby cheeks, and her lips are thin as though she is trying to suppress her smile. She is 13in (33.0cm) tall on a composition body and is incised with the square mark. Unfortunately, we were not able to obtain her mold number, if indeed she had one, as many of the Heubachs simply do not. Also, as Heubach mold numbers are done in very small letters up high on the back of the head at the crown opening, it is often difficult to determine just exactly what the numbers are, even with a magnifying glass, if they smear or do not print plainly. Sometimes, of course, they are covered with glue from the wig which makes the numbers impossible to read. *Richard Wright Collection.*

Illustration 74. Certainly a unique doll is this "winker," as I do not know of any other company which made one like this! This little doll has short molded hair and is more often made up as a roguish boy, although this little girl appears to have her original clothes, a gauze dress with red felt hat and coat. She has one blue glass eye and one eye closed, a raised eyebrow on the open eye and a down-slanting eyebrow on the closed eye. Her mouth is also raised on the left side. She is incised only with Germany done in the Heubach manner and is 8in (20.3cm) tall. *Mackemull Collection.*

Illustration 75. This illustration is from our files and goes back a long way so we were unable to obtain the information about the marks, but decided to show him anyway in contrast to the "winker" with the glass eye as this one has a painted eye, with very heavy eyelashes. The other eye is not really all the way closed, either. It is open just a wee amount to allow one to see just a tiny bit of the eyeball, mostly the white part, but just a speck of color in the far corner. He is 9½in (24.2cm) tall. Interestingly enough, a photograph of a Heubach doll on page 295 of the Colemans' *Collector's Encyclopedia of Dolls* appears to be of the same mold but with both eyes painted open, looking sideways and up. Other "winkers" have been reported with mold number 9141. *Richard Wright Collection.*

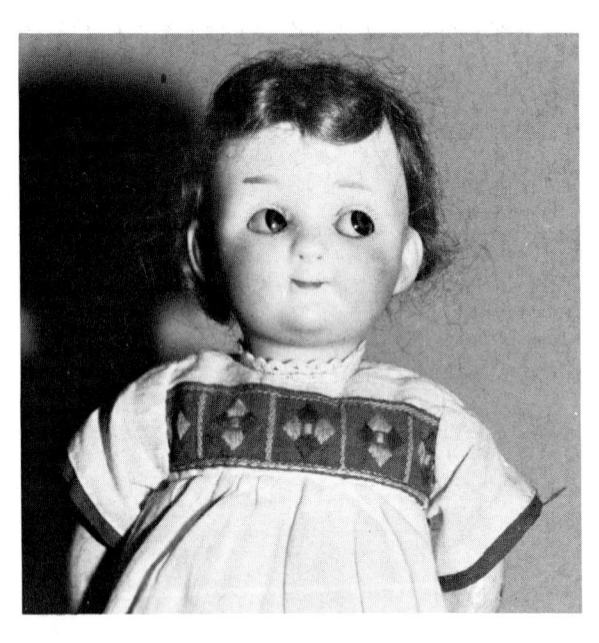

Illustration 77. A sister to the doll in Illustration 76, this one has the same mold number, but the artist treatment is a little different. The eyebrows are straight, yet feathered on the inside; the lower lip is not so wide. Also in this photograph the ears are prominently displayed, and they really stick out! Even the angle of her eyes is different. The whole doll goes to show how two faces from the same mold can be made to look different from each other. She is 9in (22.9cm) tall also, and on a papier-mâché googly body with painted shoes and socks. Her clothes appear original. *Old Curiosity Shop.*

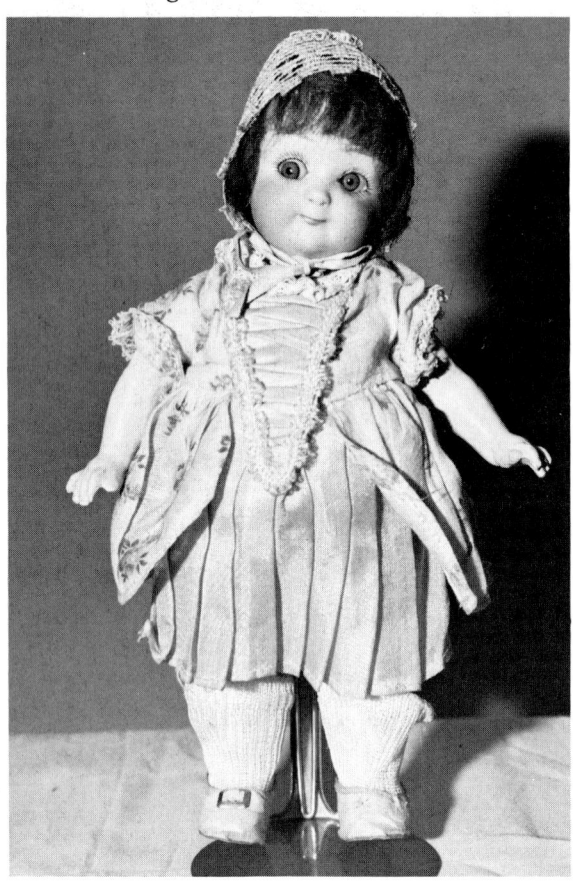

Illustration 76. This little Heubach googly appears more often than the others, but it does not diminish either her desirability or her appeal. Her little pug nose and her watermelon mouth as well as her side-glancing eyes contribute to her impish expression. (The watermelon mouth gets its name from its resemblance to a slice from a half a watermelon!) Her wig is typical of the bobbed style of mohair or sometimes human hair which was usually found on the googlies. She is dressed in what appears to be her original costume, reminiscent of a storybook character. Her five-piece body is of a better quality than is usually found on these dolls. She is incised with a square mark and 9573. (Again, there was a problem with reading the numbers and I had recorded 0573, which really does not seem a right Heubach sequence and the doll in Illustration 77 came along as 9573.) *Mackemull Collection.*

Illustration 78. This little 7in (17.8cm) googly's name is "Elisabeth" stamped right on the back of her neck in green just above the Heubach square mark. She has darling fat cheeks which take up more than half of her face. Her mouth is just a tiny thing. Her brown sleep eyes look to the side, and she has fairly heavy painted lashes. She is on a typical five-piece papier-mâché body and is wearing her original dress and hat of orange cotton. *Richard Wright Collection.*

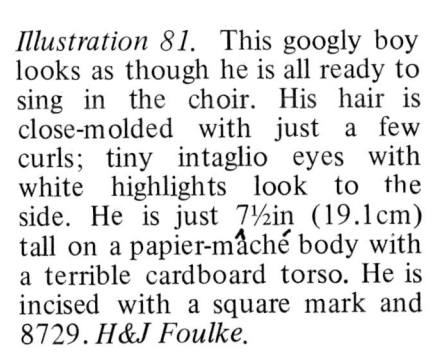

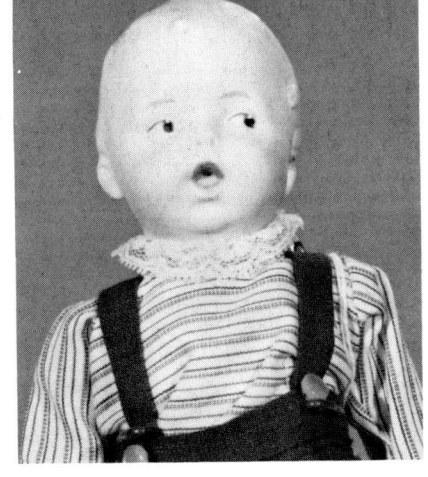

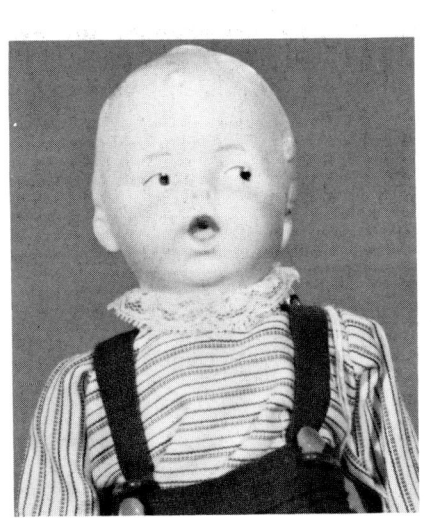

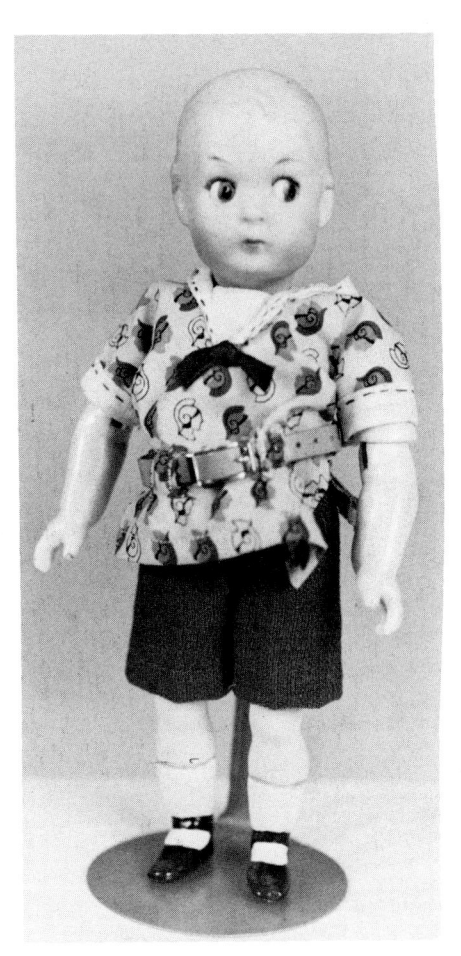

Illustration 81. This googly boy looks as though he is all ready to sing in the choir. His hair is close-molded with just a few curls; tiny intaglio eyes with white highlights look to the side. He is just 7½in (19.1cm) tall on a papier-mâché body with a terrible cardboard torso. He is incised with a square mark and 8729. *H&J Foulke.*

Illustration 79. The head of this boy is reminiscent of those on the all-bisque characters. He has an almost bald head with just a hint of molded curls at the forehead and above his ears. His brown eyes are large, painted to the side, with quite heavy upper lashes; his eyebrows are just lines; his mouth is closed. The most outstanding feature about him is his body, which is made of unusually good composition jointed at the shoulders, elbows, hips and knees with lovely molded and painted one-strap shoes and socks. He is 9in (22.9cm) tall and is incised with a square mark and 8589. *Richard Wright Collection.*

Illustration 80. This is the same mold as the boy in Illustration 79. However, the painting treatment is different. The eyebrows are heavier, the eyes are just a little larger, the eyelashes are heavier and the lips are broader. He is 7in (17.8cm) tall on a chubby googly-type composition body. He is incised with a square mark and 8589. *H&J Foulke.*

Illustraton 82. Perhaps this girl is joining the little boy in Illustration 81 in the choir; if so, she looks a little surprised to know that she can sing! Then again maybe she is just looking at a doll in a store window! She is on a five-piece composition body instead of the usual fatter papier-mâché one on which most of these googlies are found. Just 8in (20.3cm) tall, she is incised with a square mark and 9081. She appears to be wearing her original clothes. *Richard Wright Collection.*

Traditional Styles

The output of the Gebrüder Heubach factory included very few of the "dolly-faced" girls or ordinary character dolls. These types of dolls were the staple products of most of the other German doll factories. Even after the coming of the character doll, though the dolly dolls remained very popular, the brothers Heubach made very few models of this type of doll. One of which we do not have a photograph to include is a shoulder head girl doll with an open mouth, sleep eyes and wig. Impressed with the mold number 10633 and the Heubach square mark, she is like millions of her sisters turned out by the run-of-the-mill German factories. This one was marketed by Sears, Roebuck & Co. as one of their "Dainty Dorothy" dolls. It is almost a shock to see the Heubach mark on her!

ABOVE: Illustration 83. One of the more ordinary-looking dolls made by Heubach is this little child incised with a square mark on the neck and numbers which look like 7711. (Again Heubach used tiny numbers high on the crown opening of these dolls that wore wigs, and often they are only lightly impressed or blurred.) She has sleep eyes and an open mouth with four upper teeth. As with other Heubachs, her ears are not pierced. Her eyebrows are nicely feathered in the Heubach manner, and her eyelashes are also well done. She is on a rather ordinary jointed composition body. Her wig needs a little attention, but appears to have been styled in a bob. *Old Curiosity Shop.*

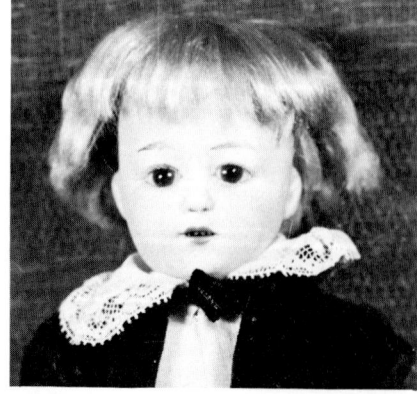

Illustration 84. This boy mold number 10532 is just 8½in (21.6cm) tall on a fairly standard papier-mâché body of five parts. *H&J Foulke.*

66

Another open-mouth Heubach is this attractive mold number 10532. This doll has been recorded in sizes from 8in (20.3cm) to 22in (55.9cm), the latter being a fairly large size for a Heubach as most tend to be smaller. Judging from the numbers seen, it was a popular model as it does turn up quite often. The doll does not have the vacant look of many open-mouth German dolls, and, in fact, has quite a sweet face. Four examples of this model are shown in Illustrations 84 through 87. All dolls of this mold usually have sleep eyes, feathered eyebrows and four upper teeth. All are incised with the square mark on the neck and 10532 at the crown opening.

Illustration 85. This fellow is 11½in (29.2cm) tall on a good quality jointed composition body. *Mary Goolsby Collection.*

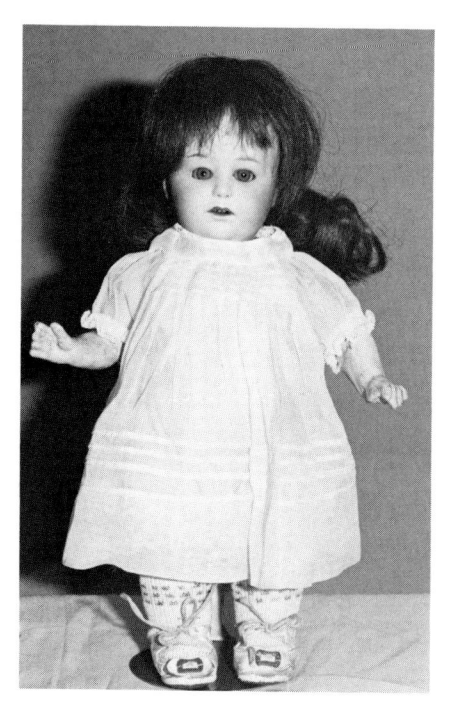

Illustration 86. This little 11in (27.9cm) girl shows that this face can comfortably be either a boy or a girl according to the owner's preference. Her wig is new, and the clothes, while old, are not original to her. She is on a chunky five-piece toddler body of medium quality. *Mackemull Collection.*

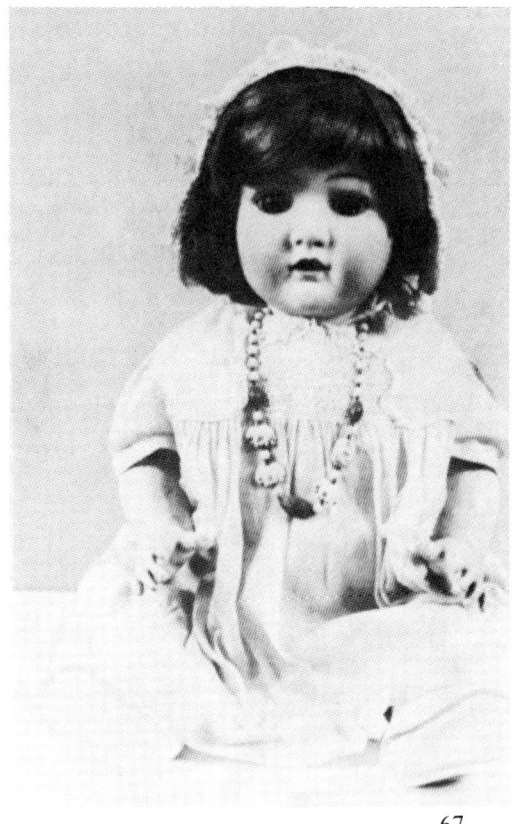

Illustration 87. The beautiful complexion of this doll can be seen in the color section on page 29. His eyes are brown and his mohair wig is auburn. In this illustration it looks as though his mouth is closed, but it is not; the lips are slightly parted, but the teeth are set back fairly far and do not show here. He is 22in (55.9cm) tall on a very good quality composition toddler body. *Ruth Noden Collection.*

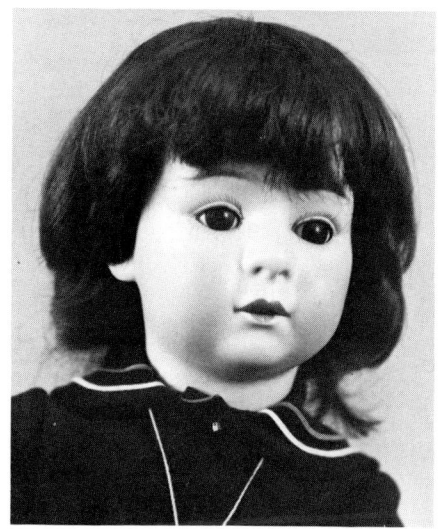

RIGHT: *Illustration 88.* This 23in (58.4cm) baby is not only an unusually large size for a Heubach, it has an unusual mark. Along with the incised square mark and the number 10586 are inscribed a large W u Z over I, indicating that the doll was made for another company, perhaps Wagner & Zetzsche of Ilmenau, Thüringia. Again the face is sweet, but not outstanding as far as character dolls go. She has blue sleep eyes, an open mouth with four upper teeth, nice fat cheeks and pretty eyebrows. Her clothes and hair are old. She is on a bent-limb baby body of excellent quality. *Ruth Noden Collection.*

Another open-mouth Heubach which turns up fairly regularly but still seems to maintain a good price is mold number 8192, which seems to be a favorite of many collectors of cute dolls. These dolls nearly always have excellent quality heads with rosy complexions. They have large soulful eyes which sleep, chubby cheeks and open mouths with four upper teeth. The eyebrows and eyelashes are always well painted. The odd thing is that they are found on a variety of bodies of different quality, perhaps indicating that this was a standard head which Heubach sold to other companies which produced the complete doll. Heads with this mold number have also been found on excellent quality five-piece composition bodies with painted shoes and socks, up to about a 12in (30.5cm) size, as well as on the slim composition bodies with the high knee joints, indicating these dolls were made until about 1930.

Illustration 89. A beautiful number 8192 head done up as a girl with replaced wig and clothes. *H&J Foulke.*

Illustration 90. This boy and girl pair of dolls are both marked 8192. They are on very nice good quality jointed composition bodies. The boy has a replaced wig and clothes. The girl has a replaced wig and hat, but may have original clothes. This pair can also be seen in the color section on page 27. *Rosemary Dent Collection.*

Christmas Novelties

For the doll makers, Christmas was the big season. They prepared over a year ahead, as companies placed their Christmas orders during the first three or four months of each year. And, of course, the wider range of goods at varying prices which a company could offer, the greater would be their sales potential. The Christmas novelties are often in the form of candy box containers, some of the smaller ones possibly meant to be hung on the Christmas tree. Some of the tiny children were often used in Christmas scenes under the tree.

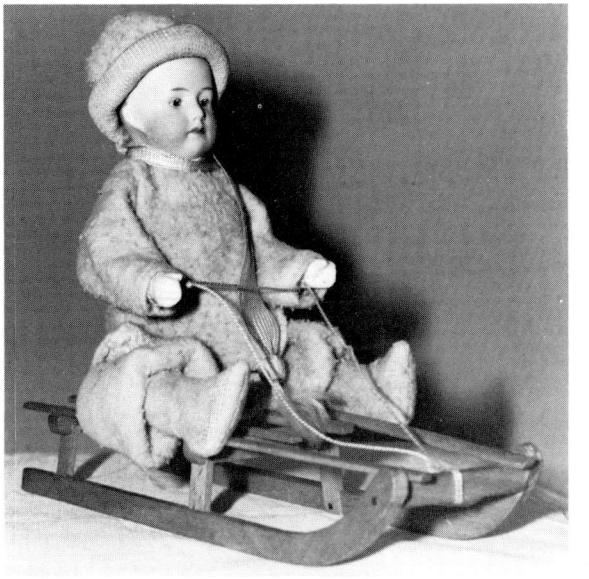

LEFT: Illustration 92. Here is another tiny Heubach boy made up with a candy box inside his torso. His head, lower arms and legs are bisque. He is wearing his original fleece or felt snow suit, cap and muffler. Including the sled, he is just 6in (15.2cm) tall. *Ruth Noden Collection.*

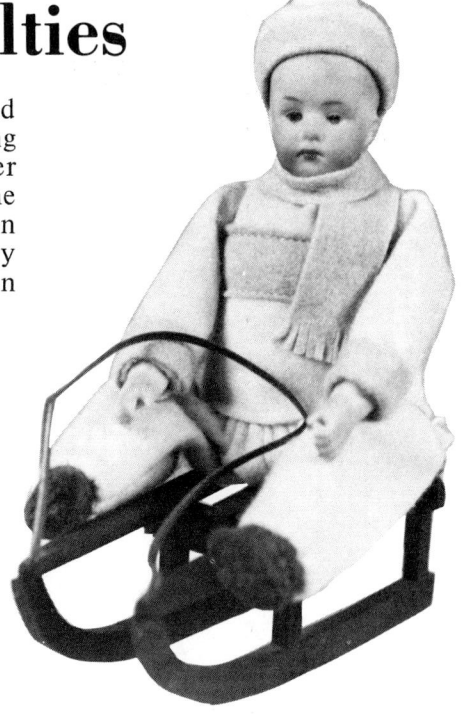

Illustration 91. This delightful pouty boy riding his wooden sled is actually a candy box. A round cylinder forms his torso which lifts off to reveal a compartment to fill with candies. He is wearing his original fleece outdoor clothes. Just 7½in (19.1cm) tall including the sled, he is impressed with the sunburst mark. *Mackemull Collection.*

Illustration 93. This 8in (20.3cm) tall pouty-faced boy is also a candy box, coming apart so that the torso holds the candies. He is wearing his original white plush suit with blue trim. His hands are bisque. *Mackemull Collection.*

Many collectors feel that these tiny bisque faces used to make up children as decorations on Christmas candy containers or as ornaments to hand on the Christmas tree were also made by Heubach. Although they are unmarked, many Heubach characteristics are apparent in these little faces. The little bodies of these dolls are made of wire covered with layers of crepe paper or cotton batting or a combination of both. The clothes actually form the covering of the wire.

ABOVE: Illustration 94. This sweet-faced googly-eyed girl sitting on a square candy container is just 4in (10.2cm) tall. She is dressed in blue and white cotton batting and holds a bunch of red berries. *Mackemull Collection.*

UPPER RIGHT: Illustration 95. It is doubtful that this little girl is really as mean as she looks, but possibly someone is trying to push her off the log as she is really getting close to the edge. The log forms a candy container. She is dressed in blue cotton batting and is 5½in (14.0cm) tall. *Mackemull Collection.*

Illustration 96. The child riding the front of this sled is an all-bisque nodder, probably not a Heubach. The child in the rear is of the type attributed to Heubach. He is wearing his original snow suit of cotton batting. *Mackemull Collection.*

LEFT: Illustration 97. Just 4in (10.2cm) tall including the base is this candy box with a little girl ornament. Judging by the expression on her face, she is taking herself quite seriously. She is dressed in a red and blue Christmas outfit which is original. *Mackemull Collection.*

All-Bisque Characters

Molded Shoes

Tiny dolls have always been popular with little girls. There is something special and cozy about a doll which is just small enough to fit comfortably in one tiny hand. These are the treasured dolls of childhood, and today many are found which have been packed away in small boxes, often with complete wardrobes of handmade clothes, many times the loving labor of a small girl just learning to use a needle. These small dolls illustrate again the infinite number of faces of varying expressions which appeared on the dolls of the Brothers Heubach, surpassing those by any other doll producer, ever. These small dolls must have been a popular product and a good selling one also, or it would not have been profitable for the company to produce so many different dolls since mold making was one of the most costly items in doll production.

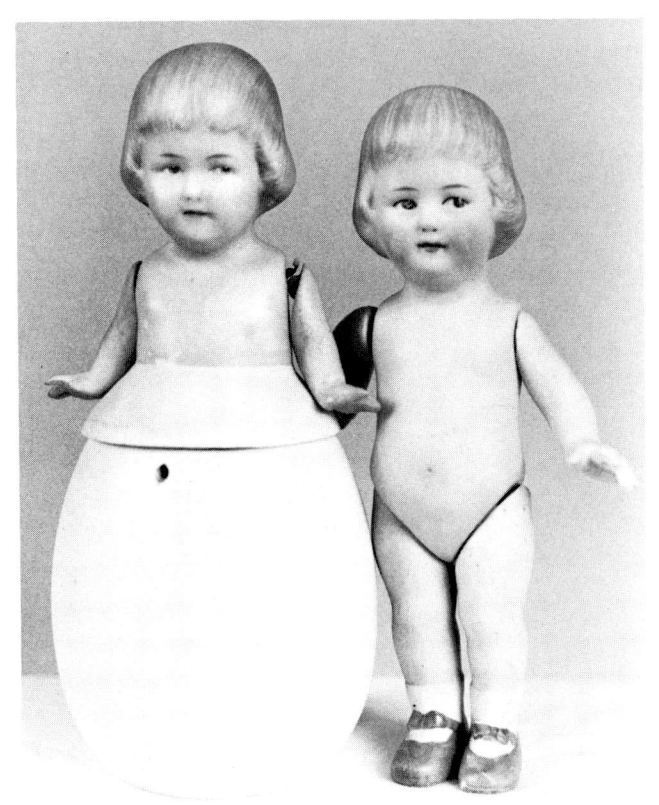

Illustration 99. The doll on the right has the same limbs as her larger sister in Illustration 98. Her fingers are delicate and her molded shoes are identical, but her socks are not so finely ribbed. This doll has also been found with stationary pedestal legs. Her bobbed hairdo is not fancy, but nicely and and cleanly styled. Her hair color is sandy with darker brush marks to provide shading. These two items make an interesting pair because, while the molding is the same, the decoration of the facial features of the doll is done with much more care than those of the girl on the egg box. The doll's eyes are larger and heavier, giving her a more alert look. Her mouth is better defined and has a shading line. The doll is 6in (15.2cm) tall and unmarked; the egg is impressed with the Heubach square mark and stands 6½in (16.5cm) tall. The *1914 Marshall Field & Company* catalog shows this doll in an 8in (20.3cm) size at the wholesale price of $6.00 per dozen. *Richard Wright Collection.*

Illustration 98. This 9in (22.9cm) girl is certainly a very desirable size in an all-bisque doll, as the majority found are much smaller. Her brown hair is lovely with brushmarks on her forehead and well-defined curls at the sides and around the back of her head. Her three hair bows are lavender and a molded ribbon runs around the back of her head to connect the two side bows. Her head is slightly turned; her brown eyes are looking to the side; and her lips are parted showing two tiny teeth. She looks like she is just getting ready to give a flirtatious response to a question. Her hands have the typical Heubach shape with the second and third fingers molded together. Her footwear is also seen on many Heubach all-bisque girls. The brown shoes have bows molded on the straps and her low white socks are vertically ribbed. She is incised 10490 over 3 between her shoulders. *Ruth Noden Collection.*

Illustration 100. This little doll is a surprising 8in (20.3cm) tall! She seems smaller because she has almost a baby look, and although she appears shy, her clenched fists indicate she is getting ready either to swing them or pound them! Her stationary pedestal legs and shoes are typical Heubach features except that her shoes are blue and the straps are narrower. Her white socks are not ribbed. A departure from the norm, her hands have clenched fists, a feature appearing on at least one other Heubach figure illustrated, and appear to be original to the doll. Her short blonde hair, wispy on the forehead with tiny side curls, indicates a much younger child than the previous dolls. Her pink cotton dress appears to be contemporary with the doll. Her eyebrow painting is interesting, as is her tiny open/closed mouth. She is incised with a square mark and 13. *Richard Wright Collection.*

Illustration 101. This little 4in (10.2cm) girl has blue slippers with pointed toes just like those of the "Chin Chin Babies." Her mouth is marvelously done in a pouty triangle shape. Her large side-glancing eyes have a lovely white highlight, as well as heavily painted upper eyelashes. She has a glossy blue bow above each ear. A boy doll with a watermelon mouth was made as a companion to her. She is incised with the Heubach square mark. *H&J Foulke.*

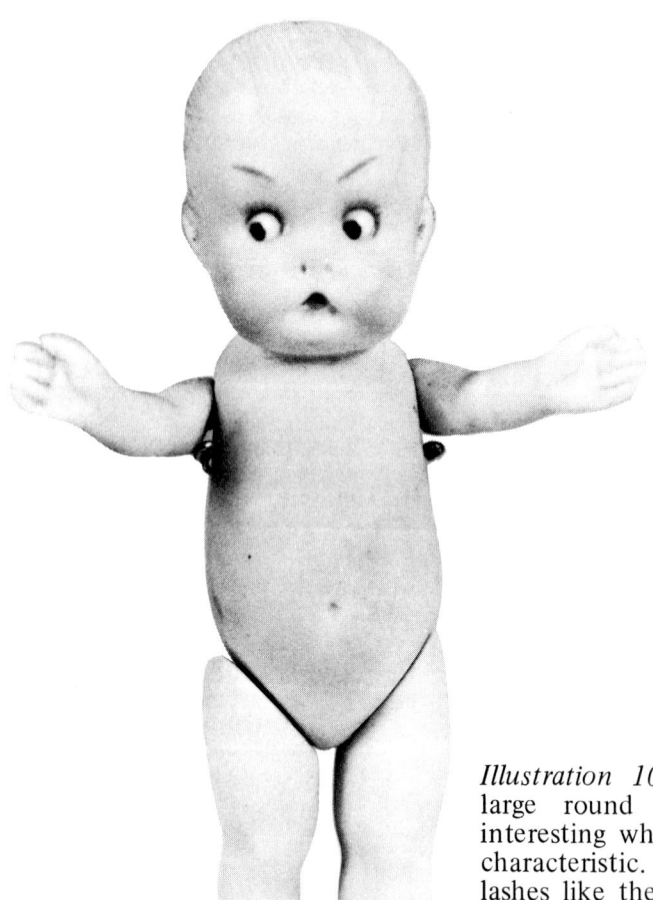

Bare Feet

Although the following three dolls are not marked, they appear to be of Heubach manufacture when the general style, construction and finishing is compared to known Heubach dolls. This is especially evident in the treatment of the large eyes with heavy upper lashes, the chubby torsos, the expressive mouths and the nearly bald heads. They were perhaps part of a series as they have many characteristics in common. They are 5in (12.7cm) tall. Their arms are alike with fingers molded together instead of separated as on the previous dolls which at first suggested replaced arms on the first that I examined. However, the next two are exactly the same which perhaps suggests cheaper production methods and perhaps later dolls. They have bare feet instead of the usual molded shoes and socks.

Illustration 102. This surprised fellow has large round side-glancing eyes, with an interesting white highlight, another Heubach characteristic. He has fairly heavy upper lashes like the previous little girl. His head is nearly bald, but he does have a few strands of hair stroked on in a sparse fashion. *Richard Wright Collection.*

RIGHT: Illustration 103. This sister is especially interesting, not only because of the smug look on her face, but for two other reasons. Although she appears to be bald, actually her hair is pulled to the back, and she has a tiny molded pony tail on the back of her head. In addition, she is one of the few all-bisques wearing her original clothes, including darling tiny black leather shoes. Her round eyes also have heavily painted upper lashes and white dot highlights. Her turned down mouth makes her especially appealing. *Richard Wright Collection.*

LEFT: Illustration 104. Also in her original clothes, a gauze chemise and cap as well as the same leather shoes as the girl in Illustration 103, is this knock-kneed, pigeon-toed child with marvelously large eyes. Her triangular shaped mouth is unusual in most dolls, but not in Heubachs. Her uplifted eyebrows add to her surprised look. *Richard Wright Collection.*

Chin Chin Babies

These appealing little Oriental characters range around 4½in (11.5cm) in height, give or take a little. Their smooth excellent quality bisque is golden yellow. The general design shows the influence of the ubiquitous Kewpie dolls by Rose O'Neill. They have chunky torsos, short fat pedestal legs and jointed shoulders with arms gracefully sloping outward. The fingers are quite distinctive, pointed, with the second and third molded together as shown in the illustration, so it is easy to tell whether or not the dolls have proper arms. Their faces are done in several styles. The molded caps vary, with at least six styles on record, including one with a molded orange cap not shown here. The boys have shiny black molded queues. The feet have molded slippers with pointed toes. The dolls are usually, but not always, stamped on the feet with a Heubach square mark. Originally the dolls wore a triangular paper label (yellow, red and black on white) on their front torsos. One little "Chin Chin Baby" that I owned had a fan-shaped label tied to her wrist.

The collector wishing to gather Heubach "Chin Chin Babies" should be careful to differentiate them from the very similar "Queue San Babies" made in Japan for Morimora Brothers. It is easy to confuse these with the "Chin Chins" because they have the same faces, hands and pointed toes, but the label of the Japanese dolls is diamond-shaped and the bisque and finishing are not so fine. However, the "Queue San Babies" while interesting in their own right, cost less than half the price of the "Chin Chins" on today's collectors' market.

Illustration 105. These two "Chin Chin Babies" have different facial expressions. The boy on the left has his head tilted to one side. The modeling detail around his eyes is very nice for such a small doll. His faintly smiling face seems to be hiding a secret! His cap is yellow with painted black trim; his shoes match his yellow cap. The doll on the right has a lavender cap with red and green trim. This headdress sometimes occurs in other color combinations. His shoes are red and his solemn face has a pouty look. Alas, he has lost his arms and is waiting patiently for a proper pair. *Mackemull Collection.*

Illustration 106. This "Chin Chin" girl also has the solemn face. Her cap is yellow with a molded decoration across the front. Black painted bands join the molded white rosettes which cover her ears. Her shoes are also yellow. *Richard Wright Collection.*

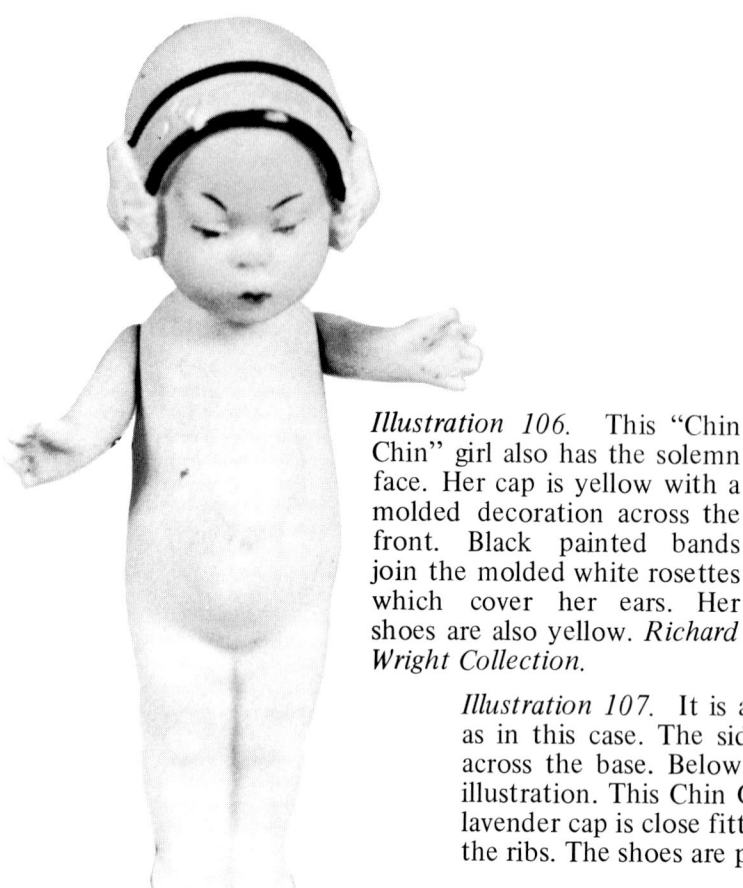

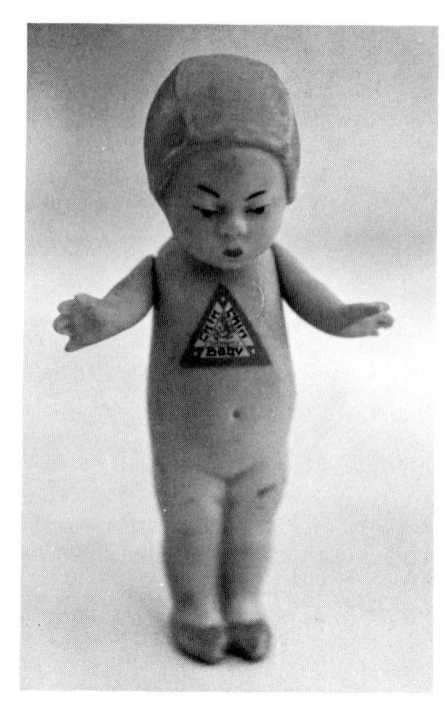

Illustration 107. It is always great to have a doll with its original label as in this case. The sides of the triangle are lettered CHIN with Baby across the base. Below Baby is Germany which does not show in the illustration. This Chin Chin also has the more common pouty face. The lavender cap is close fitting with shiny pink trim around the face and on the ribs. The shoes are pink also. *H&J Foulke.*

Position Babies

Position babies appear to be a staple item in the Butler Brothers wholesale catalog of 1899. Although the ones pictured are probably not Heubachs, they do show the apparent popularity of these little figures, either nude or in molded shifts posed in "assorted positions as natural as life." Four sets were offered: Filipino, much like the position babies pictured in Stanton's *Heubach's Little Characters* on page 39; Black; Vasser girls with wigs; and babies with molded shifts. Most came in a series of six different poses. It is interesting to note that these were included in the doll section of the catalog which seems to indicate that they were also intended as playthings for children, not simply for ornamentation.

Illustration 108. This fellow, 5in (12.7cm) tall in a sitting position, carries the square mark with 9744. He is certainly angry about something. A look at his companion in Illustration 109 might be a clue. Someone ate all of his cake! There is no molding detail in the hair except for a tiny curl on the side of his forehead, but the painting is nicely done with brush strokes indicating strands of hair. Frown ridges are molded above his eyes, and the eyebrows show careful treatment. His mouth with the turned down edges contributes to his pouty look. The ears are very small, almost an afterthought. *Richard Wright Collection.*

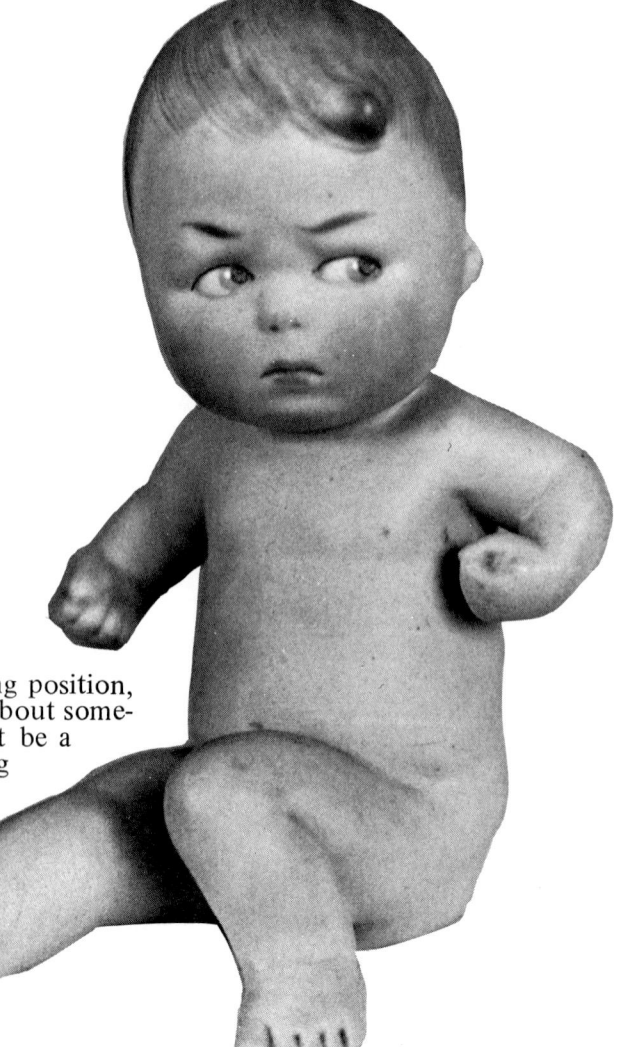

Illustration 109. Here is the same angry fellow shown in Illustration 108 with a contented-looking buddy, hands on his tummy in obvious satisfaction, mouth upturned in a smug expression, eyes squinty from his smile, almost cross-eyed really. Like his pal, his hair has no detail except for a curl at the center top of his head. He has a vase attached to his back, so was intended for some practical purpose. He is incised with a square mark and 9855. *Richard Wright Collection.*

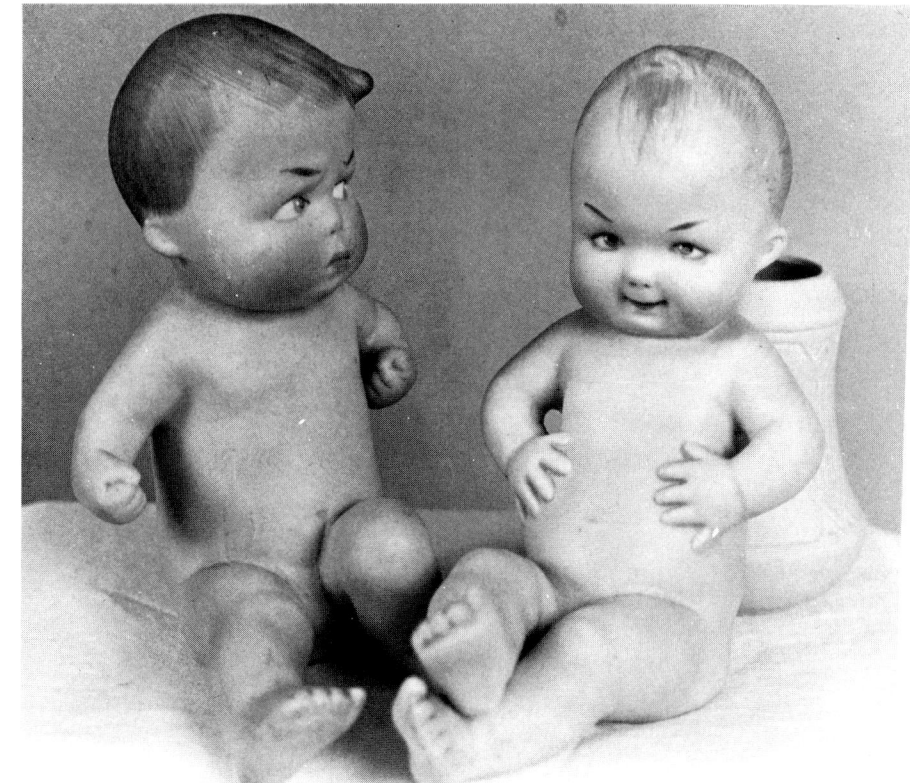

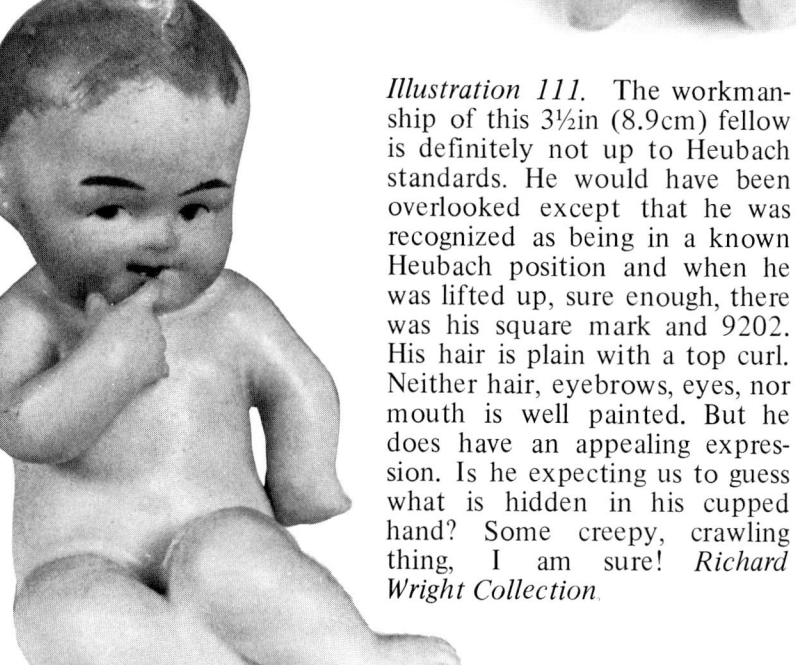

Illustration 111. The workmanship of this 3½in (8.9cm) fellow is definitely not up to Heubach standards. He would have been overlooked except that he was recognized as being in a known Heubach position and when he was lifted up, sure enough, there was his square mark and 9202. His hair is plain with a top curl. Neither hair, eyebrows, eyes, nor mouth is well painted. But he does have an appealing expression. Is he expecting us to guess what is hidden in his cupped hand? Some creepy, crawling thing, I am sure! *Richard Wright Collection.*

Illustration 110. Although unmarked, this boy is obviously another example of the boy in Illustration 109 showing that Heubach often used the same form either by itself or with a vase or box attached. However, this boy seems to have been painted by a different artist, and the overall effect is not so striking. The eyes are less dramatic, the mouth is less pronounced, and the paint strokes on the head are further apart. However, there is excellent molding on the toes, even showing the toenails. *Mackemull Collection.*

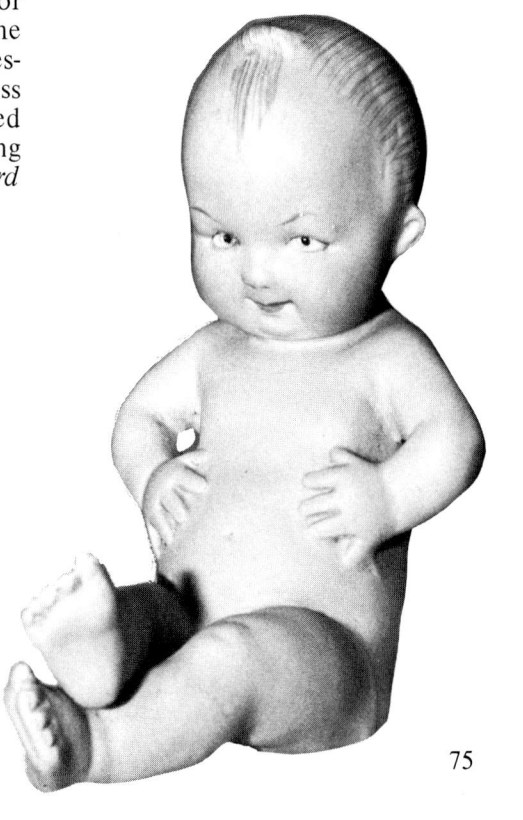

Action Figures

Heubach made a good variety of these naked figures with molded shoes or boots. Half the fun of these action figures is in imagining the circumstances which provoked their expressions. It is interesting that these children have such realistic poses and faces. Their design must have involved a good deal of work on the part of the artist, including observation of children and the sculpting of them. The facial expressions run the gamut of emotion from pensive to angry, from startled to happy, with excellent modeling detail in the faces and a fair amount in the bodies as well.

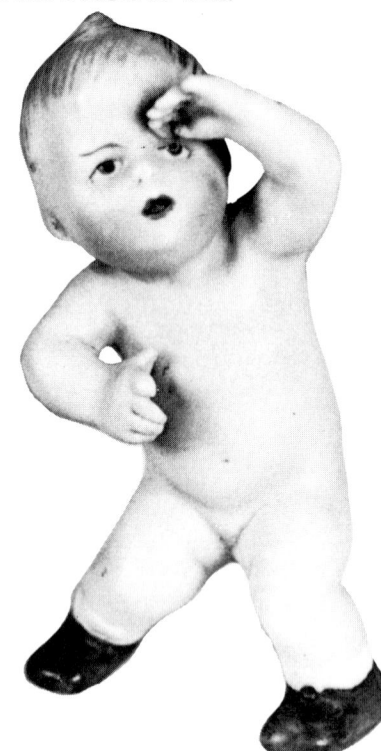

Illustration 112. What could this fellow be seeing? Something in the sky obviously -- maybe even Superman? He is 4in (10.2cm) tall with low brown oxfords and molded white socks. His open/closed mouth has a molded tongue. There is a curl on the top of his head; his hair is brush-stroked on. An unusual treatment was given to his eyebrows; the waviness gives him a frown. He is incised with a square mark and 0210, which maybe should have a 1 in front of it which did not print. *Richard Wright Collection.*

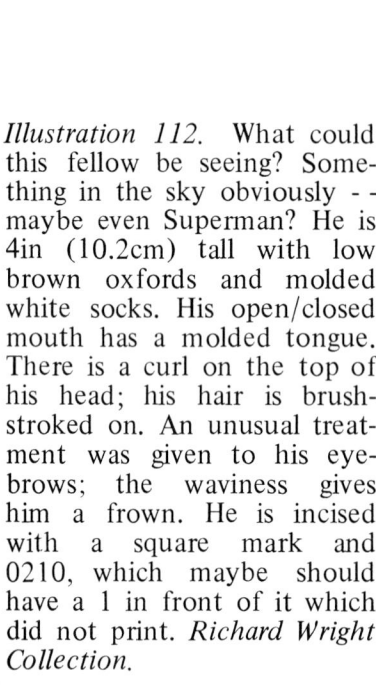

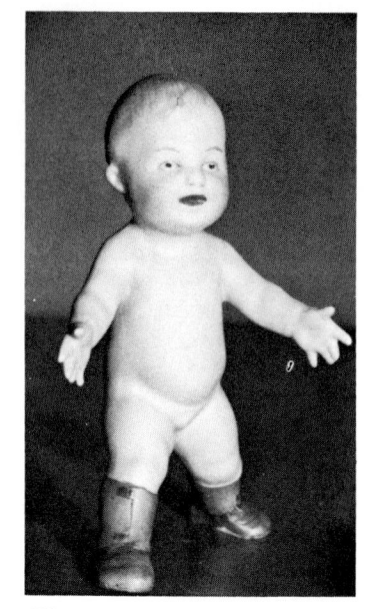

Illustration 114. This boy, 6½in (16.5cm) tall, is a slightly larger version of the boy in Illustration 113 shown here again by himself for a clearer view. He is of exceptionally fine bisque, nicely tinted with excellent molding detail. The quality of this figure is much better than the one in Illustration 113. He has a molded curl on his forehead and beautifully colored hair. The chubby legs and arms with typical Heubach fingers make him look like a healthy fellow indeed. His brown boots come just below his dimpled knee. Neither boy is marked, but both have definite Heubach characteristics. *H&J Foulke.*

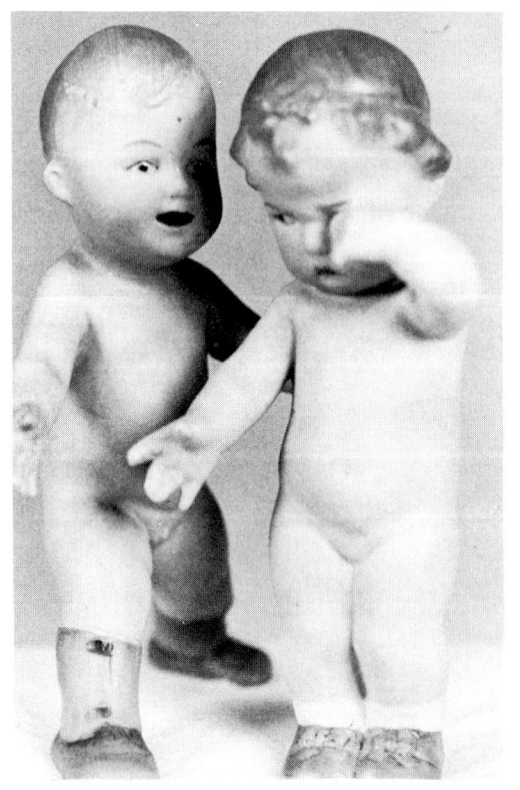

Illustration 113. The boy is imploring the girl not to cry anymore. Did he break her favorite doll? Whatever happened, she is certainly unhappy! Her molded hair is done in a sweet style, smooth on the crown and curled below her orange hair band tied in the front. She has the typical Heubach hand. Her shoes are brown with molded bows in front; her low socks are white. She is 6in (15.2cm) tall, and is incised with the square mark and 10056. *Both Richard Wright Collection.*

Illustration 115. Such a shy fellow he is as he holds his bouquet of flowers. Maybe he is thinking of presenting them to the crying girl! Apparently of the same series as the boy in Illustration 114, he has the same brown boots coming up to his knee. He is attached to a vase. Both vase and one shoe carry a square mark. The other shoe is impressed 10055. He is also 6½in (16.5cm) tall. *Richard Wright Collection.*

Easter Bunnies

Next to Christmas, Easter is probably the holiday which offers the greatest opportunity for appealing novelties. All kinds of possibilities present themselves with children, bunnies and chicks. Apparently the Heubach factory was attuned to consumers and overlooked few opportunities to create a product to fill any possible gap or to create an object to market with a seasonal theme.

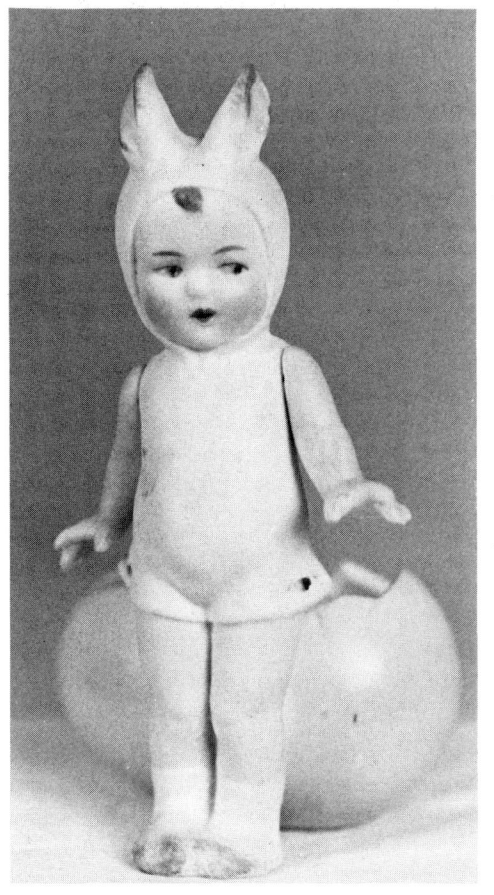

Illustration 117. The 5½in (14.0cm) companion bunny girl looks just a bit uncertain as she stands in front of her attached pink egg. Her delicately pink tinted ears are shorter than the boy's, and a tiny lock of hair peeks out from under her cap. Her bunny costume stops in a short skirt with holes into the bisque on both sides for insertion of a prettily tied ribbon. Her jointed arms are flesh-colored with hands outstretched in a pert attitude. She is incised 10540 with a square mark. *Richard Wright Collection.*

Illustration 116. This 6in (15.2cm) boy in a bunny costume was doubtless intended as an Easter novelty. The attached egg would hold tiny Easter candies. His flesh-tinted face is sweetly flirtatious with side-glancing eyes and a mischievous watermelon mouth. The molded rabbit suit is white with yellow tinted shading at the ears. His egg is pale yellow. Oddly enough, his suit is apparently sleeveless, as the jointed arms are flesh-tinted with no indication of a molded sleeve. He is incised 10539 with a square mark. *Richard Wright Collection.*

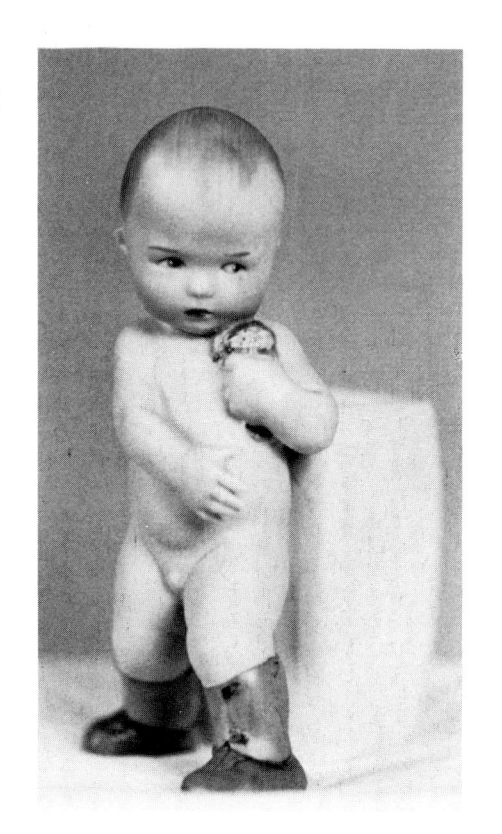

Black Position Babies

Black items were popular novelties in the last quarter of the 19th and first quarter of the 20th centuries. Apparently they were consistent sellers as a few figures and dolls were always included in the catalogs of the period. However, judging from the difficulty of finding these old items today, they were not overwhelming best sellers.

The modeling in the black figures created by the Brothers Heubach was done with great care and attention to realistic detail. The hair was given a fuzzy look by the application of tiny bisque particles, certainly a time-consuming step in producing the babies. The eyes were deeply incised with even the eyelids being carefully molded. Distinctive Negroid features include the broad noses and wide lips. Some of the figures have the sunburst mark; on others it was omitted.

These are the only figures that carry the impressed COPYRIGHTED within two circles mark. It has been suggested by Richard Wright that these figures might be based on a 1900 calendar which was copyrighted in 1899 by H. Reck.

Illustration 118. The largest of this group of four figures is 5in (12.7cm) tall. He is clutching a cob of corn as though someone might try to get it away from him. The eye detail on this fellow, which is especially good, is emphasized by interesting eyebrows. His white shift has painted blue dots. Unfortunately, the black tinting on the body and hair does not wear well and often white spots show through. *Richard Wright Collection.*

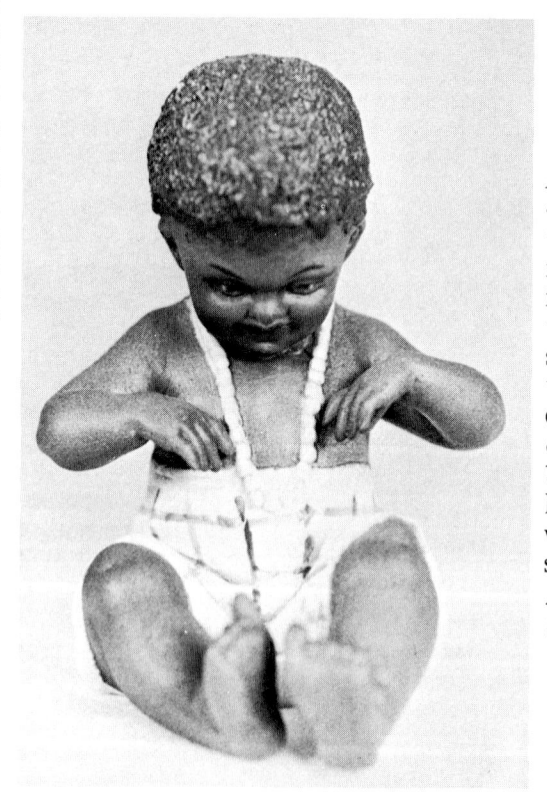

Illustration 119. This 4½in (11.5cm) fellow, wearing a molded blue necklace, seems absorbed in wiggling his two big toes which are given special definition. Again the facial modeling is excellent with emphasis on detail around his broad nose and mouth. His trousers are white with painted crossing stripes for decoration. *Richard Wright Collection.*

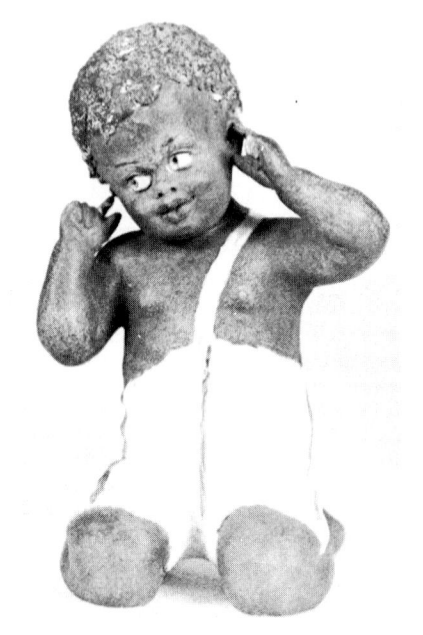

Illustration 120. The kneeling boy is 4in (10.2cm) tall, designed with fingers pointing to his ears. Perhaps the boy in the next illustration is saying things he does not want to hear! His face does not look disturbed, however, as it has a somewhat quizzical expression emphasized by the whites of his eyes which stand out on the black face. All of the detail on him is well executed with particular attention to the fingers. His white trousers with only one strap are decorated with stripes. *Richard Wright Collection.*

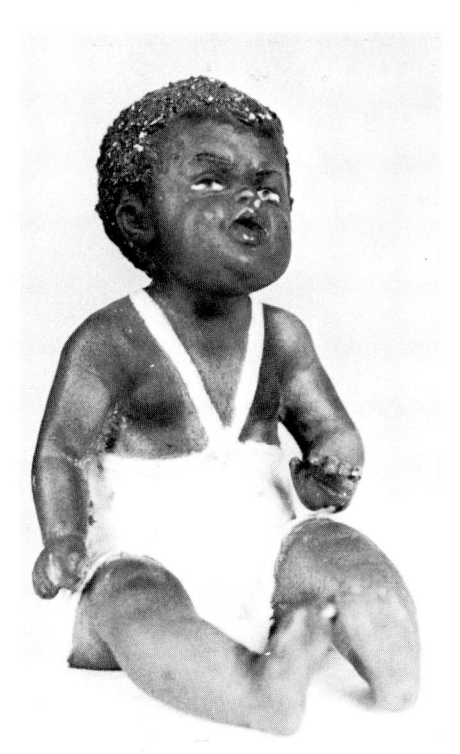

Illustration 121. This 4½in (11.5cm) boy in the V-strapped romper with turquoise polka dots certainly looks concerned about something. In fact, he is almost scowling. He has molded frown lines above his eyebrows; his eyes are partially closed with heavy lids. His mouth is partially open with two tiny white teeth showing, as though he is ready to complain. Even one hand is clenched. *Richard Wright Collection.*

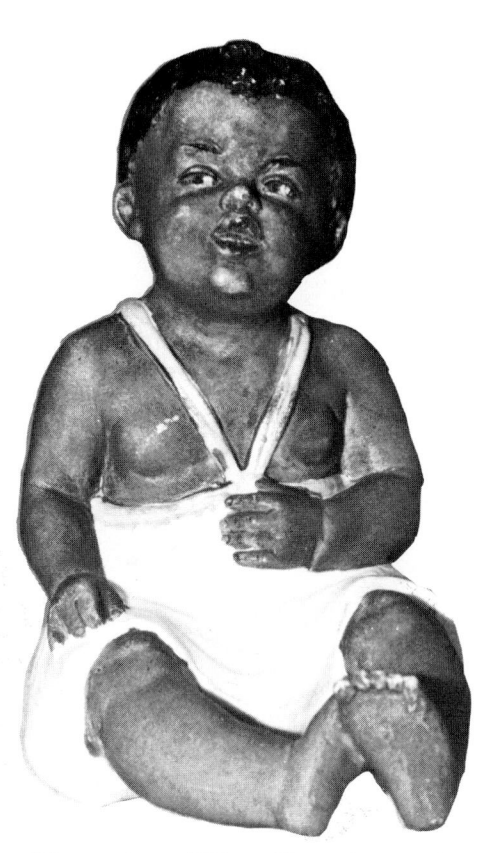

Illustration 122. Here is nearly the same baby as in Illustration 121 in a larger size. At first glance, he is the same, but closer examination shows subtle differences. He does not appear to be frowning as fiercely, and his eyes are side-glancing. Instead of being free, his arms are molded onto his body. His shift does not have the painted spots. Perhaps this was a later version of the previous doll. He is 5½in (14.0cm) tall. *Mackemull Collection.*

ABOVE: *Illustration 123.* This egg is a very rare Heubach item, indeed. Probably made as an Easter novelty, it carries the incised sunburst mark. The egg is held by one small black boy and three little black heads and one pair of arms are breaking through the shell. The egg is 5in (12.4cm) tall. Babies breaking through eggs was a popular theme for novelties of the period. These are several bisque versions of a white baby coming from an egg, as well as a lovely one done in wax. *Mackemull Collection.*

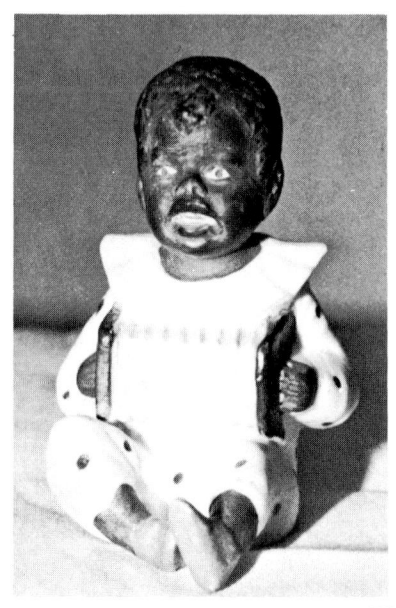

RIGHT: *Illustration 124.* This small 3in (7.6cm) black boy playing the accordian is dressed in a clown suit. Though unmarked, he is possibly a Heubach figure as he has some similarity to the other figures. His hair has good molding to give it a natural look. He was possibly one of a set of musicians. *Mackemull Collection.*

79

Piano Babies

Heubach ornamental piano babies are outstanding among the bisque figures created by the millions in the porcelain factories of Germany during the late Victorian period, the last quarter of the 19th century. There is always controversary among collectors about which came first, dolls or figures. I personally feel that the figurines came first and were the inspiration for the character dolls which came at the turn of the 20th century. Certainly a connection cannot be denied as it is easy to see family likenesses in the faces of the dolls and figures. Sometimes even the same face occurs as a figurine and as a doll. The piano babies by Heubach are outstanding because of their realistic looks and natural poses. The models were obviously done from real life, and attention was given to all of the details necessary to make the babies look alive, including toes, fingers, fat rolls, dimples, intaglio eyes and molded natural-looking hair.

Illustration 125. The baby on the left, although losing his nightgown which is trimmed with tiny beads of paint, looks happy as he reaches for his toes, a favorite preoccupation with barefooted children. He is 5in (12.7cm) tall and has the incised sunburst mark. Even among Heubach-designed babies he is outstanding for the realistic modeling in his body, arms and legs. It is easy enough to see his well-fed look with fat rolls at his ankles and wrists, as well as dimpled elbows and knees. His intaglio eyes with raised white highlights look to the side, and he has two tiny upper teeth. The crawling baby on the right is 7in (17.8cm) long and has the incised sunburst mark with 3101. His outstanding feature is his beautiful blonde hair so exquisitely molded with locks of curls on his forehead and above his ears with overall comb marks to give real texture. His white shift is trimmed with an aqua bow. *Mackemull Collection.*

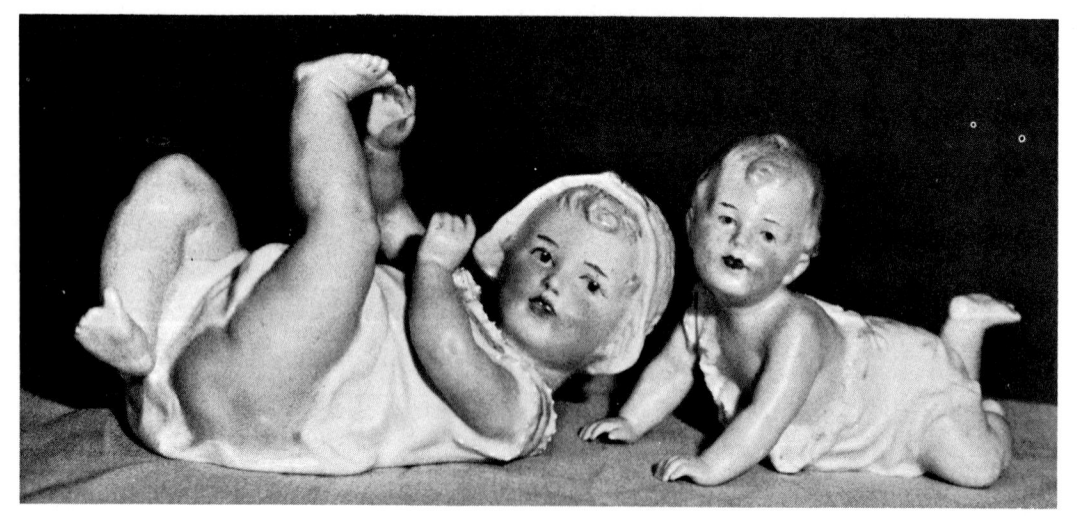

Illustration 126. The baby on the left is 6in (15.2cm) long. She is a frequently found bisque figure which came in many sizes from about 4in (10.2cm) to 12in (30.5cm). Her most outstanding feature is her molded bonnet which is done in a crocheted-type style. A molded green ribbon is threaded through the cap and ties at the top. Wisps of blonde hair peek out from under the edges of the cap. The neck and sleeves of the shift are trimmed with a molded ruffle and raised paint dots. Her open/closed mouth has two tiny white upper teeth. This baby can also be found without the bonnet, perhaps intended as a boy. The crawling baby on the right shows a family resemblance to his companion. He is just 4¼in (10.9cm) long. Both figures are marked with a sunburst. *Mackemull Collection.*

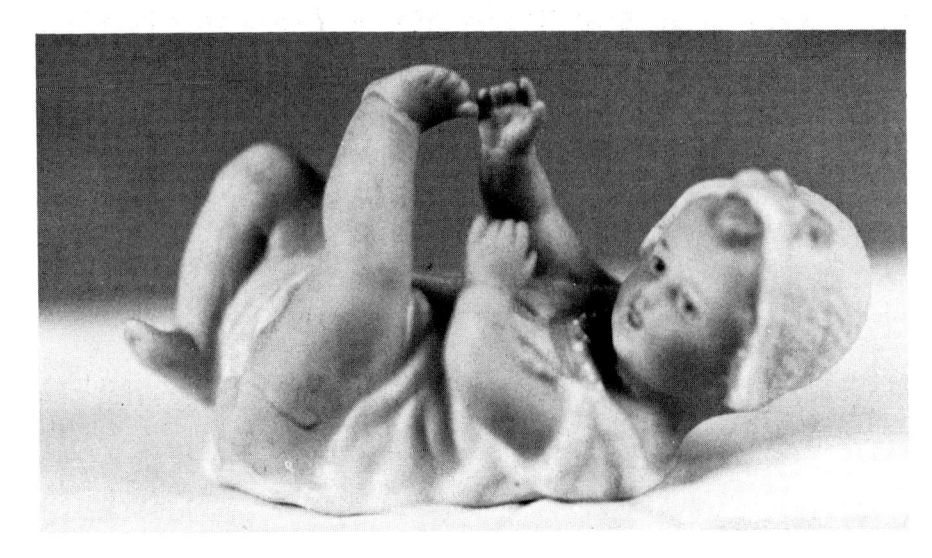

Illustration 127. This 4½in (11.5cm) long size also has a sunburst mark. Her chemise and bonnet are trimmed with blue bows. The arms and legs show almost no fat rolls; the eyes do not have much life; the cap is not very detailed and does not have a ribbon entwined around the brim. *Ruth Noden Collection.*

Illustration 128. These two children are a part of a small but interesting and unusual Heubach item, just 4½in (11.5cm) tall with green-stamped sunburst mark and 5965. The other part of the trio is a piglet! All three seem contented, even the pig. The children are nicely modeled and show a family resemblance to faces on other figurines. The soft coloring is also typically Heubach. *H&J Foulke.*

Illustration 129. A larger version of the baby in Illustration 126, this one is 9in (22.9cm) long and also has the sunburst mark. The larger size has much more detail in the modeling - - particularly on the bonnet and in the eyes and mouth. Also the fingers are much more distinctive. The eyes and the mouth have been much more carefully painted. The shading on the lips is especially nice. *Richard Wright Collection.*

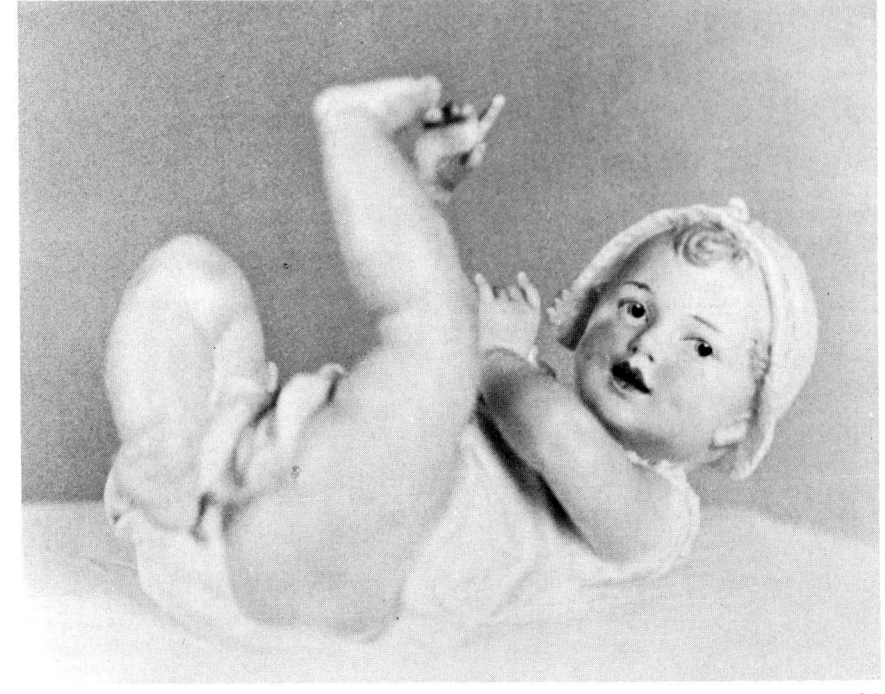

A Collector's Delight

Illustration 130A, B & C. One of the most spectacular Heubach pieces with babies is this bisque basket trinket box with a removable lid. The woven basket is tinted a natural straw color with the top edge, basket rim and clasps and hinges in a darker brown. Four blonde haired babies peek over the rim of the basket. All of the babies have the most realistic expressions with very detailed modeling. This certainly must have been a costly item to produce as the intricate detail is simply astounding. The baby on the left has an open/closed mouth with shading on his lower lip and two molded upper teeth. His eyes are dark and deeply incised. His hands are molded into clenched fists with very detailed fingers. The girl in the center has a molded fabric bonnet surrounded by a ruffle and covered with pink polka dots. A bow ties under her chin. Her lips and eyes are outstanding. The hand which rests on the hamper rim is done in typical Heubach style. The center boy has his elbow resting on the basket; his hair and hands are beautifully modeled. In the right corner is another little girl in a molded white cap. She looks a little younger than the middle girl. She has just one curl exposed under her eyelet edged bonnet. Since she does not look as happy as the others, perhaps she is feeling a little crowded with all of those larger babies in such a small basket! This rare and exquisite piece has been coveted by many Heubach collectors. The basket measures 8½in (21.6cm) long and 7in (17.8cm) high; it is marked with a sunburst. *Ruth Noden Collection.*

Flower Children

Absolutely amazing for the amount of minute detail involved in the making are these two children with large floppy hats, or what at first glance appear to be sunbonnets. However, when these are viewed from the back, they are actually inverted flowers; hence, these will be called the "flower children."

Illustration 131. The face of this baby is unbelievable for a figurine. The eyes are deeply incised and very lifelike. The eyeball is molded as well as the upper and lower eyelids; the eyebrows are not only molded, but are beautifully feathered by the artist. The open/closed mouth gives her the illusion of getting ready to speak. One expects to hear all kinds of satisfied gurgling sounds from her since she has succeeded in pulling off one stocking and has started on the second. The evenly-applied flesh tones give her a natural rosy and healthy complexion. Her dress is white with pink trim and polka dots; her hat is also pink and white. She is 10½in (26.7cm) tall and is stamped in blue with the sunburst mark. *Ruth Noden Collection.*

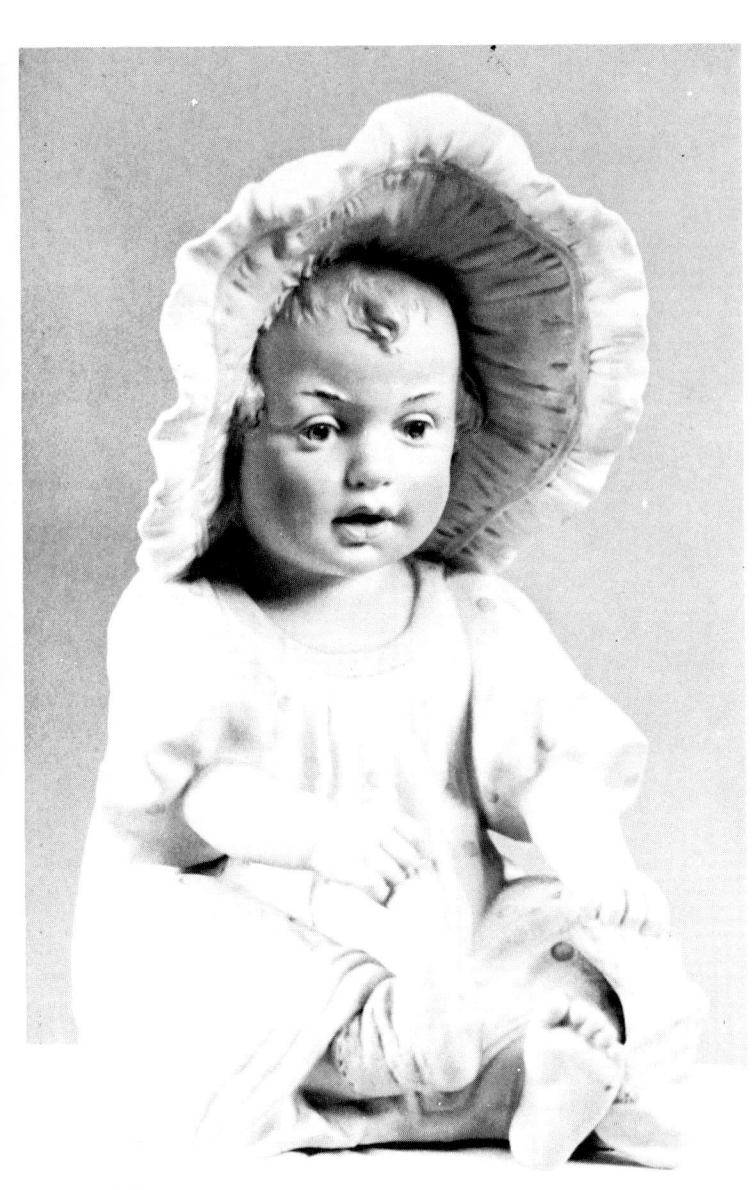

Illustration 132. An older sister of the flower baby shown in Illustration 131, the face of this little girl shows the family resemblance. She is shy, but has been caught in this tiny glance upward which may have lasted for only a few seconds at most. Her eyes are done with as much care as was lavished on the baby, but they are not as wide open, befitting her mood. Her lips are closed but give a hint of just the beginning of a smile which may be coaxed into full bloom. What a reward for the lucky recipient! Again this flower girl has the bloom of health in her rosy skin tones. As is appropriate for an older child, she is wearing a dress in a more streamlined style which hangs gracefully from a high waistline. Her dress is trimmed with turquoise as is her bonnet and she is wearing shoes and stockings. This young girl is also 10½in (26.7cm) tall, and paired with the flower baby, the two make a breathtaking impression. As with other Heubach figures, these flower children have been seen in a smaller size which, while lovely, do not have as much detail as the larger models. *Ruth Noden Collection.*

Child Figurines

Heubach was a prolific producer of not only dolls, but also figurines. Here is a presentation of some of the child figures since they are the most interesting to collectors of dolls. Most doll collectors do include a number of these child figures among their doll display since they are charming, appealing and eye-catching. Figurines were popular mantelpiece and table ornaments in the Victorian period and were carried over into the 20th century. They are difficult to date as the molds, which were expensive to produce in the first place, were undoubtedly used for long periods of time, just as with dolls. The word "Germany" had to be used on all articles for export after 1891, and does provide a dividing date of sorts. However, many times the "Made in Germany" was simply stamped on the bottom of a piece and just as easily wore off, or was possibly washed off, as bisque figures which sit out on tables or shelves exposed to the air collect a lot of dust and real dirt which makes washing them in soap and water necessary.

After becoming familiar with the Heubach style, one can almost always spot a Heubach figure, even before looking at the identifying mark. The faces always show real expressions and emotions as well as family resemblances. The clothing with frills and ruffles has fabric as well as sewing detail. The hair is usually blonde; the eyes are usually blue as one would expect of a Teutonic child anyway. The coloring of the figure is very soft. Many times a garment is left white, with color being used only for the trim of ribbons, polka dots, stripes and similar details.

Illustration 134. This little girl shows the piety expected of Victorian children who were supposed to be restrained in their manner. Anyway, it is difficult for people to resist a child who looks as angelic as this one. Perhaps she has seen the first star of the evening and is sending up her wish prayer. Her nightgown has a blue yoke and is trimmed with the gold often found on Heubach figures. She is 8in (20.3cm) tall and marked with a red-stamped sunburst. A companion piece to this one is a slightly older girl with long blonde hair, hands with fingertips together and full instead of cuffed sleeves. *Ruth Noden Collection.*

Illustration 135. This cheeky fellow is not only playing at soldier, he is taking himself very seriously about the task as he smokes on his wooden cigar. In full military dress including a sword at his side and boots, he is propped up against an attached vase in an almost "What do you think of me" attitude. This is an unusual figure. He is 5½in (14.0cm) tall and has the incised sunburst mark. *Mackemull Collection.*

Illustration 136. Many of the Heubach figures were made in pairs or series, and this fellow is half of a boy-girl pair. Leaning on his elbows, chin in hand, he has a most appealing and flirtatious look on his face. His smiling mouth has a very wide lower lip and molded teeth. His dark eyes are narrowed and side-glancing, but are deeply incised. His blouse is white with a pink collar, cuffs and polka dots. He is 6½in (16.5cm) tall and has the stamped sunburst mark. *Mackemull Collection.*

LEFT: Illustration 137. This 13in (33.0cm) figure of a girl with a dove is an example of one of the most idealistic figures produced by Heubach. It is certainly lovely, but does not seem to have as much realism as most of their other figures. The girl's hair is especially well done in a slightly different style, pulled back with a turquoise bow. Her shift has turquoise shading and tiny handpainted flower decorations. Two more realistic details appear, though, in the chubby dimpled knees and the stockings, one up and one down! *Richard Wright Collection.*

RIGHT: Illustration 138. A favorite with doll collectors is this little girl holding her doll, as many of them also like figures and pictures of children with dolls. She is 10in (25.4cm) tall and carries a red sunburst mark. Sitting on an upturned basket with feet gripping the sides for balance, she is the picture of a real little girl possibly admonishing the doll to go to sleep. Certainly, she is very serious about her task, judging from the concentration shown in her face. Her blonde hair has bangs which are gently pushed to one side and braids over and behind her shoulders. Her blue crocheted jumper and rose tam contrast with her white ruffled blouse. Her doll, which in real life would perhaps be a bisque shoulder head on a kid body, also has long blonde flowing hair, stiff arms and a lovely yellow dress with white ruffle trim which appears to be a baby dress. *Ruth Noden Collection.*

RIGHT: Illustration 139. The newsboy is a popular Heubach figure, shown as he is out on the street advertising the news and selling his papers. His mouth with molded teeth is open in a calling position. His hair is short and curly brown. His face is thinner, more mature than that of the other figurines shown here, so he is an older boy. His outfit is that of a working boy with dark hat, trousers and coat, albeit edged and trimmed in gold, and white shirt. The newspaper has writing on it, but this seems to vary from figure to figure. This one is the "Telegraph." Including the stand he is 15in (38.1cm) tall, and is marked with the sunburst. *Ruth Noden Collection.*

ABOVE: Illustration 140. This 17in (43.2cm) dandy in full day dress is certainly a high point as far as Heubach figurines are concerned. His face shows that he is looking expectantly from dark side-glancing eyes for approval of his outfit. His mouth is open in expectation of replying to an approving comment. His outfit is certainly spectacular. The top hat and jacket are ivory with gold trim and buttons; his shirt is white with gold studs; his tie is burgundy as is his vest. His wide-bottomed trousers are brown with burgundy stripes. His accessories include an enameled rose in one hand, a walking stick with dog-head handle in the other hand, glasses sitting low on his nose and a fancy handkerchief in his pocket. *Richard Wright Collection.*

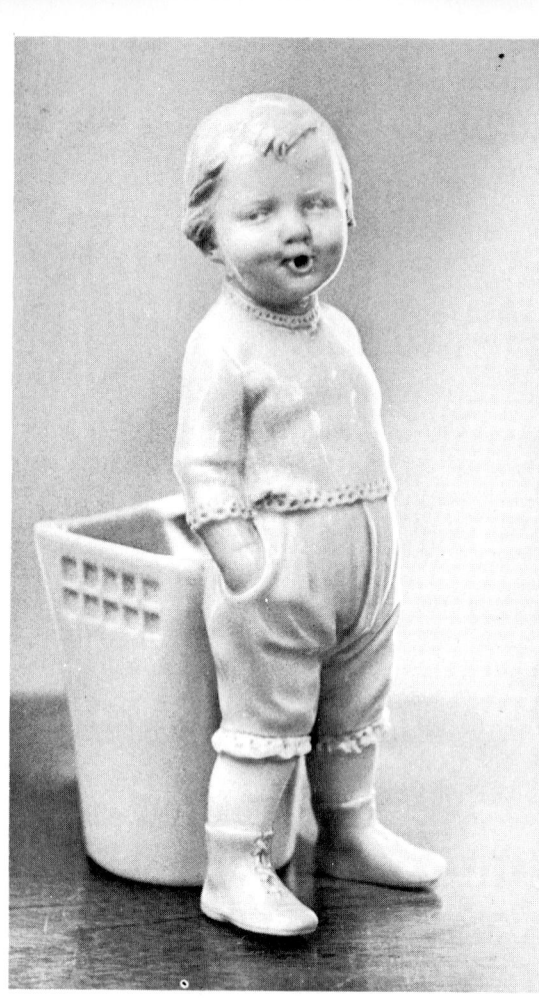

Illustration 141. Certainly a rare Heubach figure is this glazed china boy, a real departure from the myriad of bisque items made. He has beautiful molding for such a small figure with good detail in his eyes and hair, as well as the fabric of his sweater. His mouth is open as though whistling, and with hand in pocket, he presents a jaunty look. The coloring is interesting as it is reminiscent of the Royal Copenhagen figurines, gray white with just a hint of color in his pale gray suit and tan shoes. The vase against which he is leaning is like that of the boy with the cigar in Illustration 135. Just 6½in (16.5cm) tall, he is marked with a green stamped square mark, the only item shown here marked in such a way. However, quite a few glazed china animals finished in this same style stamped in the same way have been seen. *Mike White Collection.*

Illustration 142. This acrobatic fellow is a part of a series of boys at various types of play and came in both the large 12in (30.5cm) size as this one, and a smaller size of about 8in (20.3cm). He has a face typical of the Heubach company, a smiling mouth with teeth showing, deep cheek dimples, eyes just glancing up at the viewer as though looking for approval of his stunt. His blue shirt, a hole torn in the sleeve, has white beaded accents; his purple trousers stop at the knee. His position is so real; all of us have seen children acrobatting around like this. The base of the figurine is green and grassy; in the background is what is probably a bush. He is marked with the sunburst as well as the red Made in Germany circle. *Mike White Collection.*

Illustration 143. Heubach figures are known for catching emotions from serious as shown in Illustration 134 to frivolous as this little girl with the powder box in one hand and the puff in another. She flirts with herself in the mirror as she pretends to be very grown-up. Her blonde hair is long and wavy, and her face is older than that of the child in Illustration 134. Her undergarment is trimmed with gold, and the turquoise polka dots are surrounded with tiny raised paint dots, often a Heubach decorative technique, but one which does not usually show up in photographs. Again notice the raised big toe, also often seen on Heubach figures. Behind the girl is an attached vanity stool in dark turquoise. Its lid removes to reveal a trinket box. She is 10in (25.4cm) tall and stamped in blue with the sunburst. *Richard Wright Collection.*

Focusing On...

Early Unmarked Dolls Attributed to J. D. Kestner, Circa 1880 to 1892

The two doll sisters (shown in **Illustrations 5** and **6**) stood looking serenely down from their high shelf. Their exquisite features soft, melting and blending into an almost perfect countenance. Their beautifully sculpted faces, faintly brooding, faintly quizzical, perhaps shielding some secret emotion, speak to the beholder who almost expects them to come alive.

"Who," we are asked, "has created these charming dolls? Are they marked?"

"No," we reply, "but they are early German dolls now generally attributed to Kestner, although at one time dolls like these were thought to be French because they are of such fine quality — much finer than most marked German dolls."

"Oh, I must have a doll like that. Such a face!"

And so, just that easily, another collector has fallen under the spell of these fabulous dolls attributed to Kestner!

The firm of J.D. Kestner, Waltershausen, Thüringia, Germany, was already well-established in the manufacture of dolls with papier-mâché or wax-over-composition heads before Kestner acquired his porcelain factory in 1860 where he could make his own china and bisque heads. Kestner made both heads and bodies and sold doll parts separately. The early bisque dolls are not marked with any maker's identification. The Kestner crown and streamers was not used until 1895 and it was not until the 20th century that the initials "J.D.K." were incised on dolls' heads. Most Kestner dolls must be identified by known mold numbers or Kestner's size number system which seems to date from about 1892, although it wasn't registered until 1897. Obviously this firm was making bisque dolls long before. What of those dolls? How can they be identified?

Most collectors today feel that the dolls shown here, though unmarked,

ABOVE: Illustration 1. 12in (30cm) child; shoulder head on typical German kid body with bisque hands; original plaster pate with replaced blonde wig; gray sleep eyes with wide-stroked blonde eyebrows; closed mouth has a darker red line separating the lips; fat chubby face with double chin and rosy cheeks. Her clothes, except for the hat, are believed to be original and consist of a long baby's dress with a complete set of underwear. Marked only with a size number. *H&J Foulke, Inc.*

RIGHT: Illustration 2. Shown without clothes, this 19in (48cm) doll's sturdy composition body is typical of that of the dolls shown in **Illustrations 4, 5, 7, 9** and **10**. Note the excellent proportion and construction and the broad shoulders. There is a separate ball to join shoulder and elbow; the wrists are solid; the knee ball is a part of the lower leg. These bodies typically have an elongated rear. The limbs are quite shapely; note the molding of the upper leg, upper arm and calf. The face of this doll is very similar to that of the doll shown in **Illustration 10.** Her eyes are small and blue and seem to look up, but the eyebrows are shaped differently at the inside. She has the same two tiny square-cut teeth in her open mouth. Her human hair wig appears to be original. She is marked only: "12." *Sue Bear Collection.*

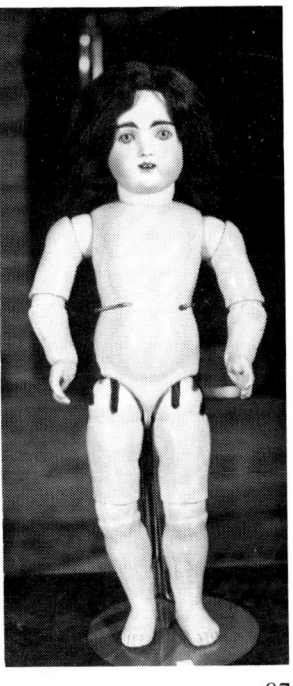

December 1975 Doll Reader

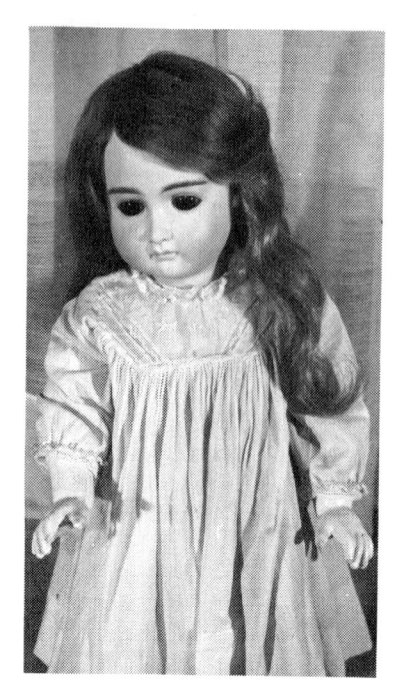

ABOVE: Illustration 3. This 17in (43cm) doll is a shoulder head on a well-constructed kid body with beautifully detailed bisque hands; lovely quality small brown eyes with eyebrows and delicately painted eyelashes; darker line between her closed lips; original plaster pate is intact. Her bisque is exquisite and of a finer texture than that of the doll shown in **Illustration 6**. *H&J Foulke, Inc.*

RIGHT: Illustration 5. This wistful child is a sister of the one shown in **Illustration 4** with the same facial characteristics and body. *Sue Bear Collection.*

are Kestner dolls of the 1880 to 1892 period. Characteristics which these dolls seem to share are listed below.
1. Squared-off mouth.
2. Shape of eye — arched and breaking toward nose.
3. Modeling through lower cheeks and chin (plump cheeks, double chins).
4. Narrow delicate aristocratic noses.
5. Heavy prominent eyebrows ending abruptly and curving down toward nose.
6. Fat round neck with bulge in back.
7. Plaster pate.
8. Usually gray or brown eyes.
9. Darker red line separating lips.
10. Eyes tinier than those of French dolls.

RIGHT: Illustration 4. This 21in (53cm) doll looks like an ancestor of the German pouties of the 20th century. Her body is sturdy, of a good strong composition, ball-jointed except at the wrists which are molded onto the lower arms; replaced wig; brown sleep eyes with irises of a deeper set amber color, prominent eyebrows painted on in many strokes. Her bisque is pale and exquisite. Marked: "14." *Sue Bear Collection.*

RIGHT: Illustration 6. This 17in (43cm) doll is on a good strong composition body completely jointed except for the wrists; the fingers are not molded separately; the legs are elongated; her plaster pate is still intact as well as her original curly blonde mohair wig; gray sleep eyes with painted eyelashes. She has a socket head with a longer thinner face, perhaps representing an older child than the doll shown in **Illustration 1**. Her hat of lovely lace and ribbons is believed to be original. *H&J Foulke, Inc.*

LEFT: Illustration 7. Still another face is represented by this appealing 15in (38cm) child; body is of good composition with unjointed wrists and fingers molded together; her legs are not as elongated as those of the doll shown in **Illustration 6**; original plaster pate; tiny deep brown sleep eyes under heavy eyebrows; puffed-out cheeks and double chin. Her clothes are replaced. *Sue Bear Collection.*

RIGHT: Illustration 8. This small 13in (33cm) child in a pout is on a Kestner marked body of more delicate construction than those of the other dolls shown and is completely jointed, even at the wrists; the fingers are delicate and separated; her eyes are different from the others shown as they are a true blue color and paperweight; she has a protruding upper lip, even more accentuated because the lower lip is molded in; pronounced double chin. Her wig and clothes are replaced. Marked: "8." *Sue Bear Collection.*

BELOW: Illustration 9. This 22in (56cm) child's oblong face with thinner cheeks gives her quite a different appearance from her sisters. Yet she has the same brown amber-flecked eyes and eyebrows as the dolls in **Illustrations 4** and **5**. She is a later doll for she has an open mouth, actually a small slit with molded, almost buck teeth and tiny thin lips. She is on a sturdy composition body. Wig and clothes are replaced. Marked: "14." *Sue Bear Collection.*

RIGHT: Illustration 10. This 25in (63cm) child has a shorter face and chubbier cheeks than the child in **Illustration 9**. She has an open mouth with full lips and two square upper teeth. Her brown sleep eyes are accented by especially long painted eyelashes. Her body of sturdy composition has straight wrists, but separated fingers. Her wig is a replacement. Marked: "15." *Sue Bear Collection.*

RIGHT: Illustration 11. These 6½in (16cm) twins are members of the same family. Compare their tiny faces with that of the doll shown in **Illustration 1**. They are all-bisque with swivel necks and peg joints at the shoulders and hips. They both have sleep eyes and the blonde mohair wigs and clothes are original. Their boots are blue with molded heels and tassels. *Becky Roberts Lowe Collection.*

Focusing On...
Many Faces of Simon & Halbig

Illustration 1. Mold 950. This is a shoulder head number with a closed mouth and is on a pink cloth body with bisque lower arms and black cloth lower legs. Many of those of this number are smaller dolls dressed in regional costumes, and this one has on what is apparently an original costume, possibly part of an historical series. He has a pale blonde curly mohair wig and pierced ears. He stands 10in (25cm) tall. This head also could appear on a kid body and have a closed or open crown. *H&J Foulke, Inc.*

The mark of the Simon & Halbig firm is certainly one which is highly regarded by doll collectors and connoisseurs. Their factory, located in Thüringia, Germany, a thriving doll center in the "heyday" of the bisque doll was founded in 1869. Historical information about the operations of the company is very limited, but much can be learned from examination of the doll heads themselves. Simon & Halbig was in the doll head business during the whole gamut of bisque-head production as their mark has been found on all types of bisque heads from the molded hairdos and bald-head ladies of the 1870s to the ruddy-cheeked dolls of the 1930s. Most are a solid "middle-class" doll of very good quality bisque, falling somewhere between the coarse cheap German and the fine expensive French.

Simon & Halbig made heads only which were sold to other companies, such as Heinrich Handwerck, Cuno & Otto Dressel, Kämmer & Reinhardt, and Jumeau, who made the bodies and otherwise assembled the doll for sale. In 1920 Kämmer & Reinhardt purchased the Simon & Halbig factory, but they also still made heads for other companies, for instance, the heads marked "AHW//S&H" are of this later period.

Presented here are illustrations and descriptions of only a handful of the more than 100 molds used by this most prolific company. This figure includes molds marked with the firm initials "S & H" only, as well as those marked "S & H" with another company. Generally speaking the numbers ending in "9" are socket heads and the numbers ending in "0" are shoulder heads with stationary necks. Mold number 1079 is the most frequently found, and examination of many of these heads shows that this number was used for over 30 years.

Illustration 2. Mold 1249. This socket head is very popular with collectors today and is sometimes also incised "Santa." It was first made in about 1900 for Hamburger. The bisque is usually good quality with molded eyebrows, an open mouth and pierced ears. This particular doll is 27in (69cm) tall and has her original pale blonde mohair wig in original curls, never combed! The lower lip on this model usually has a red triangle painted in for shading. *H&J Foulke, Inc.*

Illustration 3. Mold 1009. This mold number is a socket head, which is used on either a jointed composition body or a kid body with shoulder plate. This particular doll is of smooth bisque with an open mouth, brown sleep eyes, and pierced ears. Her wig is a replacement. Her body is the kind collectors refer to as the "German fashion type." It has an elongated torso of cloth with kid legs, kid-covered wood upper arms, pinned elbow joints and lovely modeled bisque lower arms. Her socket head is inset in a bisque shoulder plate; the opening is kid lined. She would date about 1889 and is 17in (43cm) tall. *H&J Foulke, Inc.*

Illustration 4. Mold 949. This mold number is also for a socket head and is used on both composition and shoulder plate kid bodies. It can have a closed or open mouth. This particular doll with pale smooth early bisque is on an all-kid body of fine quality with bisque lower arms. She has a solid dome head, stationary brown eyes, pierced ears and original pale blonde mohair wig. This mold can also have the usual cut head. This doll would probably be considered a product of the late 1880s because of her solid head, closed mouth and lack of the word "Germany" on her head. (After 1891, products coming into the United States had to be marked with country of origin.) *H&J Foulke, Inc.*

Illustration 5. Mold 939. This is a socket head number which appears on a composition body. It can have a closed or open mouth with one or two rows of teeth. This particular doll has blue sleep eyes and an open mouth of upper teeth only, pierced ears and apparently an original wig of pale blonde mohair. Her body is of jointed composition with straight wrists. The lack of the word "Germany" on the head, the open mouth and the unjointed wrist suggest a date of about 1890 for this doll. She is 13in (33cm) tall. Early versions of this mold with pale bisque, paperweight eyes and a closed mouth are easily mistaken for French dolls. *H&J Foulke, Inc.*

Illustration 6. Mold 1109. This socket head mold is one of the rarer numbers and has a longer and thinner face than number 1079. This particular doll is 15in (38cm) tall with a decided ruddy tone to the cheek tinting. *H&J Foulke, Inc.*

Illustration 7. Mold 1159. This one is the popular Simon & Halbig lady doll socket head. She is referred to as the S & H "Gibson Girl" when she appears on the jointed composition lady body with molded bust and shaped waist (also called the pregnant doll). This head is also used on the "flapper-type" body with flat chest, and long thin arms and legs with feet molded to wear high-heeled shoes. The particular doll shown is a 14in (36cm) flapper. She has a brown human hair wig, blue sleep eyes and an open mouth. She is wearing a blue silk flapper dress and hat, possibly original. *H&J Foulke, Inc.*

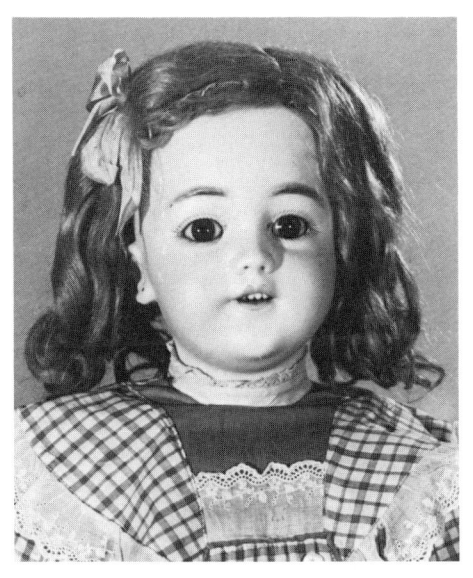

Illustration 8. Mold 1248. This one is definitely a sister to number 1249, seen in **Illustration 2**, but she is found far less frequently. Her face is smiling a little more than her sister. She also has the molded eyebrows and red triangular shading on her lower lip. Her dark blonde mohair wig is very full and made with good quality hair. She is 24in (61cm) tall. *H&J Foulke, Inc.*

Illustration 9. Mold 1299. This mold number, which is fairly hard to find, is a darling character face, so appealing! She has a different mouth, narrow and bow-shaped with only two wide-spaced upper teeth. Her wig of blonde mohair appears original. He is 20in (51cm) tall. *H&J Foulke, Inc.*

```
SIMON & HALBIG
      1249
      DEP
    Germany

S & H           S & H 1009
                  DEP
 939                St.
```

Illustration 10. Three examples of Simon & Halbig marks.

91

Focusing On...

German Characters

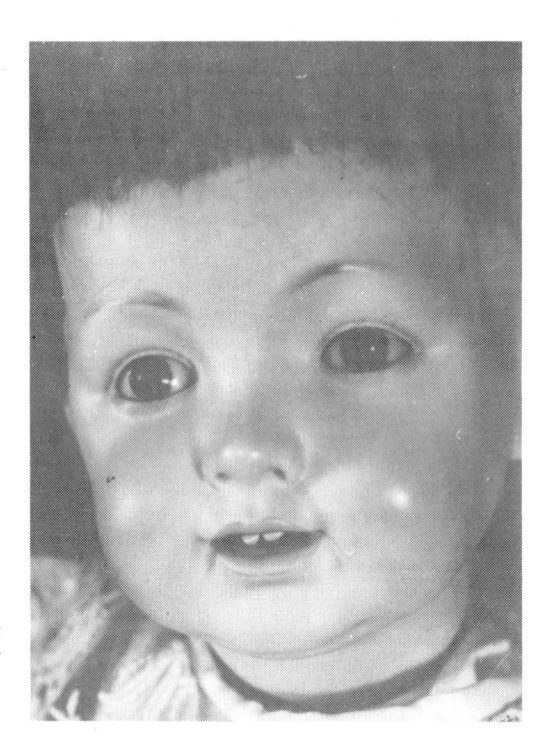

Illustration 1. "Herbie;" rare J.D.K. 220 with jointed toddler body. *Jan Foulke Collection.*

"Herbie" sits in an armchair in my living room. About the size of a 14- to 16-month-old child, he has caused many visitors to do a quick double take for a few seconds wondering whether my nephew or a neighbor's son is visiting until they realize, somewhat dismayed, that he is only a doll. Then follows the inevitable comment: "Oh, my, I thought he was a real little boy!" Then, as if in justification: "Well, he looks just like one."

But visitors are not the only ones taken in by "Herbie." To me, too, he has a reality. He is one of the few dolls I talk to — just cannot help myself since it seems natural to talk to him as I pass him sitting there with his smiling face beaming up at me. (This, in spite of the warning of an old gentleman friend: "Well, deal in dolls if you want to, and good luck to you, but don't get so funny over them that you *talk* to them!" Obviously, he had never met "Herbie.") Also, to our Siamese cat, he must seem real, since he curls up in the chair to sleep with "Herbie" when we are away. And then there is my father, who complains when he sits in the living room that he feels as though someone is watching him. Then, of course, my husband introduces "Herbie," just as if he were a real person, to all of our visitors. So, here sits "Herbie," actual proof of the skill of the German doll makers of the early 20th century in achieving their goal of creating a doll which was so lifelike that it looked like a real child.

A severe departure from the stereotyped "dolly faces," these new character dolls with their natural, expressive features were modeled by artists from real babies and children. Generally, Marion Kaulitz, with her "Munich Art Dolls" in composition, is credited with beginning this important reform in dolls' heads. Käthe Kruse and Steiff with their cloth character dolls followed closely. Character heads in bisque were first produced by Gebrüder Heubach, Kestner and Kämmer & Reinhardt, whose first character doll was the famous "Baby" mold number 100, introduced about 1909. Other manufacturers soon joined them, for the market in these new dolls was brisk. The lifelike faces became very popular and provided new impetus to the sagging German doll industry.

The character heads of the babies were larger in proportion to the bodies, as is natural with small children. Usually, the ears were more detailed and stood out further from the head. The forehead had the typical baby bumps on front and side depressions. The nose was flatter and broader, sometimes turning up on the end. The cheeks were fuller and chubbier, with a more pronounced double chin. The mouth was wider open and more natural with fuller lips. The heads had natural-looking molded hair or wigs, usually of soft mohair. Many of the character dolls had painted eyes. Gebrüder Heubach dolls, especially, are noted for their lovely intaglio eyes, painted with iris and pupil concave.

However, not all of the character heads portray babies. Many of them are faces of older children expressing many moods — smiling, frowning, pouting, and crying.

The first character heads seem to have been placed on leather or ball-jointed bodies. About 1909 Kämmer & Reinhardt developed their bent-limb composition bodies, which helped make the baby doll character even more lifelike. These new bodies really resembled those of chubby children with molded rolls of fat, fat stomachs, creases at wrists and so on. The arms and hands were molded in natural poses with fingers curving in or stretching out. The legs and feet were molded with dimpled knees, thick ankles and often a turned up big toe. These new bodies were much more realistic than the ball-jointed bodies formerly used with hardly any shape to the limbs.

Looking at the accompanying illustrations, it is easy to agree with one manufacturer's statement: "A photograph of this doll is really a photograph of a baby."

Illustration 2. Kämmer & Reinhardt; open mouth with four upper teeth; sometimes has flirty eyes; marked: K★R 117n." *Helen Teske Collection.*

Illustration 3. Kämmer & Reinhardt: pouty face; painted eyes; very desirable; marked: "K★R 114." *Helen Teske Collection.*

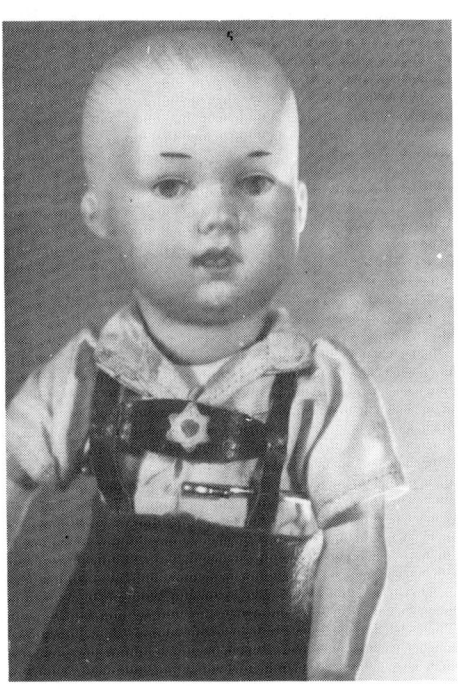

FAR LEFT: Illustration 4. J. D. Kestner; typical Kestner composition arms and hands; marked: "J.D.K. 226." *H&J Foulke, Inc.*

LEFT: Illustration 5. Armand Marseille; unusual mold; ball-jointed body; intaglio eyes; open/closed mouth with molded teeth; original clothes; marked: "GB 250 AM." *Betty Harms Collection.*

ABOVE: Illustration 6. Alt, Beck & Gottschalck; perky face; flirty eyes; marked: "ABG 1352." *Terry O'Kolowich Collection.*

RIGHT: Illustration 7. J. D. Kestner; ball-jointed body with especially long legs appropriate for a boy; marked: "J.D.K. 257." *Helen Teske Collection.*

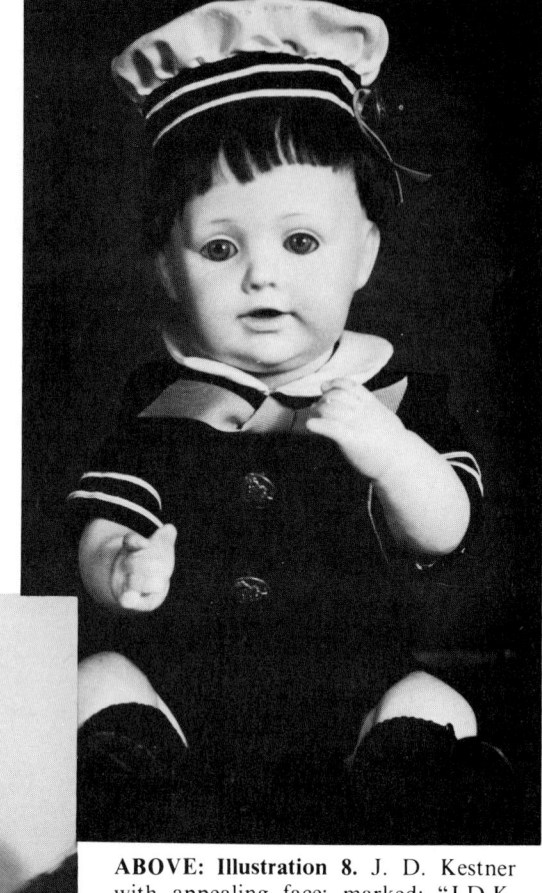

ABOVE: Illustration 8. J. D. Kestner with appealing face; marked: "J.D.K. 247." *H&J Foulke, Inc.*

RIGHT: Illustration 9. Bähr & Pröschild; fine bisque with mohair wig; marked: "B.P. 585." *H&J Foulke, Inc.*

FAR RIGHT: Illustration 10. Bähr & Pröschild for Kley & Hahn; lovely molding; beautiful intaglio eyes; marked: "531." *Anna Buhlman Collection.*

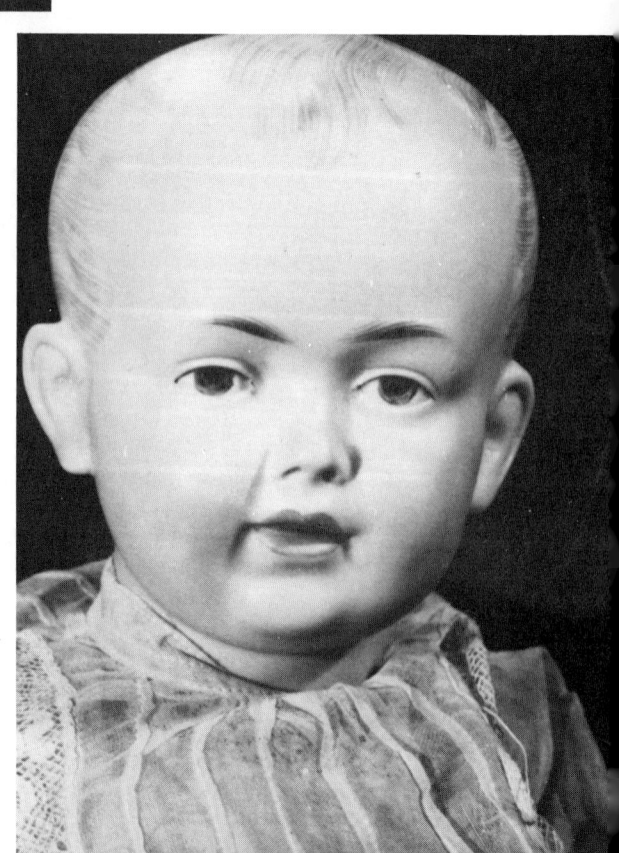

Focusing On...
German Character Children

The creation of the character dolls — dolls which were modeled after real children — was an innovative development of the German doll industry, a refreshing and new doll concept after so many years of following in the footsteps of the French doll makers. The character doll movement began in Munich in 1908 with a group of artist-designers who conceived the idea of making dolls which were more real-looking and childlike than the pretty "dolly faces" which represented an idealized rather than a real child. Gebrüder Heubach and Kämmer & Reinhardt were among the first firms to produce these character dolls with bisque heads, but within a very short time other progressive firms had joined in.

Because of their artistic qualities and general appeal, these German character children are very desirable and quite sought-after by doll collectors. For some unexplained reason (perhaps economic, as these new dolls were not an immediate success with the general public) most companies went into rather heavy production of the character babies instead of the children, which causes the latter to be even more rare and desirable today.

No detailed descriptions have been given for these dolls, as the photographs speak for themselves, showing dolls which are superb examples of this period in the German doll industry; truly these character children are its crowning achievement.

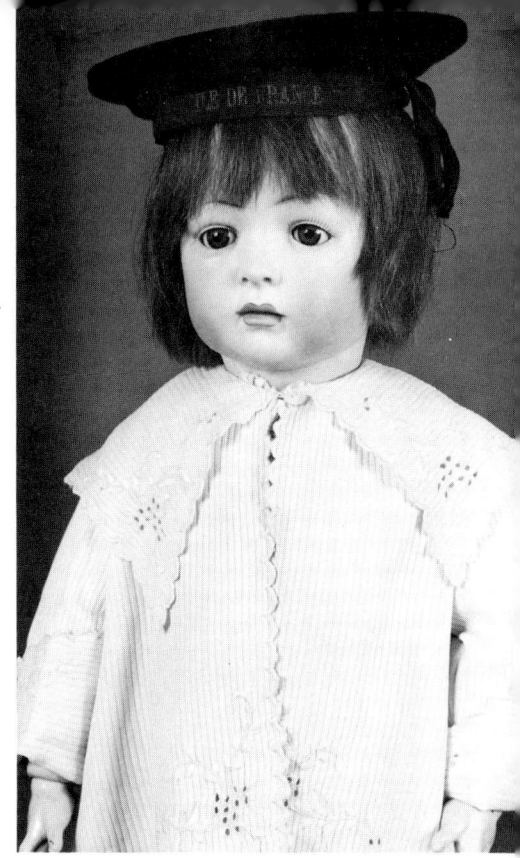

Illustration 2. The Kley & Hahn factory also produced this boy with mold number 169; he is on a composition ball-jointed toddler body. *Richard Wright Collection.*

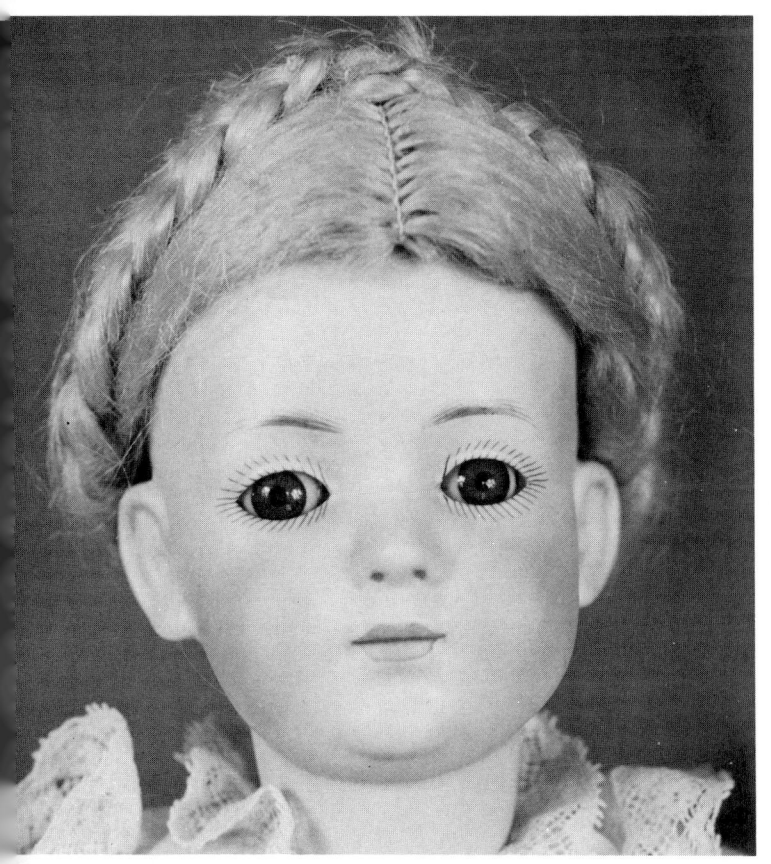

Illustration 1. A product of the Kley & Hahn factory in Ohrdruf, Thüringia, Germany, this 15in (38cm) character girl from mold number 546 has glass eyes and her original blonde mohair wig. She is on a composition ball-jointed body. *Jane Alton Collection.*

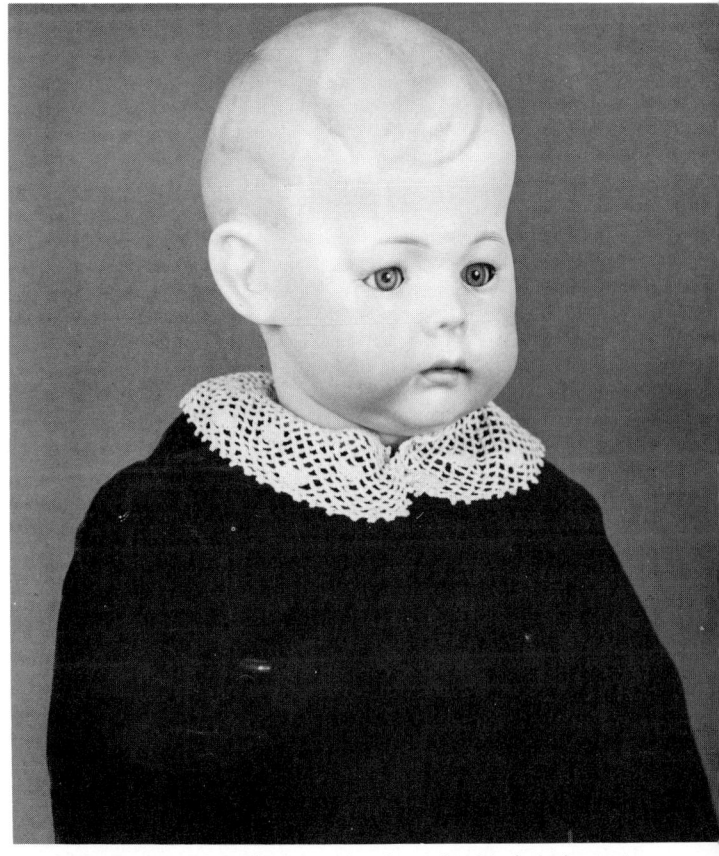

Illustration 3. This child with blonde molded hair is from the Armand Marseille factory in Köpplesdorf, Thüringia. He is "Fany," mold number 230 and is on a composition ball-jointed toddler body with unjointed wrists. *Richard Wright Collection.*

August/September 1982 Doll Reader

ABOVE: Illustration 4. The Gebrüder Heubach factory in Lichte, Thüringia, made the head of this 27in (69cm) pouty girl, mold number 6969. She has beautiful feathered blonde eyebrows and a decidedly down-turned mouth. She is on a composition ball-jointed body. *Richard Wright Collection.*

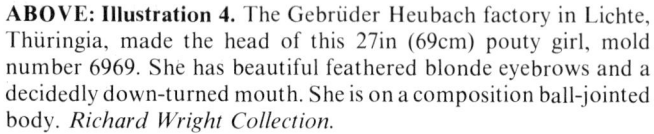

ABOVE RIGHT: Illustration 5. The Simon & Halbig factory also produced this very black character child with Negroid features, mold number 1358. She is on a black composition ball-jointed body. *Richard Wright Collection.*

BELOW: Illustration 6. A very rare doll from the Armand Marseille factory is this 16½in (42cm) girl with gray intaglio eyes and very full lips; she has no mold number. *Richard Wright Collection.*

BELOW RIGHT: Illustration 7. This 13½in (34cm) boy by Simon & Halbig of Gräfenhein, Thüringia, has beautifully modeled blonde hair, blue painted eyes and eyebrows of one wide stroke. He is mold number 153 on a jointed composition body wearing original clothes. *Richard Saxman Collection.*

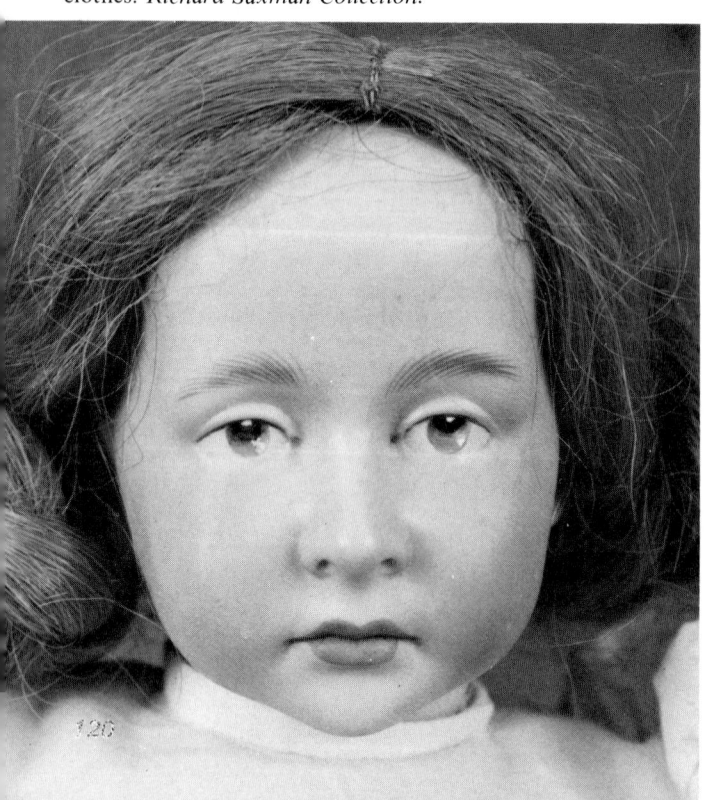

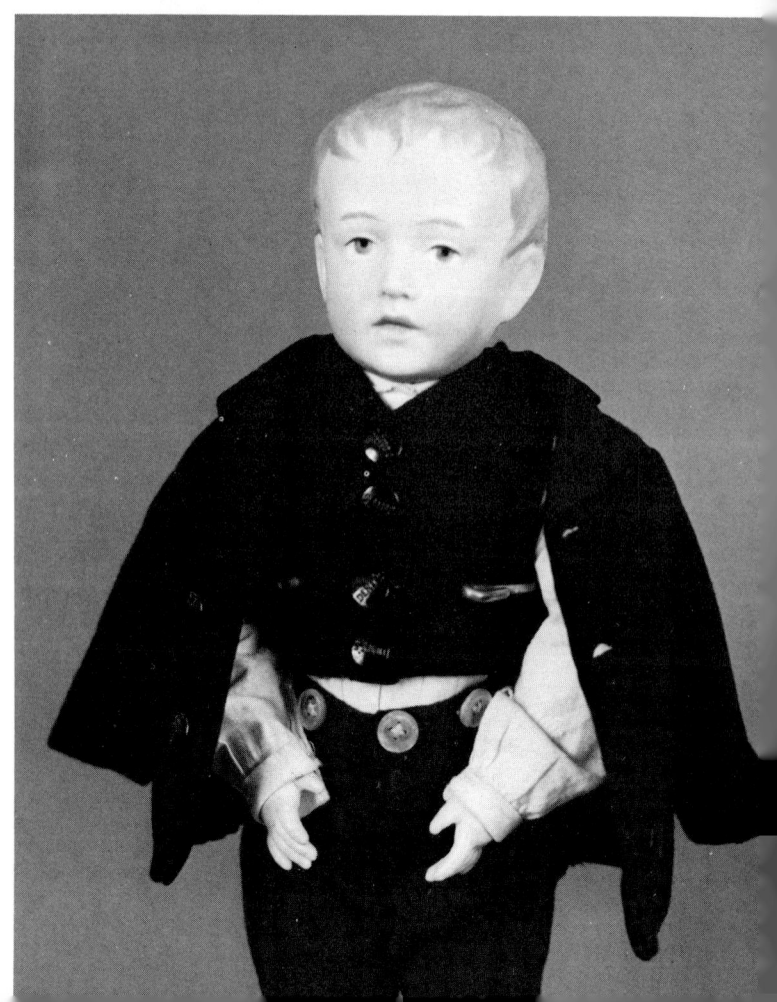

Color Illustration 1. From the factory of J. D. Kestner in Waltershausen and Ohrdruf comes this 16in (41cm) girl from mold number 189 with dimples, glass eyes and her original blonde mohair wig with coiled braids. She is on a pink composition ball-jointed body with the red "Germany" stamp used by Kestner and also has a paper label from G. A. Schwarz toy store in Philadelphia, Pennsylvania. *Richard Wright Collection.*

Color Illustration 2. This 19in (48cm) boy is another doll from the Simon & Halbig factory; his long face, full lips and sharp nose are distinctive characteristics. His mold number is 150. *Richard Wright Collection.*

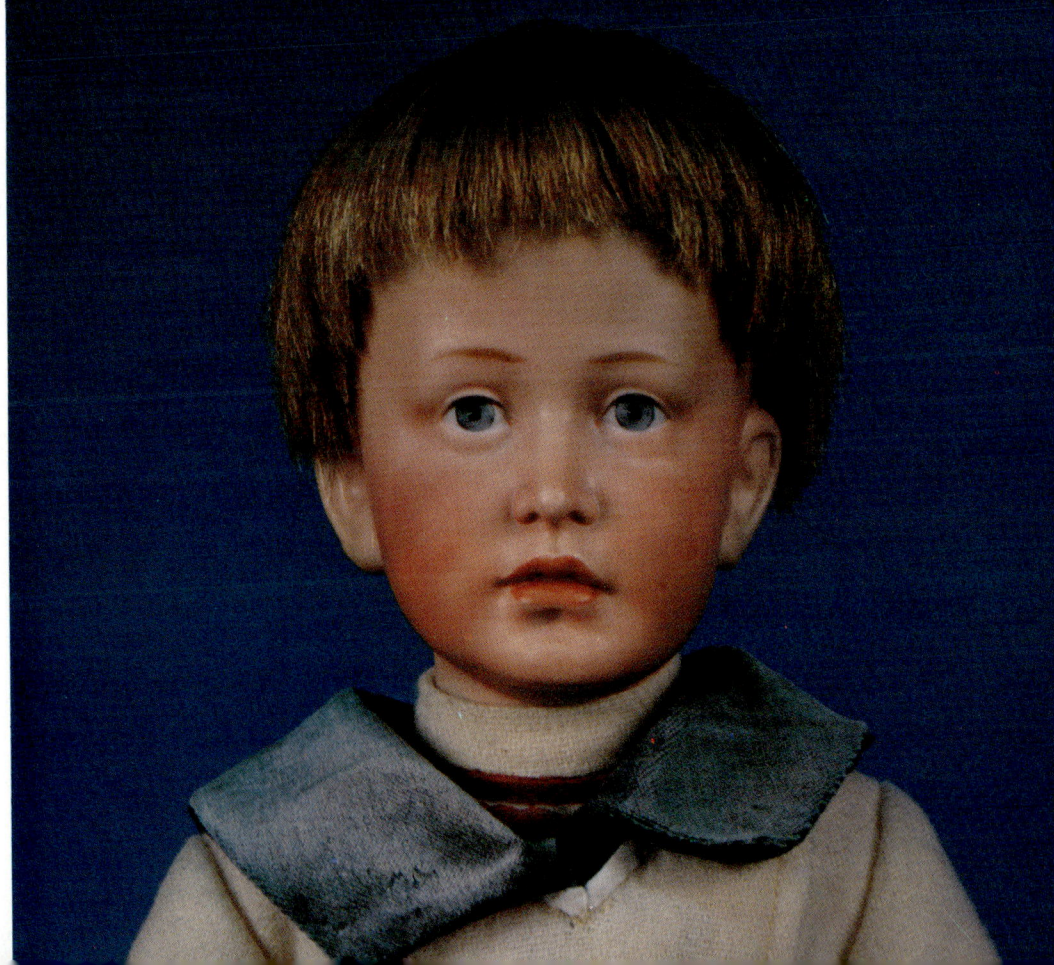

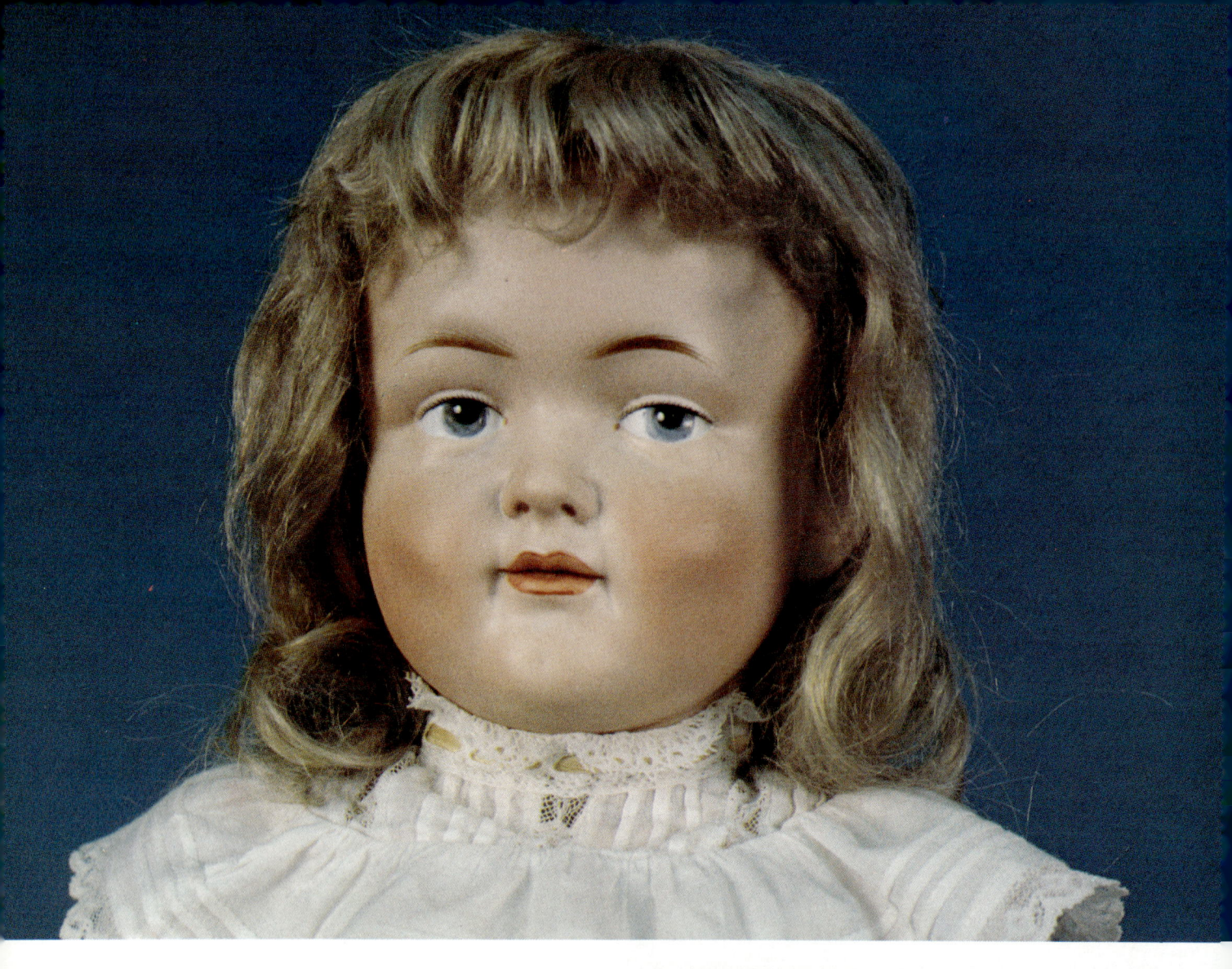

ABOVE: Color Illustration 3. A very rare doll from the Kley & Hahn factory is this 21in (53cm) girl with gray intaglio eyes looking to the side; very tiny upper lashes are painted across her eyelid. With incredible detail in the modeling, she is from mold number 549. *Richard Wright Collection.*

RIGHT: Color Illustration 4. Another doll produced by Kämmer & Reinhardt with a head made by Simon & Halbig is this 12in (31cm) boy from mold number 107. He is on a composition ball-jointed body and is wearing his original clothes. *Richard Wright Collection.*

Focusing On...

Hertel, Schwab & Co.: A New Name for a Familiar Face

Illustration 1. Mold number 141 character child with closed mouth. *Esther Schwartz Collection.*

As a result of the voluminous research presented in the new *German Doll Encyclopedia, 1800-1939,* by Jürgen and Marianne Cieslik, recently translated into English and published by Hobby House Press, Inc., doll collectors must accustom themselves to many new names of German porcelain factories, doll factories, **verlagers,** exporters and patent holders. Foremost of newly-discovered porcelain factories is that of Hertel, Schwab & Co. owners of Stutzhauser Porzellanfabrik located near Ohrdruf, Thürginia. Most of the dolls revealed by the Ciesliks to be from this porcelain factory have long been attributed to Kestner & Co., Kling & Co. or Bähr & Pröschild. Interestingly enough, all four of these factories are located near the small town of Ohrdruf. All of them produced bisque of generally the same quality as can be seen by examining the ubiquitous *Bye-Lo Baby* which was made by all of these factories excluding Bahr & Proschild and including Alt, Beck & Gottschalck. It would be impossible to pick up a *Bye-Lo* and determine which of the four factories made the head. Therefore, although the Hertel, Schwab & Co. heads have been attributed to the wrong factories (Whoever had even heard of this company?), they were attributed to the right **Location.** It is probably no coincidence that various factories in the same geographic area produced heads with characteristics so similar as to be confusing. In such a small town, there must have been a lot of interaction between the factories with sculptors, artists, mold makers and decorators transferring from one place of work to another at different times.

J. D. Kestner pioneered and established the doll industry in the Waltershausen area, near Ohrdruf. It was solely due to his efforts that Waltershausen became a thriving center for making dolls. His first factory was built in 1816. His early dolls were jointed wooden ones, or papier-mâché heads on leather bodies, and later cloth bodies with wax-over-composition heads. His business kept growing and he developed overseas markets, particularly an American trade. In the 1850s other doll factories opened in Waltershausen. In 1860 Kestner bought his own porcelain factory in nearby Ohrdruf. This factory produced, in addition to doll heads, tea sets, knickknacks, bathing dolls, small all-bisque dolls, bathing beauties and pincushion heads. Other doll factories which sprang up in Waltershausen were C. M. Bergmann, Kämmer & Reinhardt, Kley & Hahn, Koenig & Wernicke, Bruno Schmidt and Franz Schmidt. Porcelain factories located nearby which supplied heads to the doll makers were Simon & Halbig (1869), Hertel, Schwab & Co. (1910), Kestner & Co. (1860), Kling & Co. (1834), Bähr & Pröschild (1871), and Alt, Beck & Gottschalck (1854).

February/March 1986 Doll Reader

Illustration 2. Mold number 165 googly made for Strobel & Wilken. *Richard Wright Antiques.*

Illustration 3. Mold number 154 character child. *Dr. Carole Stoessel Zvonar Collection.*

Illustration 4. Mold number 152 character baby on toddler body. *Private Collection.*

Illustration 5. Mold number 99 character baby for Koenig & Wernicke. *Dr. Carole Stoessel Zvonar Collection.*

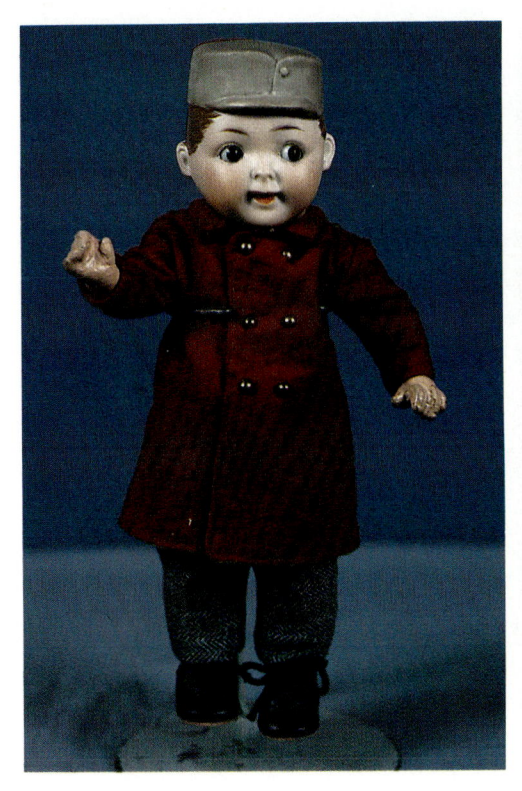

FAR LEFT: Illustration 6. Two-faced googly, one side with a Turkish soldier's cap, the other with an Austrian soldier's cap. This doll was apparently made by an Ohrdruf porcelain factory, possibly Hertel, Schwab & Co. This view shows the Austrian soldier's cap. *Esther Schwartz Collection.*

LEFT: Illustration 7. The two-faced googly, seen in *Illustration 6,* showing the side with the Turkish soldier's cap. *Esther Schwartz Collection.*

Waltershausen dolls became known on the world doll market for their fine quality and excellent craftsmanship. They were generally far superior to the products produced by the Sonneberg doll makers who specialized in mass-producing dolls for cheaper prices. Sonneberg was known for its wood products as early as 1500, but by the late 1700s, these had been superceded by articles for the toy trade. Large Sonneberg area doll factories were owned by Cuno & Otto Dressel, Arthur Schoenau, Heinrich Stier and F. M. Schilling; later, large porcelain factories were owned by Armand Marseille, Ernst Heubach, Porzellanfabrik Mergersgereuth (P.M.), and Schoenau & Hoffmeister. The majority of Sonneberg dolls do not approach the quality of the Waltershausen ones but, of course, there are individual exceptions, particularly with a few of the dolls made by Armand Marseille.

Hertel, Schwab & Co., compared to other Ohrdruf porcelain factories, was a relative newcomer, founded at the late date of 1910. It seems very strange that the name, even the existence of this company remained unknown to doll collectors until 1984 in spite of their fairly large production of character babies in particular. No trademark has been found registered to them, and they apparently never placed their name or initials on any of their products. What ties their heads together and identifies them for collectors is a very consistent number series and their very distinctive "Made in Germany" signature.

The Hertel, Schwab & Co. designs are, for the most part, extremely well executed. The techniques are very similar to those of Kestner & Co., hence the confusion of the products of the two companies. The Ciesliks say the factory was founded by August Hertel, Heinrich Schwab, Friedrich Müller and Hugo Rosenbusch. All were sculptors and the last was also a porcelain painter. Perhaps the presence of the artists in the company accounts for the extremely high level of the designs and the wonderful execution.

The bisque from the Hertel, Schwab & Co. factory is consistently of excellent quality; seldom does one find heads which are grainy, full of imperfections or off-color or splotchy. Of course, every factory let a few duds through, but considering the output of the factory, the quality is very high. The process of making porcelain heads is very complex and problems can arise at any step of the process from preparation of the slip to the final firing. However, as with dolls from other Ohrdruf area factories, Hertel, Schwab & Co. heads are made with smooth bisque, well sanded, containing no bumps or imperfections in the biscuit. The decoration is artistically handled. Apparently the factory decided on a style which all of the artists followed, painting according to a model. The complexion tinting is a natural peachy color, and cheeks have a healthy ruddy look. One distinctive decorating feature is the "wavy" or "flyaway" eyebrows sometimes found on the character dolls, although Bähr & Pröschild characters also sometimes have these eyebrows making it dangerous to attribute heads only on this feature. Hertel, Schwab & Co. dolls that do not have "wavy" eyebrows have arched ones with individual brush strokes at the inner and outer corners. Some of the child character dolls have faintly molded eyebrows. The mouth painting is done very well in a soft red tint, with the upper lip having upturned corners and a pronounced bow. Often there are shading strokes at the peaks of the upper lip and at the bottom of the lower lip. Some characters have closed mouths; some are open with teeth, and many have open/closed mouths with molded teeth and tongue. In 1913, Hertel, Schwab & Co. advertised a doll head with movable tongue. The black eyelashes are long and finely painted with one light brush stroke each. Some dolls have real upper eyelashes. Each nostril opening is shaded with a red dot, and one is also placed at the inner corner of the eye; the red color usually matches the lip color.

Many of the character children come in two versions, either wigged or with

101

RIGHT: Illustration 8. 23in (58.4cm) mold number 98 character baby with pierced nostrils and "follow eyes" which look at you from whatever position you view the baby; made for Koenig & Wernicke. *Dr. Carole Stoessel Zvonar Collection.*

FAR RIGHT: Illustration 9. Mold number 100 character baby on toddler body with flirty eyes. *Dr. Carole Stoessel Zvonar Collection.*

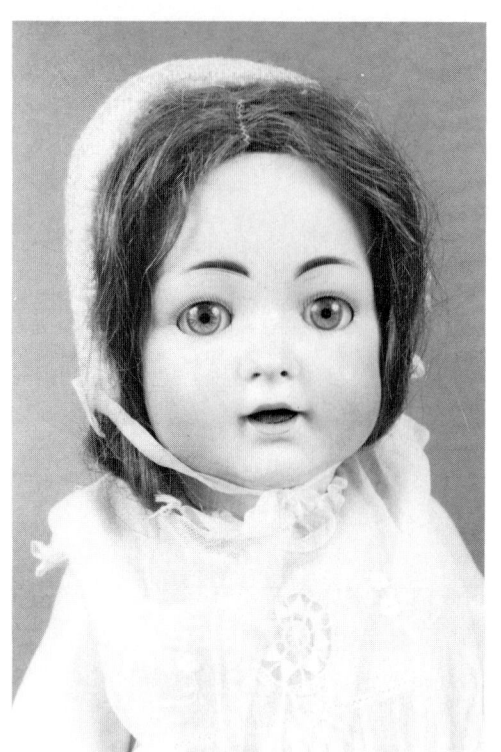

molded hair, such as 166 and 169. Character babies, particularly 150 and 152, have nice soft mohair or angora fleece wigs in bobbed style which are often blonde and are sewn onto a cloth wig cap, just like those on Kestner dolls, not merely a clump of hair pushed into a hole or glued on the crown and fluffed out. Many of the toddler characters have human hair wigs with braids, especially those for Koenig & Wernicke. However, it is possible that doll factories could purchase heads only and supply their own wigs in whatever medium or style they preferred. Hertel, Schwab & Co. made quite a few dolls with molded hair. Some of these were babies, molds 138, 142, 151, 158, 167 and 176, nearly bald with just a molded curly forelock and the remainder of the hair indicated by brush strokes painted naturally, the way hair would grow. One favorite character boy which collectors refer to as *Tommy Tucker,* molds 154 and 166, has side-parted hair painted blonde overall, and wispy bangs combed to the side. One googly, mold 163, has molded orange-blonde hair in a "Campbell Kid" style; another, mold 172, has molded side and forelocks with painted strokes overall.

Most Hertel, Schwab & Co. dolls have glass eyes of very nice quality; some are gray, a color seldom used by other makers. It was formerly thought that these gray-eyed dolls were Kestners. A few of the Hertel, Schwab & Co. character babies and children, usually molds 142, 151 and 138, have painted or glass eyes. Of course, all the character children had painted eyes at first as there was so much molding detail around the eyes, makers could not figure out how to insert glass eyes. Additionally, it was cheaper to produce dolls without glass eyes, as it reduced the labor required to cut the eye sockets, make the glass eyes and inset them. Those dolls which have painted eyes are quite artistic. The eye is done to look very natural with a black pupil and shaded iris, and with a white enamel highlight. The complete eyeball and socket are molded; the upper eyelid is molded and indicated by a black brush stroke directly above the eye topped by a light red one. One rare googly-eyed doll, mold 175, is winking with one round glass eye, and a partially closed painted eye!

All of the Hertel, Schwab & Co. dolls that I am aware of are socket heads except for the *Bye-Lo* which has a flange neck, but in 1925 Hertel, Schwab & Co. advertised "shoulder heads with sleeping eyes and wig." These have not yet been identified and are perhaps the character shoulder head mold 200.

Hertel, Schwab & Co. made heads for quite a few factories and exporters, among whom were Koenig & Wernicke; Kley & Hahn; Rudolph Walch; Albert Schachne; Wiesenthal, Schindel & Kallenberg; George Borgfeldt & Co.; Louis Wolf & Co.; and Strobel & Wilken. Known molds for the foregoing companies are detailed in the mold number chart.

When discussing character babies with mold number 150, 151 and 152 in our book, *Kestner, King of Dollmakers,* we stated that we did not know who made the heads, but we felt that they were probably not by Kestner for a variety of reasons listed there. Now it is nice because of the Ciesliks' research to be able to identify the maker of this popular group as Hertel, Schwab & Co. The character baby with mold number 152 is plentiful on the doll market and appears to have been the most widely distributed of the Hertel, Schwab & Co. babies. This doll was retailed as *Our Baby* by Louis Wolf & Co. However, not all of this mold number are incised with Wolf's mark, so perhaps this was a stock model which Hertel, Schwab & Co. sold to many producers. It has always been attributed by doll collectors to Kestner and has brought a good price considering its widespread availability. It remains to be seen if it can hold its market value with this new identification.

Marked Koenig & Wernicke bodies have been found using heads 98 and 99, so finally it is good to know the porcelain factory responsible for these perky character faces. There is also a number 100 which appears to belong to this group. This identification has been possible because of the distinctive "Made in Germany" mark on these and the 151 mold character baby. The Kley & Hahn doll factory appears to have been one of the largest customers of Hertel, Schwab & Co. Kley & Hahn had 14 known character children and babies made for them, including the two-faced baby, mold 159. Kley & Hahn also bought heads from Kestner, as well as Bähr & Pröschild (500 series).

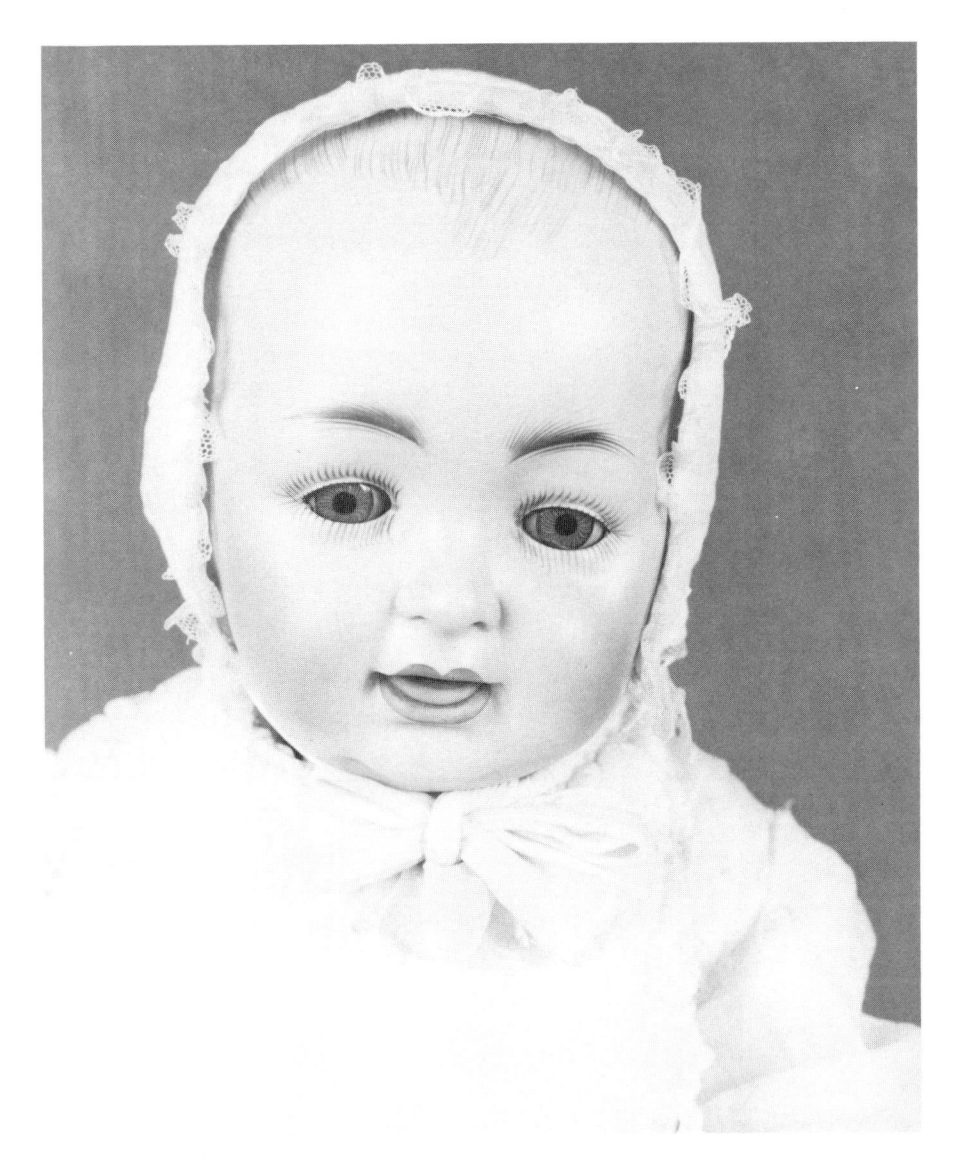

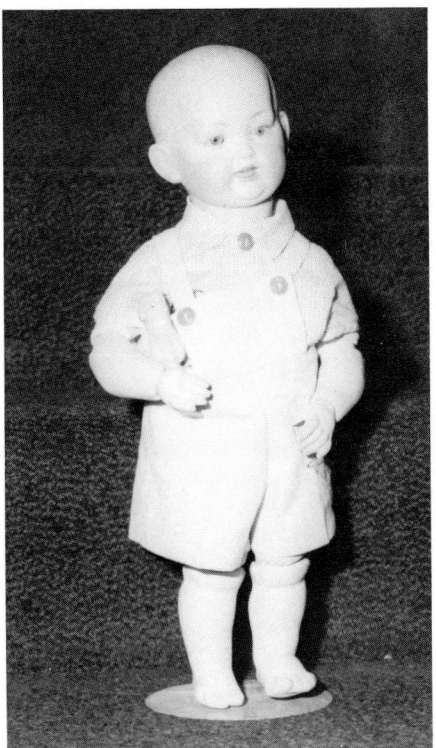

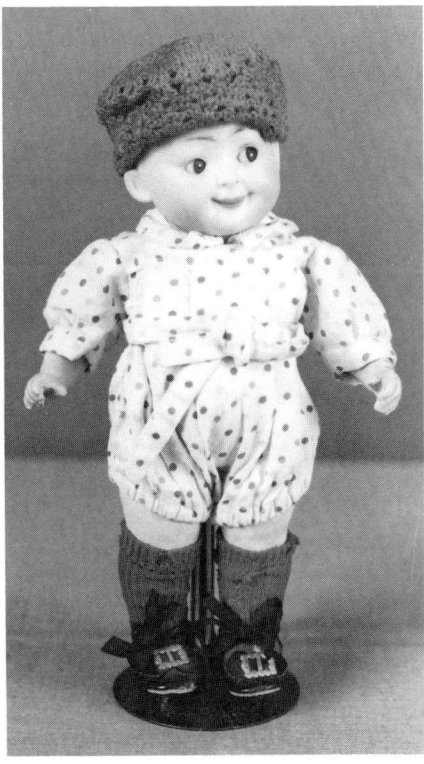

Again, it is satisfying to know at last the maker of the googly numbers so popular with collectors. These dolls had always been attributed to Kestner: number 165 with wig and 163, its counterpart, with molded hair; number 173 with wig and number 172, its counterpart with molded hair. These four googlies were made for Strobel & Wilken, New York importers, and were just a part of their "Jubilee" line. Googly number 178 is another molded hair model, this one for Kley & Hahn and rarely found. Number 175 is another rare googly, this one winking, and is shown by the Ciesliks. Further, regarding the googlies, it is interesting to speculate whether or not Hertel, Schwab & Co. made the very interesting series of googlies with molded hair and hats which have recently turned up from a German source as old factory stock, most of which was purchased by a California dealer. These faces bear a very strong resemblance to googlies 165 and 173 and appear to have been made by an Ohrdruf porcelain factory. In addition to the two-faced dolls shown in *Illustrations 6* and *7* with one side a Turkish soldier, the other side an Austrian, the series includes a German soldier, a British one (cap looks like a bellhop, but is not), and an Uncle Sam with blue top hat.

The Ciesliks list several known mold numbers for Hertel, Schwab &

TOP: Illustration 10. Mold number 151 character baby with molded tongue. *H&J Foulke, Inc.*

BOTTOM LEFT: Illustration 11. Mold number 158 character toddler made for Kley & Hahn. *Lesley Hurford Collection.*

BOTTOM RIGHT: Illustration 12. Mold number 173 googly with flirty eyes on toddler body made for Strobel & Wilken as part of their "Jubilee" line. *Richard Wright Antiques.*

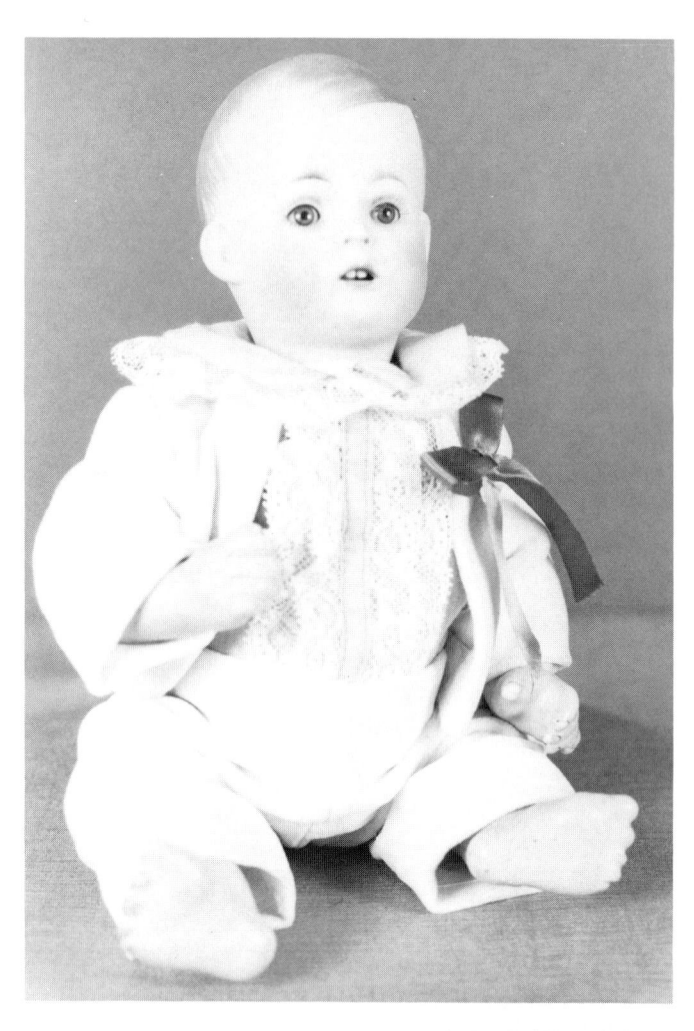

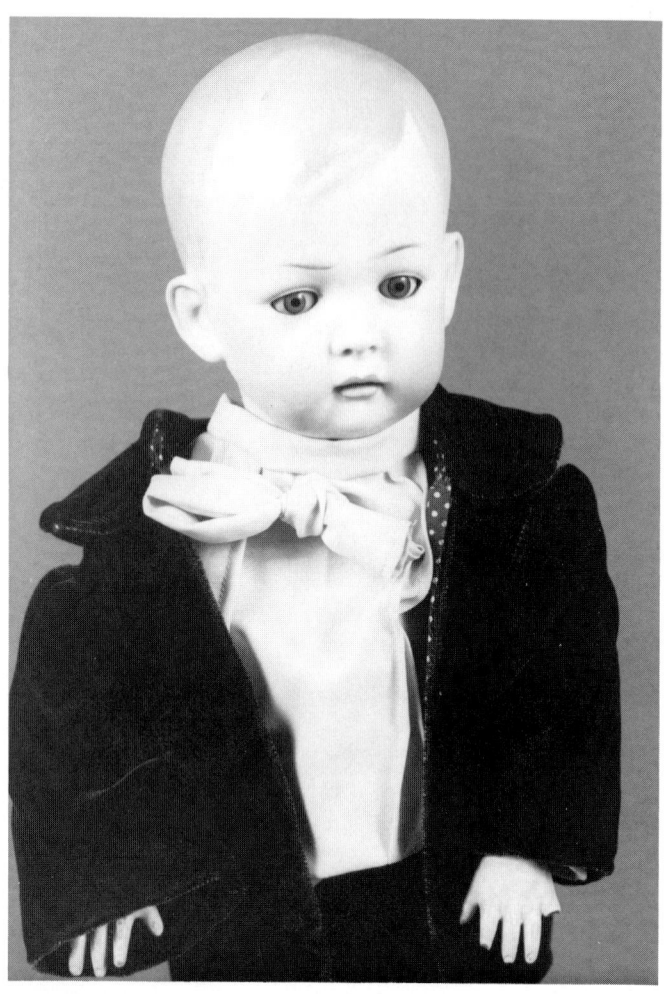

TOP LEFT: Illustration 13. Mold number 166 character with molded hair and open mouth made for Kley & Hahn. *H&J Foulke, Inc.*

TOP RIGHT: Illustration 14. Mold number 166 character child with molded hair and closed mouth made for Kley & Hahn. *Esther Schwartz Collection.*

BOTTOM LEFT: Illustration 15. Mold number 169 character child with closed mouth made for Kley & Hahn. *Richard Wright Antiques.*

BOTTOM RIGHT: Illustration 16. Mold number 167 character with open/closed mouth made for Kley & Hahn. *Dolly Valk Collection.*

104

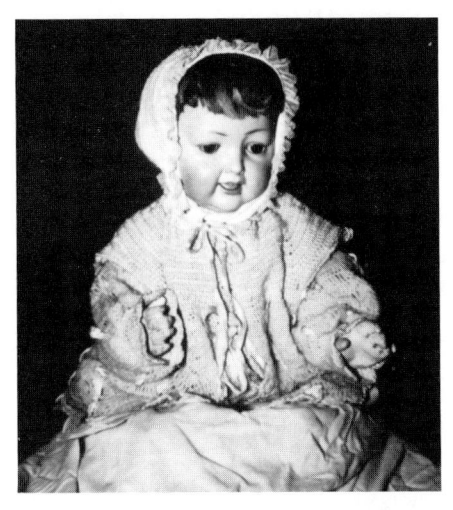

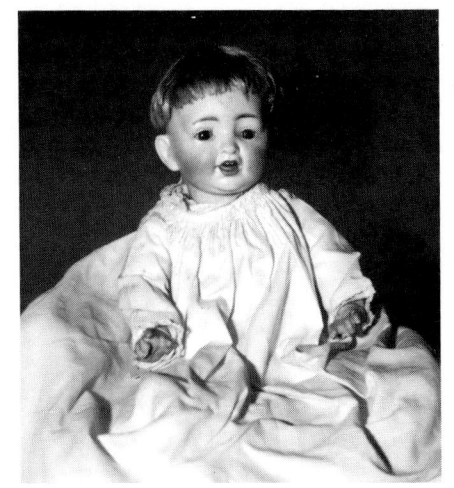

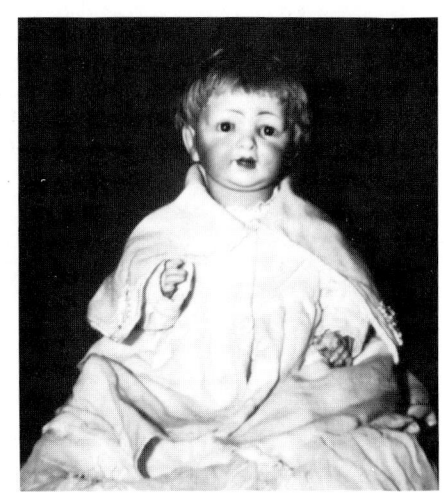

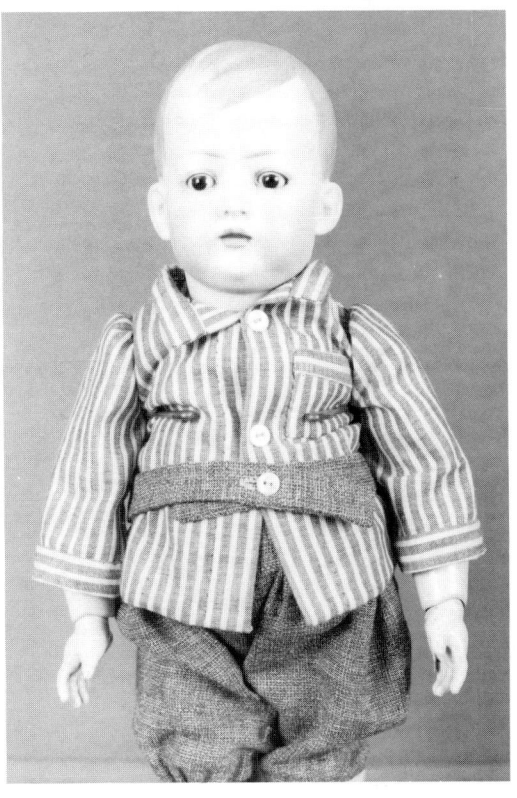

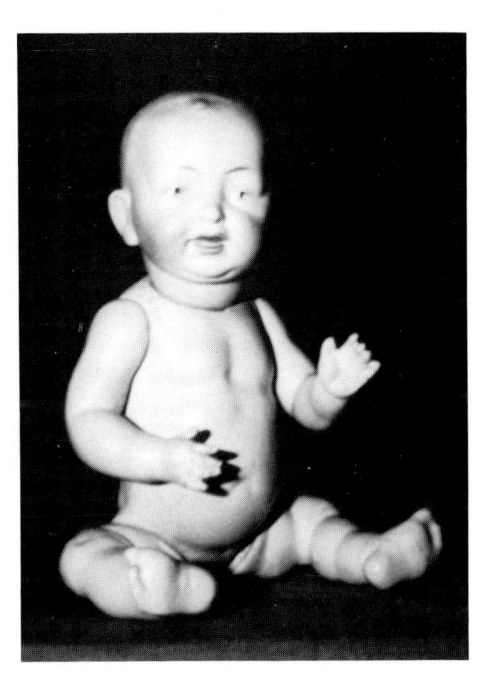

TOP LEFT: Illustration 17. Mold number 160 character baby with open/closed mouth and two molded teeth for Kley & Hahn. *Private Collection.*

TOP MIDDLE: Illustration 18. Mold number 152 character baby for Louis Wolf & Co. *Private Collection.*

TOP RIGHT: Illustration 19. Mold number 152 character baby. *Private Collection.*

BOTTOM LEFT: Illustration 20. Mold number 154 character child with closed mouth and molded hair. *Richard Wright Antiques.*

BOTTOM RIGHT: Illustration 21. Character baby with painted eyes of the type produced by Hertel, Schwab & Co. *Private Collection.*

Co. all-bisque dolls. Numbers 208 and 217 are very confusing, since Kestner also used these numbers on all-bisques. Number 217 for Kestner is a googly, according to Cieslon the Geniene Angione attributed the 217 googly to Wm. Goebel based on the fact that the molded shoes and stockings match those of a marked Goebel doll. The Cieslikslist Hertel, Schwab & Co. 217 as a "doll with sleeping eyes" which could also be a googly. Number 208 all-bisque doll turns up frequently, sometimes as a swivel neck, sometimes stiff-necked, with glass or painted eyes, and with open or closed mouth. My book, *Kestner, King of Dollmakers*, contains a good selection of these dolls. Obviously, more study needs to be given the 208 dolls to determine which models are Kestners and which belong to Hertel, Schwab & Co. The Cieslons list mold number 220 as an all-bisque doll, but I have not found this doll yet. Number 222, they give as *Our Fairy*, a googly with wig. For an illustration of this doll, see our *5th Blue Book Of Dolls & Values* page 267. *Our Fairy* was made in 1913 for Louis Wolf & Co.

Collectors interested in historical research pertaining to their German dolls will find a wealth of information about doll makers and their products in the Cieslikss' *German Doll Encyclopedia, 1800-1939*. Some mold numbers can now be assigned to factories, especially of the earlier dolls where makers did not place their marks on the heads. Many doll marks previously attributed to the wrong makers have been correctly identified. Many factories hitherto unknown which made papier-mâché and early dolls have been listed. The *German Doll Encyclopedia, 1800-1939* provides page after page of information and is high on my suggested reading list for doll students. □

See chart on page 106.

Hertel, Schwab & Co. — Stutzhauser Porzellanfabrik
Stutzhaus near Ohrdruf — Founded 1910

Mold Number	Description	Verlager	Picture Source
98	character baby — sleep eyes, wig, open mouth	Koenig & Wernicke	Article illustration
99	character baby — sleep eyes, wig, open mouth	Koenig & Wernicke	Article illustration
100	character baby — sleep eyes, wig, open mouth		Article illustration
*130	sleep eyes, open/closed mouth		
*132	sleep eyes, open mouth w/tongue		
*133		Kley & Hahn	
134	character child — sleep eyes, wig, closed mouth		*4th Blue Book Of Dolls & Values*®, p. 142
*135		Kley & Hahn	
136	dolly face — sleep eyes, wig, open mouth		*Kestner, King of Dollmakers*, p. 64
138	character baby — molded hair, painted eyes, standard model	Kley & Hahn	
141	character child — painted or sleep eyes, closed mouth, wig		Article illustration
142	character baby — molded hair, painted or sleep eyes, open or open/closed mouth	Rudolf Walch	*Kestner, King of Dollmakers*, p. 171
*143	glass eyes, closed smiling mouth w/molded teeth		
*147	Googly — open/closed mouth		
148	character baby — doll cries real tears, wig, glass eyes, open/closed mouth	"Weinde," Albert Schachne	Ciesliks' *German Doll Encyclopedia*, p. 157
149	character child — painted or sleep eyes, wig, closed mouth		*6th Blue Book Of Dolls & Values*®, p. 157
150	character baby — domed head or wig, painted or sleep eyes, open or open/closed mouth	Some for Wiesenthal, Schindel & Kallenberg	*Kestner, King of Dollmakers*, p. 168
151	character baby — domed head, painted or sleep eyes, open or open/closed mouth		Article illustration
152	character baby — sleep eyes, wig, open or open/closed mouth	*Our Baby*, Louis Wolf & Co.	Article illustration
154	character child — molded hair, sleep eyes, closed mouth		Article illustration
157	character child — wig, sleep eyes, closed mouth	Kley & Hahn	Ciesliks' *German Doll Encyclopedia*, p. 117
158	character baby — molded hair, sleep eyes, open/closed mouth	Kley & Hahn	Article illustration
159	two-faced character baby — laughing, crying	Kley & Hahn	
160	character baby — wig, sleep eyes, open/closed mouth	Kley & Hahn	Article illustration
161	character baby — wig, sleep eyes, open/closed mouth	Kley & Hahn	
*162		Kley & Hahn	
163	Googly — molded hair, closed mouth	"Jubilee Doll," Strobel & Wilken	*5th Blue Book Of Dolls & Values*®, p. 158
165	Googly — wig, closed mouth	"Jubilee Doll," Strobel & Wilken	Article illustration
166	character child — sleep eyes, molded hair, open or closed mouth	Kley & Hahn	Article illustration
167	character baby — wig, sleep eyes, open/closed mouth	Kley & Hahn	Article illustration
169	character child — wig, glass eyes, closed mouth	Kley & Hahn	Article illustration
*170	sleep eyes, open/closed mouth		
172	Googly — molded hair, glass eyes, closed smiling mouth	"Jubilee Doll," Strobel & Wilken	
173	Googly — wig, glass eyes, closed smiling mouth	"Jubilee Doll," Strobel & Wilken	Article illustration
175	Googly — molded hair, closed mouth, winking		Ciesliks' *German Doll Encyclopedia*, p. 117
176	character baby — sleep eyes, wig, open mouth		
178	Googly — molded hair, glass eyes, open mouth	Kley & Hahn	Gladyse Hills Hilsdorf
*180		Kley & Hahn	
*200	character — smiling shoulder head	Louis Wolf & Co.	

*These are numbers recorded by the Ciesliks but I have not located dolls with these numbers.

Focusing On...

Simon & Halbig Faces

Among collectors and connoisseurs of antique German bisque dolls, the products of the Simon & Halbig porcelain factory of Gräfenhain, Thüringia, Germany, are held in very high esteem. Simon & Halbig heads are regarded as superior to those of other German producers not only because of the consistently high quality of their workmanship, but also because of their designs. Even during the early years of bisque doll head production when the same basic insipid dolly face was produced for over 30 years, the majority of Simon & Halbig designs were more distinctive in a subtle way very difficult to pinpoint or define.

The Waltershausen area in which the Simon & Halbig factory was located had

Illustration 1. The heads on this darling pair of toddlers were made for Kämmer & Reinhardt by Simon & Halbig. Their chubby cheeks are dimpled; their open mouths have two upper teeth and separate tongues. These smiling faces with glass eyes became very popular and quickly replaced the more realistic faces of the character children shown in **Illustrations 8** and **11**. *Mary Lou Rubright Collection.*

Illustration 2. Simon & Halbig produced several models of Oriental heads with pale yellow complexions and matching jointed composition bodies. These three all-original examples are all from mold 1199. Their outstanding modeling features narrow slanted eyes and eyebrows. *Regina Steele Collection.*

a reputation for producing the finest German dolls. Known for their excellent craftsmanship, Waltershausen dolls were identified as such in contemporary advertising, and the term **Waltershausen** came to indicate a doll of very good quality.

The Simon & Halbig firm was a porcelain manufactory which produced doll heads, arms and probably legs as well as full porcelain dolls. They sold their heads to other companies who made or provided bodies and completed the doll. Some of these companies had heads especially made by Simon & Halbig from their own molds, hence the heads carry two sets of identifying marks. Some of these factories were C. M. Bergmann, Heinrich Handwerck, Kämmer & Reinhardt, Cuno & Otto Dressel, Adolf Hulss, Franz Schmidt, and Wiesenthal, Schindel, & Kallenberg, and an unidentified company using the initials S & C. Many other companies used the Simon & Halbig stock heads (so, sometimes, did these named companies) which carried only the S & H trademark and the mold number. Quite a few French firms also used stock Simon & Halbig heads including Jumeau, Roullet and Decamps and E. Daspres.

Originally published in **Simon & Halbig Dolls, The Artful Aspect** *by Jan Foulke.*

May 1984 Doll Reader

Illustration 3. This beautiful 24in (61cm) lady is an example of mold 1159, a very popular model with today's collectors as the face is that of an adult, providing a nice change from all of the dolls with child faces. The doll dates after 1900 and has features typical of this period — molded eyebrows and real rather than painted upper eyelashes, although hers are missing. These heads came on lady bodies with molded bosom and nipped-in waist as well as slender arms and legs. *Mary Lou Rubright Collection.*

Illustration 4. This fine 14in (36cm) example of Simon & Halbig's mold 939 appears to have been made for the French trade. Like the French dolls, the bisque is very thin; there is no lip on the crown opening. Her mouth is closed, but a white space separates upper and lower lips. Her blue paperweight eyes are threaded and have a larger blue shading. Her ears are pierced and she has a cork pate. Her totally original outfit is similar to those featured on French dolls of the early 1880s period. *Lorna Lieberman Collection.*
Originally published in **Simon & Halbig Dolls, The Artful Aspect** *by Jan Foulke.*

I have always admired doll heads made in the Simon & Halbig factory. Their craftsmanship is outstanding; their faces unmistakably expressive. The obvious care and attention accorded to each head is amazing considering the quantity of the factory's production. I began to notice a wide assortment of mold numbers and face styles which lead me on a search of just how many different mold numbers this firm produced. My study is presented in a new book in which over 150 molds are listed and discussed along with over 550 photographs. Of course, one never considers a book of this type finished, as hopefully other unrecorded numbers will surface in the future.

Illustration 5. This petite 12in (31cm) dolly is incised: "Simon & Halbig//600//Germany," and is a very difficult-to-find model. She has brown sleep eyes and molded upper eyelids. Her short lightly-stroked eyebrows and lack of special shading on her lips probably place her at a later period than the doll shown in **Illustration 7.** She is all original. *Regina Steele Collection.*

ABOVE LEFT: Illustration 6. This 25in (64cm) doll is a typical example of a head from the Simon & Halbig factory which would date in the mid 1880s. She is incised: "S 15 H//949." The fine quality bisque of this period is given only a light complexion tint with slightly rouged cheeks. The eyebrows are very long and quite heavy with many individual brush strokes noticeable at the inner and outer edges. The eyes are small, usually stationary, with a molded upper eyelid and generously painted eyelashes. Her mouth is closed with quite full lips which have special shading strokes, one on each bow of the upper lip and one on each side of the lower lip. A shading line also divides the upper and lower lips. Her chin sports a deep dimple, and her ears are pierced. *Betty McSpadden Collection.*

LEFT: Illustration 7. This lovely all-original 20½in (55cm) doll is an example of a typical Simon & Halbig doll face head. It is from mold number 1009, one of the first numbers to be made only in the open mouth style. The German factories turned out dolly faces by the millions, yet those with Simon & Halbig mold numbers have a distinctive personality. Their faces are pert, almost smiling, with lively eyes. This doll has the usual Simon & Halbig almond-shaped sleep eyes; her painted eyebrows are long and curved with no molding. Her parted lips show four upper teeth; they also have the four special shading strokes seen on the earlier closed mouth dolls. Her cheeks are full and her chin is dimpled. She also has pierced ears. This doll is totally original with her blonde wig and red satin dress with fancy matching hat trimmed with ruffles and bows. *Ralph's Antique Doll Museum.*

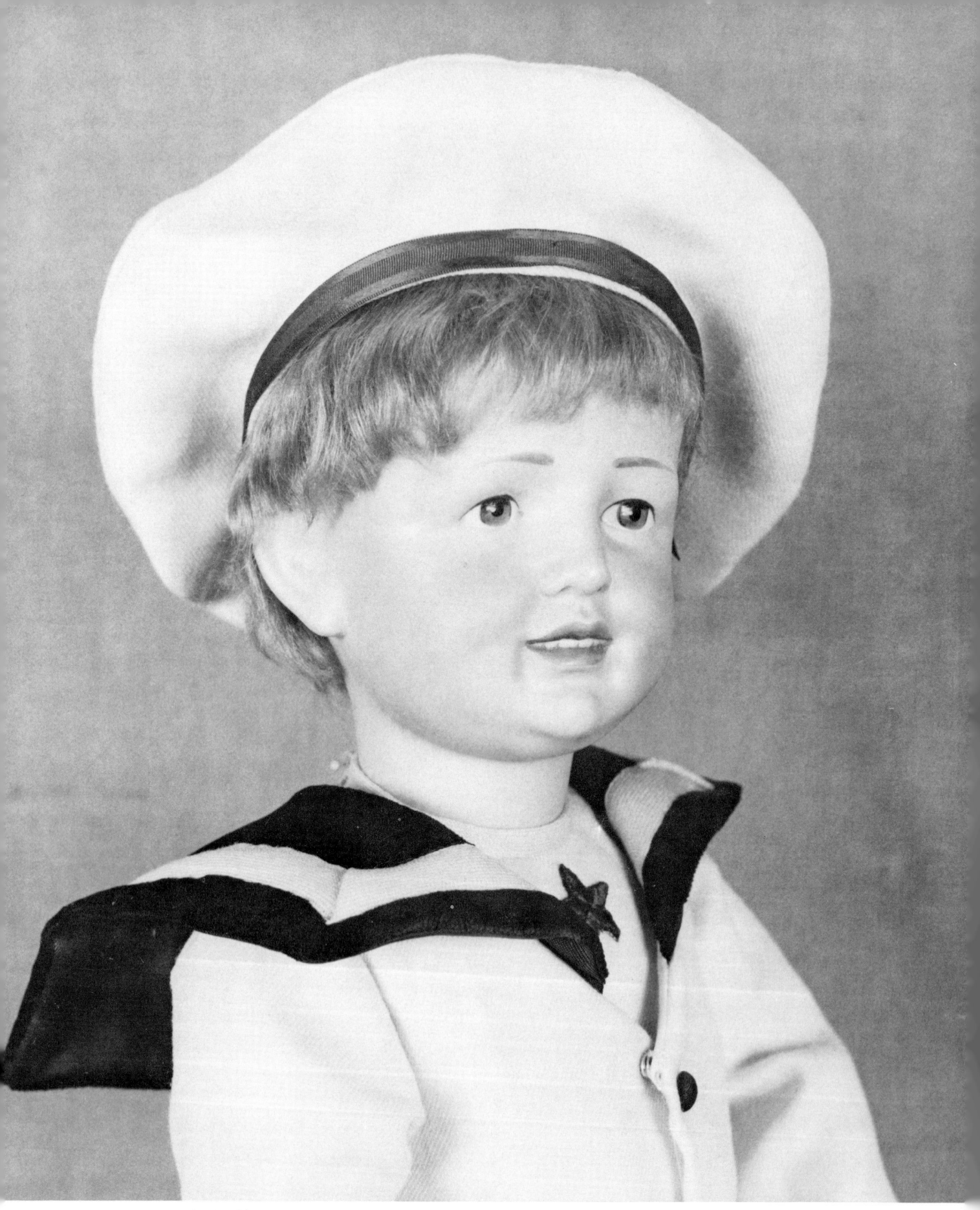

Illustration 8. This marvelous and rare 22in (56cm) boy is from mold number 151. His real-looking face is a result of the German character doll movement which places his date at about 1910. The molding detail around his eyes and mouth makes him so alive that his photograph looks like that of a real child. He has painted eyes with molded upper teeth. His very large ears are notable. *Roberts Collection.*

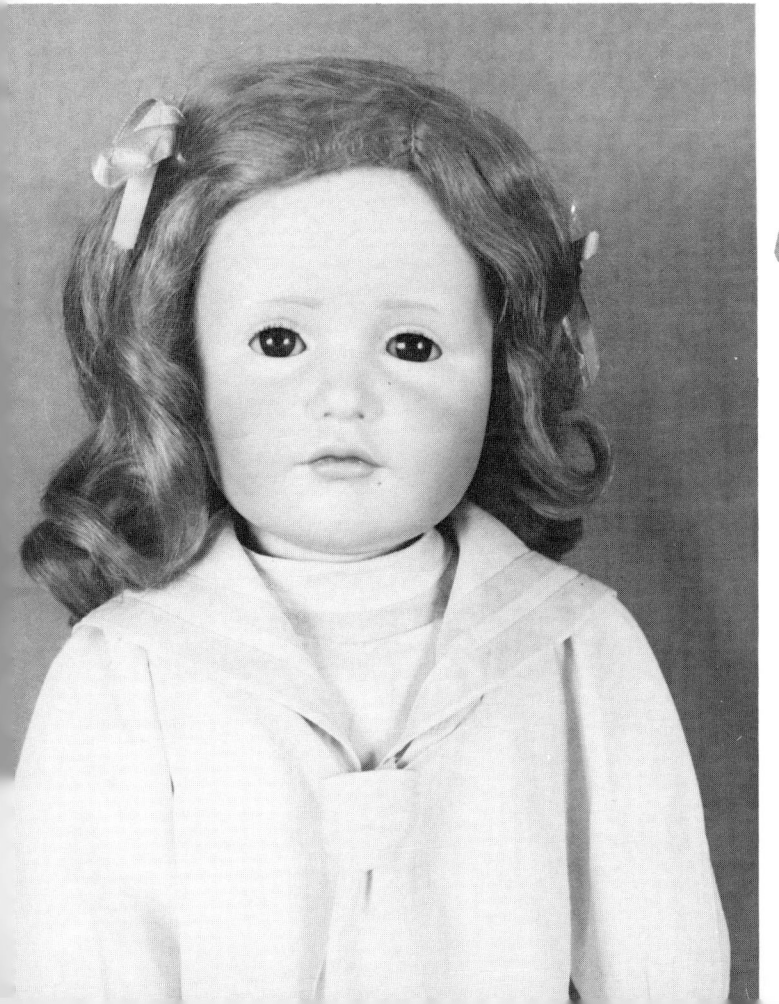

Illustration 9. The Simon & Halbig factory produced many dolls with brown and black tinted complexions. Some of these were standard models simply tinted dark; some of them were especially designed models with Negroid features, such as this example of mold 1358, which has full lips as well as a broad nose. This very sought-after doll was finished in black as well as several shades of brown. The example here has a very light facial complexion, but a darker jointed composition body, a not unusual combination. She is 20½in (52cm) tall dressed in clothing of her period, but not original. Six upper teeth show between her full orange lips. *Lorna Lieberman Collection.*

ABOVE LEFT: Illustration 10. This 19½in (50cm) example of mold 1305 is one of the rarest Simon & Halbig models. In realism she excels with her long protruding nose, her sharp jutting chin, and her witchy eyebrows. The smile, however, makes her a good witch rather than a sinister one. *Ralph's Antique Doll Museum.*

LEFT: Illustration 11. Simon & Halbig made the bisque heads for the very popular Kämmer & Reinhardt character dolls. This is a rare glass-eyed version of mold 114 *Gretchen*. Collectors are particularly fond of dolls with pouty faces like *Gretchen's*. This example is 22½in (57cm) tall on a chunky jointed body. *Roberts Collection.*

Focusing On...

A. M. Lady Dolls

Illustration 1. 13in (33cm) lady doll.

RIGHT: Illustration 2. 12in (31cm) lady doll.

LEFT: Illustration 3. Close-up of the lady doll in **Illustration 2**.

The lady or so-called flapper dolls of the post World War I period are fairly difficult to find on today's doll market. Probably there are not as many available today because they were made for such a short period of time, when compared to the production period of child dolls. Several German companies including Cuno & Otto Dressel, Simon & Halbig and Armand Marseille made the lady dolls during this era. Both of the ladies pictured here are by Armand Marseille, mold 401.

Their bodies are of good quality composition with joints at shoulders, elbows, hips and knees. The torsos are flat-chested. The long, slender limbs have shaped unjointed wrists and ankles; the feet are shaped for high-heeled shoes. Their bisque heads have oval faces with high cheek coloring, thin brown eyebrows, gray sleep eyes with real lashes and bow-shaped mouths with parted lips and four upper teeth.

The lady in **Illustration 1** has brown mohair pulled back in a low bun, probably a replacement. She is wearing her original white lace-trimmed cotton undergarment with blue ribbons. She is the proud possessor of the wardrobe of original clothes. Her height is 13in (33cm).

The lady in **Illustrations 2** and **3** is 12in (31cm) tall. She has her original blonde mohair wig in bobbed style. Her white silk stockings and white leather high-heeled shoes are original, but her dress, hat and parasol are borrowed from the other lady's wardrobe. The outer dress is made of yellow crepe with lace and aqua bead trim draped over an underdress of lace, also with bead trim. Her flower-trimmed hat and parasol match her dress.

The trousseau which belongs to the brown-haired doll shown in **Illustration 1** was apparently made by a professional dressmaker or seamstress, judging from the couturier styling and the finishing and the trimming details. No shortcuts were taken to hasten the job, and some of the detail sewing must have been very time-consuming. Her hats were also professionally made. We do not know whether this lady was purchased from the store with her wardrobe or whether she was purchased in chemise only and the dresses subsequently ordered. Whichever, it goes without saying that the trousseau would have been a costly item. The doll and clothes were found in the trunk with humped lid shown in **Illustration 8**. The trunk, however, predates the doll by at least 20 years, and we do not know whether it was always with her or if it was a later addition.

Now for a description of the trousseau. Only one dress is not pictured since it was too fragile to remove from

June 1978 Doll Reader

Illustration 4. Dresses and accessories from the trousseau belonging to the doll in **Illustration 1**.

Illustration 5. Dresses and accessories from the trousseau belonging to the doll in **Illustration 1**.

Illustration 6. Dresses and accessories from the trousseau belonging to the doll in **Illustration 1**.

Illustration 7. Dress and accessories from the trousseau belonging to the doll in **Illustration 1**.

Illustration 8. The trunk in which the doll in **Illustration 1** and her clothes were found.

Armand Marseille
Germany
401
A 7/0 M

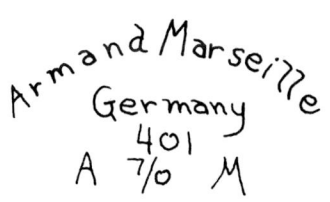

Illustration 9. Marking on dolls.

its plastic bag. It is a lovely red satin straight-line dress with sheer blue overdress with lace trim. It has a long blue sash, also tiny glass buttons.

In **Illustration 4**, the dress on the left is of white silk with lavender stripes. It has lavender piping for trim, also lace trim on neckline and sleeves. The dress has a matching belt. The middle dress is of dusty rose velvet with chiffon insets. Jet beads dangle from a high waist. There is chain-stitched trim, a lace underdress and a train with a large black bead butterfly. The dress on the right is of dusty rose silk, A-line style. It has black silk collar and cuffs, white lace detachable collar, black covered buttons and bogus buttonholes. The extra back panel is pointed with button trim also. The hat is of natural straw with lavender ribbon and flowers.

In **Illustration 5**, the dress on the left is of rose wool with a brown silk blouse with lace inset. Brown buttons and braid trim are on the wrap-style skirt. The matching jacket/cape comes to a long point in the back. In the middle is a dress with a pink satin skirt and lace blouse and overskirt. There is a large pink satin bow at the waist in back and a smaller one further down the back. Flower trim is on the front belt. The hat is of natural straw with pink silk lining and covered with pink flowers. On the right is a bronze velvet straight dress with green beaded trim. The dress has a velvet inset with tassels and a light brown taffeta fringe overskirt. There is a pleated inset in the back of the dress. A green satin parasol and hat of tan velvet and natural straw with a feather complete the outfit.

In **Illustration 6**, the dress on the left is A-line and of black wool with velvet and lace trim. The net bodice was once lined with red silk. There is a matching jacket, and a hat of black plush with fuschia ribbon and jet bead trim. The middle dress is of aqua silk with pink crepe sleeves and neck trim. There is an overlay of metallic lace with sequins and the train peaks in the back. The dress has a pink crepe bow with long ends and cut steel decoration and there is a matching parasol with flowers. The dress on the right is of gray silk with brown velvet ribbon trim and a lovely lace vest. There is a brown velvet belt. A hat of blue straw with blue velvet lining, ribbon and blue and white flowers can be worn with this dress.

In **Illustration 7**, the dress is of white cotton with ecru embroidery and openwork with scallops at waist and hem. The hat is of natural straw with a plaid multi-color ribbon band and a red feather. Other articles from her trunk are clockwise: red shoes and clutch bag, white leather high heels, white silk stockings, mirror, embroidered handkerchief, comb and scissors which work.

Both of these dolls are from the collection of Mike White, and we appreciate his kindness in being willing to share them with others.

113

Focusing On...

German Dolly Faces

Produced over a period of nearly 50 years with little change, the German "dolly faces" were the perennial favorites of our mothers and grandmothers. They were made by the millions which accounts for the fact that they are the dolls which are today so readily available. The Colemans say that the "dolly faces" were "treated in the image of 'beauty' exemplified by Lillian Russell in her era (1879 to 1912) and thereafter." They are the pretty dolls, and nearly every collector first becomes interested in dolls because of the beauty in the faces of these appealing German dollies.

Though most of these dolls were popularly priced, the cost did vary according to the quality, size and clothes of the dolls, starting at 25¢ and going up. Here are some examples of prices from catalog reprints, just for fun.

1895 Butler Brothers
  Finely dressed dolls, no maker given
    21in (53cm) $2.75
    27in (69cm) $5.50
    29in (74cm) $7.75
1903 Montgomery Ward
  Kid-bodied Kestners, undressed
    8½in (22cm) "Baby-type Body"
      (short and chubby) $0.25
    23in (58cm) $3.75
    28in (71cm) $5.75
  Finely dressed, no maker given
    16½in (42cm) $1.50
1909 Macy's
  Handwerck
    22in (56cm) Undressed $1.24
    18in (46cm) Finely dressed $4.49
    22in (56cm) Undressed,
      no maker $0.98
1924 Montgomery Ward
  Kämmer & Reinhardt, undressed
    18in (46cm) $2.19
    25in (63cm) $3.89
1930 Montgomery Ward*
  Slender girl doll, no maker given
    14½in (37cm) $1.44
    24½in (62cm) $2.69
  Kidiline body, jointed, undressed
    20in (51cm) $2.23

*In this same catalog Effanbee's *Patsy* was selling for $2.75!

Here are some guidelines which are important for investing in German dollies at the least risk — and any investment is just that — a risk!

First, watch your makers. It seems to me dolls sell best in this order.
1. Simon & Halbig; Kämmer & Reinhardt; any good doll of good quality with a slightly different face.
2. Kestner.
3. Handwerck; Bergmann; Walkure, A.M. 1894; Kley & Hahn.
4. Schoenau Hoffmeister, Heubach Köppelsdorf, A.M. 390, AW Special, and so on.
5. Name dolls, such as *Alma*; kid-bodied dolls of mediocre quality.

(Generally speaking, the dolls with jointed composition bodies sell better than the kid-bodied dolls.)

Second, be very particular about the quality and condition. When many of the same type are available, you have more time to look around and be sure that the dolls have good eyes and wigs and that the body is in good condition. Normal wear is acceptable; an old doll is not supposed to look brand new!

Third, be sure that the doll has appropriate clothes unless you are planning to dress it yourself. Collectors are becoming more interested in dolls which have old clothes, or at least clothes of the proper material and style for the period of the doll.

Many collectors have asked my advice about buying dolls at auctions. Now that doll collecting is so popular, many auction houses are including dolls in the regular auctions or having special doll auctions. You are more likely to get a good buy on a common doll at auction than on a rare one. Obviously more people are after the rarer dolls and bidding is tighter on them. Sometimes a nice, but common, doll is overlooked in the scramble and comes out a good buy.

However, again there are several cautions about buying at auction, especially if you are a new collector.

First, always examine the dolls personally *before* you bid. Sometimes

Illustration 1. 13in (33cm) 192 Kämmer & Reinhardt. *H&J Foulke, Inc.*

from a distance, a doll looks cute, but close inspection reveals poor bisque, a banged-up body and other possible flaws.

Second, if you get the top bid, always double-check the doll as soon as it is placed in your hands to make sure no damage occurred from the time you first examined it until it came up for auction. Most auctions will take an item back immediately, but as soon as you leave, you have no recourse even if there is damage you did not see.

Third, be cautious if you are a beginner and your knowledge is limited. The large doll auction houses write a detailed catalog listing damage, but do not guarantee the bodies are proper or original to the doll. The small general auction houses who do not know anything about dolls can present problems for the beginner, in the way of mismatched heads and bodies, representing a doll as rare when it is not, and above all...reproductions.

Fourth, when deciding what to bid for a doll, take into consideration whether or not the doll is going to need a wig, clothes or body work. All of these items can add up.

In my opinion, good buys can be found at both shows and auctions. Both are fun and exciting. A doll collector never knows what "treasure" awaits wherever dolls are gathered together.

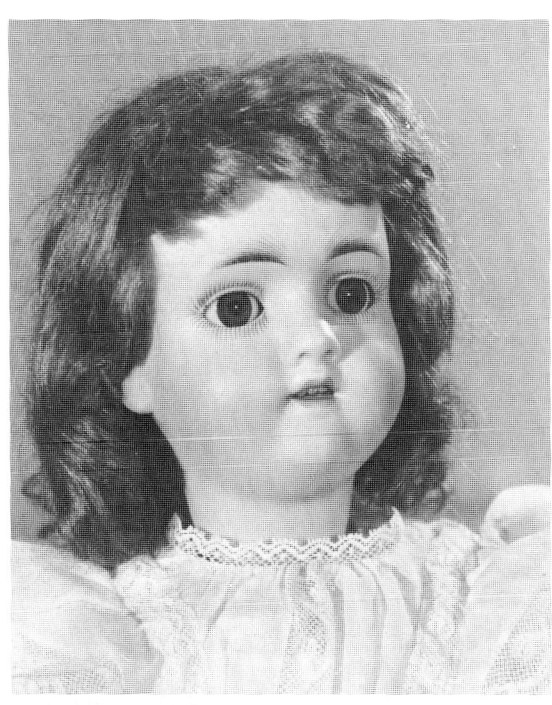

LEFT: Illustration 2. 18in (46cm) Kley & Hahn. *H&J Foulke, Inc.*

BELOW: Illustration 3. 14in (36cm) 1009 Simon & Halbig. *H&J Foulke, Inc.*

Illustration 4. 13in (33cm) 224 Bähr & Pröschild. *H&J Foulke, Inc.*

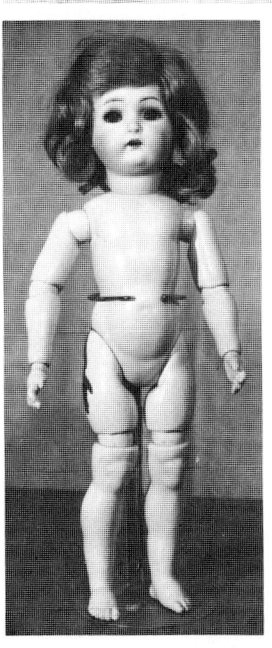

FAR LEFT: Illustration 5. Kämmer & Reinhardt with teen-type body. *H&J Foulke, Inc.*

LEFT: Illustration 6. 14in (36cm) Schoenau & Hoffmeister, all original. *H&J Foulke, Inc.*

RIGHT: Illustration 7. 30in (76cm) Handwerck. *H&J Foulke, Inc.*

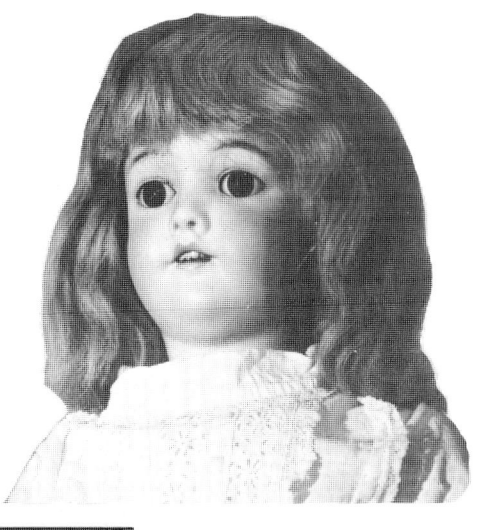

FAR LEFT: Illustration 8. *Miss Viola* on a body made in Germany. *H&J Foulke, Inc.*

LEFT: Illustration 9. 19in (48cm) mystery girl, maker unknown. *H&J Foulke, Inc.*

Focusing On...

Young Baby Dolls

Although dolls down through the ages have been dressed as infants or young babies, few of them were really designed after real babies. Dolls which were dressed in infant clothes were of the same type as those dressed as children or sometimes even adults.

In the 18th century a few of the peg-wooden Queen Anne-type dolls were dressed in infants' clothes. During this period also the poupards were very popular; these were infant dolls made of one piece of wood dressed in swaddling clothes.

In the early 19th century some of the peg-wooden dolls were dressed as infants, as were some rag dolls. The Taufling dolls of the 1850s were dressed in baby clothes. The regular model china, composition and wax dolls of this period also sometimes wore baby clothes, as did the *Frozen Charlottes*.

The English poured wax dolls of the last half of the 19th century had specific models to represent babies which were dressed in very elaborate infant outfits as many of these were luxury dolls. Other infants of the 1870s were the London Rag Baby dolls with their muslin over wax mask faces. Also used as infants during this period were the bisque shoulder head dolls on cloth or kid bodies. In 1878, Bru brought out their *Bébé Teteur*, a nursing doll which was dressed in infant clothes. With the advent of the jointed composition body, even some of those dolls were dressed as infants.

In the 1890s, Martha Chase developed her cloth baby dolls, and the *Philadelphia Baby* came out at about the same time. These types of dolls are often dressed as infants.

In about 1900, Horsman and other manufacturers of composition dolls were offering models dressed as babies. In 1908 rag and celluloid dolls were dressed as infants. The bent-limb composition body developed in 1910 increased interest in infant dolls. The character doll head gave a more realistic baby look, and many of these character babies were dressed in long baby clothes. However, these did not have the faces of newborn infants.

The first firm to produce a real infant head in bisque was Louis Amberg & Son. The heads which were designed by Jeno Juszko were made in Germany by several firms: Recknagel, Herm Steiner and Armand Marseille. They represented two- or three-day-old infant under the trade name *New Born Babe*. Apparently the time was not right for this innovation and the doll was not an overwhelming success.

In 1924 Grace S. Putnam's *Bye-Lo Baby* came on the market. After a slow start, perhaps it was too realistic for some buyers at first look, it became a huge success. The first Christmas George Borgfeldt, the distributor, could not get enough of the dolls on the market and people had to stand in line to buy one; thus it received the nickname "Million Dollar Baby." The *Bye-Lo* heads were made by J. D. Kestner as well as at least five other German porcelain factories.

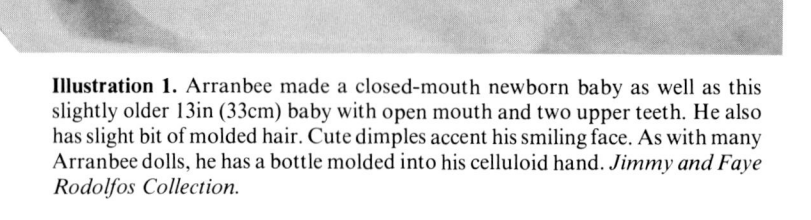

Illustration 1. Arranbee made a closed-mouth newborn baby as well as this slightly older 13in (33cm) baby with open mouth and two upper teeth. He also has slight bit of molded hair. Cute dimples accent his smiling face. As with many Arranbee dolls, he has a bottle molded into his celluloid hand. *Jimmy and Faye Rodolfos Collection.*

Illustration 2. A 14in (36cm) Simon & Halbig mold number 1079 dolly-face on a jointed composition body in original infant clothes. *H & J Foulke.*

Thus, the infant doll as a separate doll form was established in its own right, and by 1925 all of the doll manufacturers were making newborn dolls. These infants generally were characterized by tiny sleep eyes, bald heads with no molded hair but sometimes a fontenal, usually a frowning expression, large ears, broad nose, usually a closed mouth and sometimes a thrust-out chin.

A Checklist of Infant Dolls (Illustration reference given unless included in article.)
1. Amberg's *New Born Babe* (open and closed mouth models) (*5th Blue Book of Dolls & Values*, page 42)
2. *Bye-Lo Baby* (*5th Blue Book of Dolls & Values*, page 75)
3. *My Dream Baby*, A.M. 341 and 351 (*4th Blue Book of Dolls & Values*, page 6)
4. A.M. 347
5. Arranbee (open- and closed-mouth models)
6. A.M. *Kiddiejoy* (*2nd Blue Book of Dolls & Values*, page 175)
7. Orsini *Kiddiejoy* (*5th Blue Book of Dolls & Values*, page 266)

ABOVE: Illustration 3. Horsman's 12in (31cm) *Tynie Baby* designed by Bernard Lipfert and issued in 1924 has a bisque head, cloth body and composition hands. He is distinctive because of the frowning expression and the deep molding around his mouth. This baby wears his completely original labeled outfit. *Jimmy and Faye Rodolfos Collection.*

RIGHT: Illustration 4. This nice large 20in (51cm) long baby with a 14in (36cm) head circumference is by Armand Marseille from his mold number 347, a fairly difficult one to find. He has very small sleeping eyes and an open/closed mouth. His body is pink cloth with composition hands. *Jimmy and Faye Rodolfos Collection.*

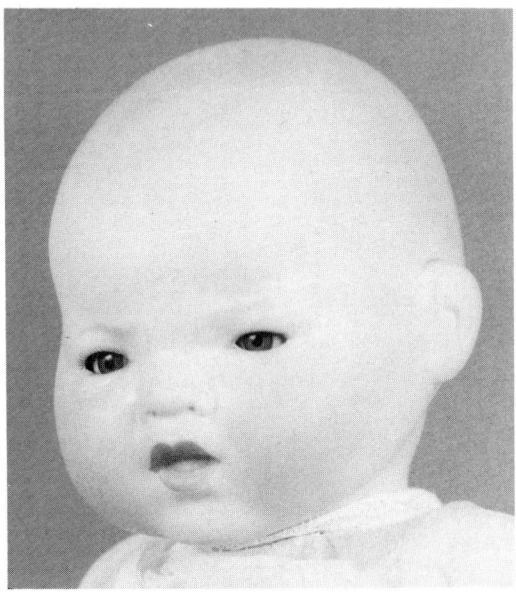

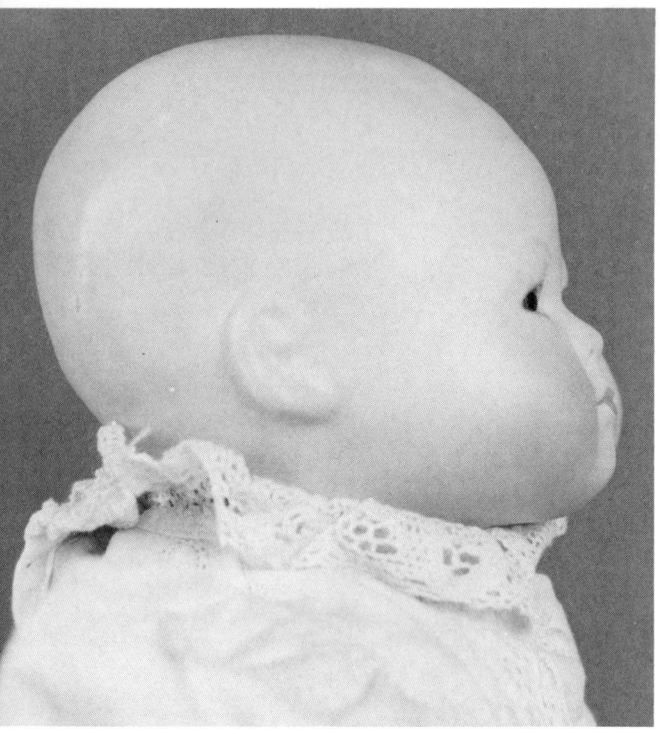

Illustration 5. A profile view of the Arthur A. Gerling baby showing his quite elongated head and thrust-out chin. He is also characterized by his open or pierced nostrils. For a front view of this doll, see the *5th Blue Book of Dolls & Values*, page 144. *Jimmy and Faye Rodolfos Collection.*

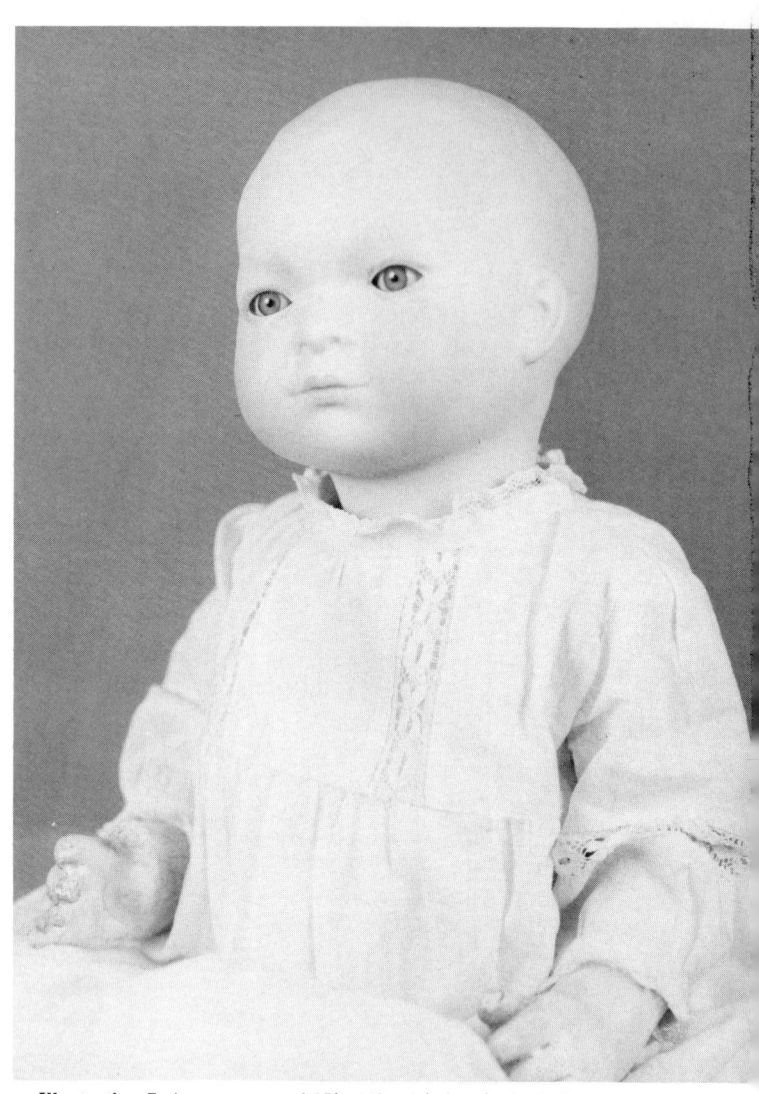

Illustration 7. A very unusual 17in (43cm) infant incised "800," has a socket head on a composition body. *Jimmy and Faye Rodolfos Collection.*

8. Kämmer & Reinhardt (*4th Blue Book of Dolls & Values*, page 206)
9. Schoenau Hoffmeister Pouty Baby
10. Siegfried (*Wendy & Friends*, page 74)
11. Arthur Gerling Baby
12. Horsman's *Tynie Baby*
13. *Baby Gloria* (*5th Blue Book of Dolls & Values*, page 56)
14. *Baby Phyllis* (*5th Blue Book of Dolls & Values*, page 57)
15. 800
16. OIC (*5th Blue Book of Dolls & Values*, page 262)
17. Century Doll Company (several variations)
18. Heubach Köppelsdorf 349 (*3rd Blue Book of Dolls & Values*, page 162)
19. Heubach Köppelsdorf 338
20. F.S. & Co. 1285 (*Antique Collectors Dolls,* Series I, page 251)
21. R.A. 138 (*2nd Blue Book of Dolls & Values*, page 231)
22. Herm Steiner (open- and closed-mouth models)
23. Herm Steiner 739 and 740 two-headed doll (*3rd Blue Book of Dolls & Values*), page 307
24. P + 1002 (*4th Blue Book of Dolls & Values*, page 142)
25. Grace Putnam *Babykins* (*Handbook of Collectible Dolls I*, page 34-0)

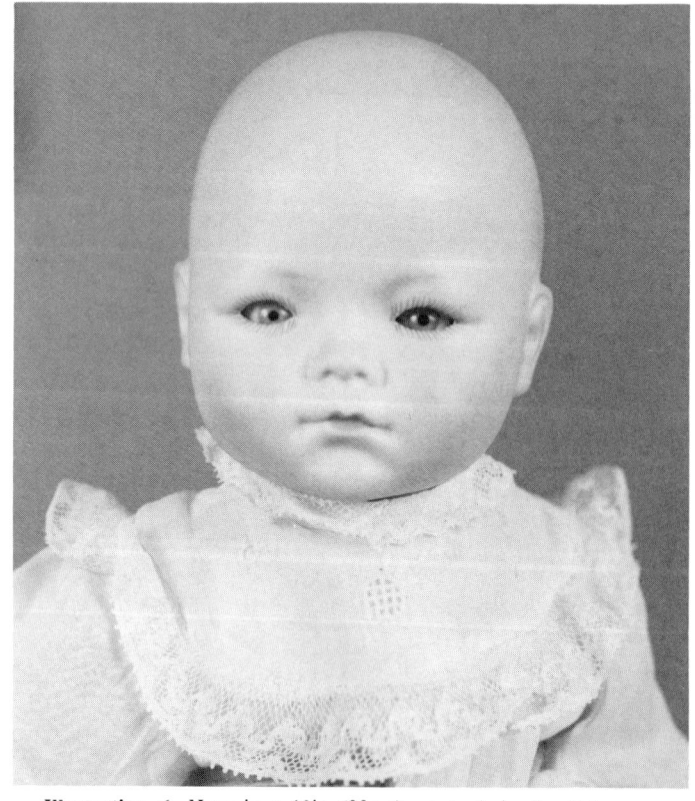

Illustration 6. Here is a 13in (33cm) pouty baby by Schoenau Hoffmeister Porzellanfabrik Burggrub. This is a rare and desirable baby. *Jimmy and Faye Rodolfos Collection.*

On the above list, I debated about including a few which had teeth. Should a doll be considered an infant if it has teeth? A baby develops bottom teeth at about six months; upper teeth at about seven and one-half months. We would be glad to hear of other newborn-type babies which are not on this list.

Focusing On...

Bathing Beauties

Although bathing beauties would more appropriately be placed in the category of figurines or ornaments, they do have an appeal for many doll collectors. The same exquisite bisque and delicate workmanship which produced the desirable all-bisque dolls went into the production of the bathing beauties. It really is not strange to see a grouping of these lovelies fitting well into a doll collection.

This collection of 13 beauties is found to be particularly interesting because, even though they are different sizes and poses, they are apparently of one individual beauty, made in a series by one company. But which company and what country remain, for the time being at least, a mystery. These girls are all in their original boxes which, unfortunately, are unmarked; it is also a problem to see whether or not there might be one lady with information incised on her, since all except one are wearing very fragile original clothes which are sewn on. The only one who has lost her clothes is not much help either, since she is incised only "4247" on her abdomen.

The background information which accompanies the ladies is interesting, though unverified. They are supposed to be various poses done of the Australian champion swimmer, Annette Kellermann. Information about her is scant, but there are articles appearing in various popular American magazines by and about her in the years 1910 to 1918.

Ladies Home Journal, July 1915, August 1910.
American Magazine, March 1917.
Bookman, 1918.
Cosmopolitan, June 1910.
Harper's Weekly, January 27, 1912. (Also on June 18, 1910, the *New York Times* reported that Miss Kellermann was fined for speeding! One wonders how fast automobiles could go in 1910.) A friend reports that he remembers seeing Miss Kellermann appear in a vaudeville swimming act in Washington, D.C. Legend also has it that as the pioneer of the one-piece figure-hugging bathing suit, Miss Kellermann was arrested on Boston's Revere Beach for indecent exposure. Again, remember that whether or not these figures are indeed of Miss Kellermann, has not been confirmed.

For such small figures, these are made with care and precision. The bisque is of better quality with even tinting. The faces are modeled in the classic oval shape with pointed chins. The decoration was executed carefully: eyebrows are usually painted brown with one stroke; lips are orange, usually slightly parted with white between, although several have completely closed lips; roughed cheeks are red-orange. The molded intaglio eyes are painted black with a white highlight, red eyeline and black upper and lower eyelids. Wigs are of soft brown wavy mohair. All together or in small groups, these figures make a stunning display.

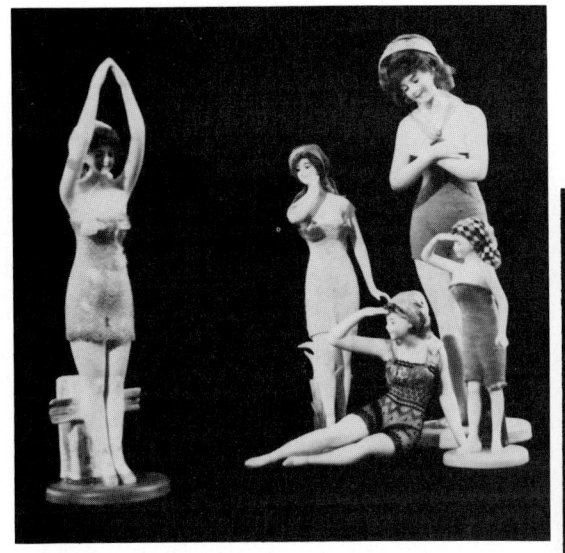

ABOVE: Illustration 1. A grouping of the bathing beauties.

RIGHT: Illustration 2. 9in (23cm) bathing beauty, the tallest of the standing poses and the only one which is barefoot. Her bathing suit is rust-colored cotton knit and her head scarf is very fragile silk, as are all of them.

Illustration 3. 2¾in (7cm) tall and 6in (15cm) long figure wearing black lace in a deteriorating condition.

October 1977 Doll Reader

Focusing On...

All-Bisque Dolls

All-bisques are a very popular specialty in the field of doll collecting. But they are purchased not only by the "all-bisque collectors" — many doll fanciers buy them as dolls for larger dolls or to put in displays with small furniture or just because of their charm and personality. Often these small dolls can solve the space problem which plagues many collectors since quite a large number of them can be attractively arranged on one shelf.

All-bisques are available in a great variety — with glass or painted eyes, wigs or molded hair, jointed at shoulders and hips or stiff limbed, long or short molded stockings, boots or Mary Janes, swivel necks or stiff, knee and elbow joints (very rare), open or closed mouth, molded clothes or undressed, beautiful little children or impish characters.

All-bisque dolls were always popular with little girls and were imported into this country primarily from Germany, by the millions. At most doll shops and shows you will be able to find quite a few all-bisques of the more common variety, but the dolls which are shown here are the harder-to-find types. They are all very desirable examples of all-bisques.

Illustration 1. A group of all-bisque dolls except for the A.M. Googly which sneaked in on the back row.

RIGHT: Illustration 2. One of the most sought-after of any of the all-bisques is this captivating 5in (13cm) googly-eyed sweetheart probably made by the German doll firm of J. D. Kestner. "Francie," as we call her, has several features that make her especially desirable — her swivel head, her googly eyes, but most of all her elbow and knee joints which are very rare in an all-bisque doll. We turned her knee joints in to give her the pigeon-toed look, and you can see one of her elbow joints. Her goo goo sleep eyes are brown with painted eyelashes. She still has her original brown mohair wig as well as original clothes, handmade by her first owner. *Jan Foulke Collection.*

BELOW RIGHT: Illustration 3. Of the many all-bisques we have seen, this lovely little girl is one of our favorites Just 6in (15cm) tall, she is outstanding for several reasons. She has the hard-to-find swivel neck; her bisque is pale and smooth; she has desirable long stockings in a pale blue shade; her dress and hat of lace and ribbon are original, as is her blonde mohair. Her black shoes have pompons molded on the toes. Altogether she is an extremely fine and exquisite little doll. She has no markings to help determine her maker, although it is probably Simon & Halbig. *Betty Harms Collection.*

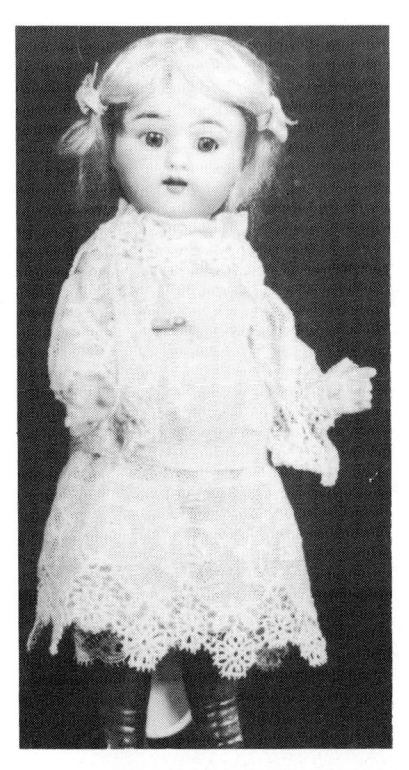

Illustration 4. This lovely 7½in (19cm) tall girl is marked to indicate that she is a product of the German firm Simon & Halbig. This is unusual in that most all-bisques are either unmarked or marked only with a stock and/or size number. She is of very fine quality and has the label of a Paris toy store on her torso. She has many desirable qualities, including a swivel neck, glass eyes, long black stockings and brown four-strap boots in addition to very good bisque as well as finely molded hands. *Betty Harms Collection.*

Illustration 5. This 4in (10cm) fellow is a desirable French-type with original clothes. Although probably of German manufacture, he is classified as French-type because he has qualities usually associated with French dolls — swivel neck, long thin face, set glass eyes, heavy painted upper and lower eyelashes and fine detail of work in facial molding, wig and clothes. *Betty Harms Collection.*

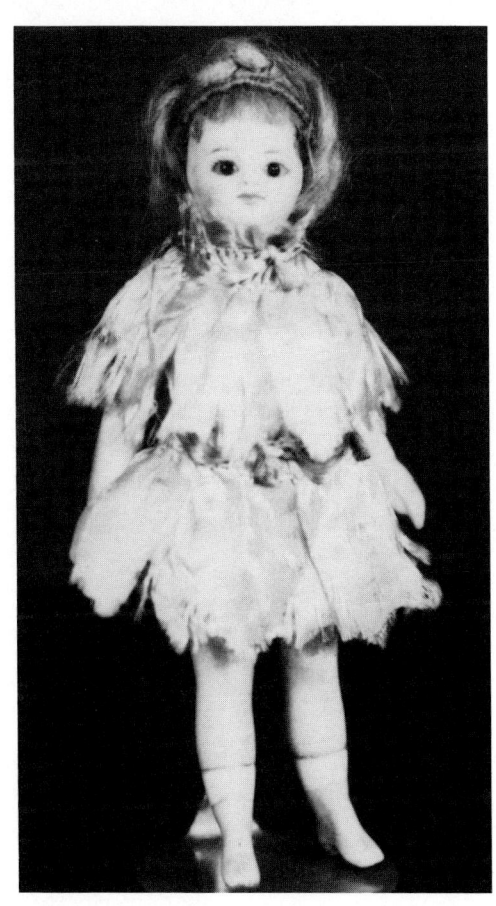

Illustration 6. Generally regarded as French, this 5in (13cm) girl has unusual blue boots. She has a long slim body which contrasts with the chubby look usually associated with German all-bisques. She has a swivel neck and beautiful stationary glass eyes. *Betty Harms Collection.*

Illustration 7. Certainly this pouty boy took our fancy the first time we saw him. Probably of German manufacture, he is 6in (15cm) tall. His eyes are painted and his neck is stiff, yet his unusual pensive expression endears him to a collector. *Betty Harms Collection.*

Focusing On...

Those Adorable Snow Babies

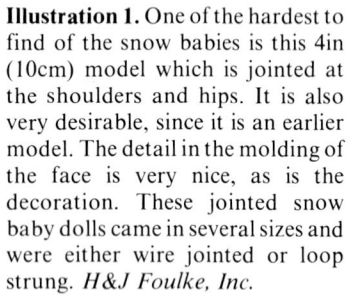

Illustration 1. One of the hardest to find of the snow babies is this 4in (10cm) model which is jointed at the shoulders and hips. It is also very desirable, since it is an earlier model. The detail in the molding of the face is very nice, as is the decoration. These jointed snow baby dolls came in several sizes and were either wire jointed or loop strung. *H&J Foulke, Inc.*

Illustration 2. This crawling snow baby is another early and very desirable one. As with other early dolls, she has no country of origin stamp; neither has she defined hands or feet. The decoration of her face is lovely; she even has red accent eye lines. The modeling of her face is sharp and clear as can be seen in the profile view. Her hood is unusual in that it is peaked instead of rounded like a helmet. She is 3½in (9cm) long. *H&J Foulke, Inc.*

Illustration 3. This 2½in (6cm) tall smiling snow baby is a real joy. His face was modeled with thought and care, and the decoration is lovely as well. There is no detail in the hands or feet, which are painted brown. He is stamped "Germany," and would be a welcomed addition to any snow baby collection. *H&J Foulke, Inc.*

Illustration 4. This 2in (5cm) tall snow baby is the director of a six member band. Other babies play drum, flute, saxaphone, tuba and concertina. His shoes are painted orange, and he is molded on a base. He is one of the few babies examined who has a stock number which is "1780." We have not figured out what the bump on his back is. *H&J Foulke, Inc.*

For many children of the first decades of the 1900s, Christmas was just not complete without the Christmas garden display under the Yule tree — and, of course, the most fun items for many children in the garden scene were the tiny snow babies. In addition to being used in the garden, these tiny children decorated Christmas cakes and other goodies. Many adults remember them also as being given as favors at Christmas parties.

While there were a few large and very beautiful bisque pieces made incorporating snow children, the majority by far are under 3in (8cm), and most just 1in (2cm) or 2in (5cm) tall. Many German companies were apparently involved in the manufacture of the snow babies, most of which are stamped "Germany" on the bottom. Of course, sometimes the stamped mark wore off, and some of the early babies were not marked at all. As is often the case with such popular items, the Japanese also entered the snow baby market. Their items are stamped "Made in Japan" and are not of the same quality in either modeling or decoration as the German pieces.

The snow babies are made of white

bisque, their snowsuits and hoods covered with tiny granules of white bisque "snow." Their faces are flesh-tinted with painted features. The quality of the decoration of the faces varies greatly; since many were not fired, the features may wear or wash off easily. Hands were not usually painted, but the shoes were. Some of the figures have only part of their costumes covered with "snow," the rest being painted with bright colors. Sometimes this color was not fired in, so one has to be careful in handling and cleaning these tiny items, so that the color does not inadvertently get washed off.

Hundreds of different pieces were made using the snow baby motif.

Illustration 5. This attractive figure presents three carolers. Two are playing instruments, a horn and a violin, and the center one is singing from his song book. Their hats are covered with snow, and they are standing on a snow-covered base. All are colorfully painted in red, blue, brown and green tones. Of course, the most rare item in this illustration is the yellow lantern, which was most often lost. *H&J Foulke, Inc.*

Illustration 6. The snow baby twins, standing with their arms around each other, are just 1¾in (4cm) tall. The faces are nicely painted, and each baby has a wisp of hair peeking out from his hood at the forehead. *H&J Foulke, Inc.*

Illustration 7. Snow babies riding sleds are fairly easy to find. The sleds, usually tan or yellow, are stamped "Germany." However, this figure is a little different in that one baby is molded atop the other, whereas usually the tiny babies are merely glued to the sled in various positions. Although this is a cute figure, the painting of the eyes is carelessly done. The whole figure measures 2in (5cm) tall. *H&J Foulke, Inc.*

Illustration 8. This little girl is called an "Alaska Tot" in the *1914 Marshall Field & Co. Catalog*. I always assumed that she was sitting, but in the catalog she is shown leaning forward on a pair of wooden skis. Probably she came both with and without the skis. She is just 1½in (4cm) tall, a little cutie with a snow sweater and cap, and a pink painted and molded skirt; her legs are white and her shoes are merely painted on. She has a little boy companion who looks just like her except that he is wearing blue molded and painted short pants. *H&J Foulke, Inc.*

Illustration 9. A favorite with collectors and a very hard snow item to find is this 3in (8cm) Santa astride a snow bear. His face is very well painted; his suit is colored red; and he carries a yellow pack on his back, out of which peep several toys. The nose and feet of the bear are tinted also. "Germany" is stamped on the bottom. *H&J Foulke, Inc.*

Illustration 10. This 2¼in (6cm) boy skater is a very well-done figure, and is another example of a child who is partly snow-covered. His red cap with a pompon sits on the side of his head to show his blonde hair with one lock hanging down on his forehead. His pants are blue and skates are gold. The base which supports his leg is stamped "Germany."

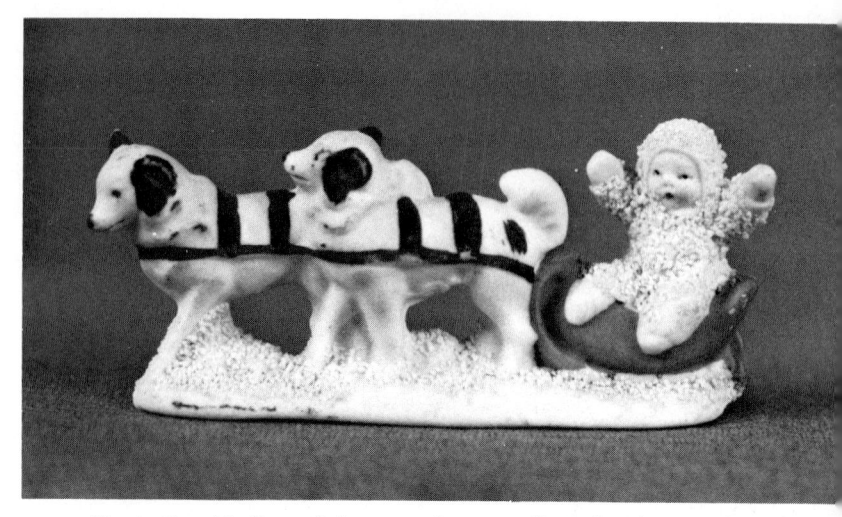

Illustration 11. One of the cutest items available is this snow baby sitting on an orange sled pulled by two husky dogs. This is really a tiny baby as the whole figure is only 1¼in (3cm) high. The huskies have black patches on their ears and bodies and are connected with a blue molded and painted harness. The figure is mounted on a snow base which is marked "Germany."

Illustration 12. This boy is particularly interesting since he is a variation of the boy in **Illustration 10** except this figure has no snow decoration at all. He is wearing a green coat, brown pants and gold skates. He is marked "460" and "Germany."

Illustration 13. In interesting contrast to the figure in **Illustration 11**, is this version of the same item which is marked "Made in Japan." It is easy to see the difference in quality even from the photographs, and even if the figure were not marked, a collector would notice that it is an inferior piece.

Focusing On...

Izannah Walker Dolls

There are many wonderful giving and sharing people in the doll world. Maurine Popp is one of them. When the *4th Blue Book of Dolls and Values* came out, she noticed that there were no pictures on page 329 of any Izannah Walker dolls. She graciously offered to bring some Walker dolls from her collection to an event where we both would be so that Howard could photograph them for future use. This was an extremely generous offer on her part, but it was not until we saw how very fragile were the dolls and clothes that we realized just how unselfish this was. I know that everyone who sees the photographs of these rare dolls will also appreciate her kindness.

There is no one positive date for when Izannah Walker of Central Falls, Rhode Island, started to make her rag dolls, but family tradition places the date in the 1840s. The 16in (41cm) Izannah Walker doll, shown in **Illustration 1**, is wearing her original plaid taffeta dress. She is regarded as one of the earlier models. Surprising to me was the fact that there was not just one Walker mold, but a fairly large family of faces. Some of the dolls have pointed noses, others flat or round; some have round alert eyes, others tiny and mysterious; some have upturned almost smiling lips, others have a pouty look. The painting of the hair style also gives variety as some have long curls, some have swirls, and some have short brush-stroked hair. In spite of all of this variation, however, it is evident that one hand created them all. The doll was made entirely of cloth with head and limbs painted in oils. The bodies were stuffed with horsehair, cotton batting, newspaper, almost anything, and contained a large stick for support. Some were barefooted and some had painted boots. These earlier dolls had no protective finish (like the Chase dolls), and as is evident in the close-up photographs (**Illustrations 2** and **3**), the paint has a tendency to dry out, crack and flake; consequently an early Walker doll must be handled with extreme care. The applied ear is characteristic of the earlier dolls and can be seen in the side view. The hair style of this particular doll has the two long side curls and short brush-stroked hair in the back. She also has

Illustration 1. 16in (41cm) Izannah Walker doll wearing her original plaid taffeta dress. *Maurine Popp Collection.*

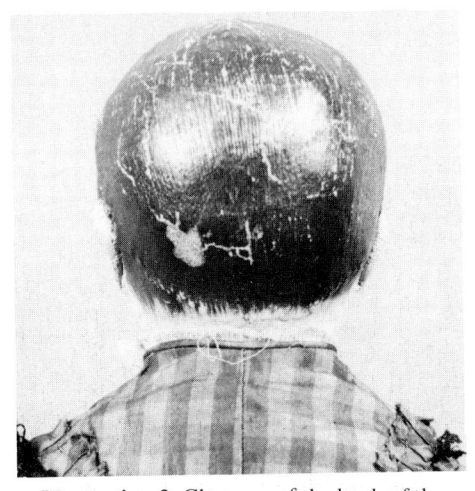

Illustration 2. Close-up of the back of the head of the 16in (41cm) Izannah Walker doll, seen in **Illustration 1**, showing how the paint has a tendency to dry out, crack and flake.

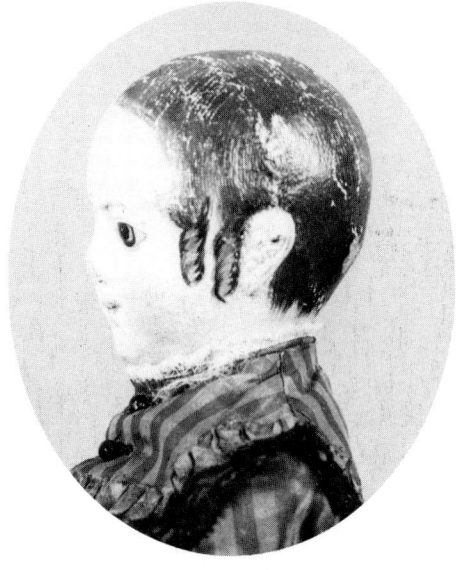

Illustration 3. Side view of the 16in (41cm) Izannah Walker doll, seen in **Illustrations 1** and **2**, showing the two long side curls.

Illustration 4. 21in (53cm) early Izannah Walker doll in her original off-the-shoulder brown cotton print dress.

February/March 1982 Doll Reader

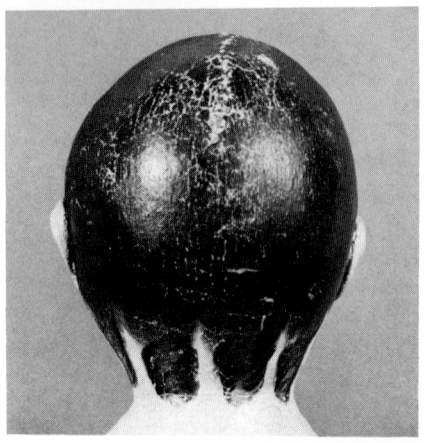

Illustration 5. Close-up of the back of the head of the 21in (53cm) early Izannah Walker doll, seen in **Illustration 4**, showing the four plump curls.

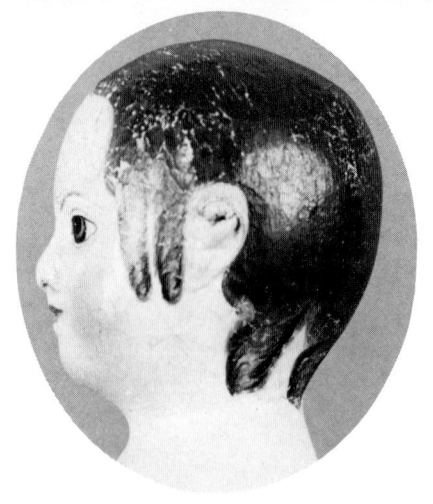

Illustration 6. Side view of the 21in (53cm) early Izannah Walker doll, seen in **Illustrations 4** and **5**, showing her two side curls.

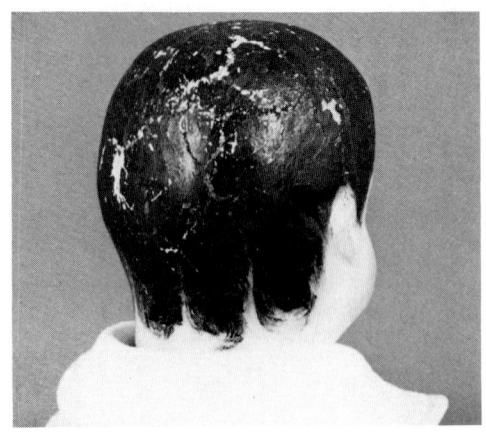

Illustration 8. Close-up of the back of the head of the 18in (46cm) boy, seen in **Illustration 7**, showing the brush marks.

Illustration 7. 18in (46cm) boy and girl pair Izannah Walker dolls with 1873 patent label.

Illustration 9. Label showing the patent date.

the painted boots, not visible because of her long dress.

Another early Walker doll, the face on the one shown in **Illustrations 4, 5** and **6**, is somewhat different in that her cheeks are not as plump and her lips are more tightly closed. Her original off-the-shoulder brown cotton print dress gives a good look at her lovely sloping shoulders as well as her arms and hands. Her hair style features two curls at each side and four plump curls at the back of her head. She is 21in (53cm) tall.

In 1873, Miss Walker was granted patent #144,373 which was for an improvement in the manufacture of her dolls which "consists, mainly, in the secondary or double stuffing next to the external or painted layer, whereby, with a sufficient soft surface, the tendency of the paint to crack or scale off is obviated." The dolls with the label containing this patent date as shown in **Illustration 9**, "I.F. WALKER'S/PATENT/NOV. 4th 1873." are somewhat different in construction than the earlier dolls. The heads were separate and could be removed; the ears were molded instead of applied, and the facial features were not as well defined. The later dolls all have painted shoes. The boy and girl pair shown in **Illustration 7** are 18in (46cm) tall with appropriate hairdos. His is short with brush marks on the sides and back (see **Illustration 8**); hers has long curls at the sides and back.

In the specifications for her patent Miss Walker made some observations about her own dolls: "My doll is inexpensive, easily kept clean, and not apt to injure a young child which may fall on it. It will preserve its appearance for a long time, as the soft secondary stuffing under the stockinet or external webbing enables it to give under pressure, so that the oil paint will not scale off. At the same time the inner and more compact stuffing prevents ordinary pressure from forcing the surface in to such an extent as to crack the paint."

For a marvelous color picture and an in-depth discussion of Izannah Walker dolls, see John Noble's *A Treasury of Beautiful Dolls*, pages 31 to 34 and 40.

Focusing On...

Babyland Rag Dolls

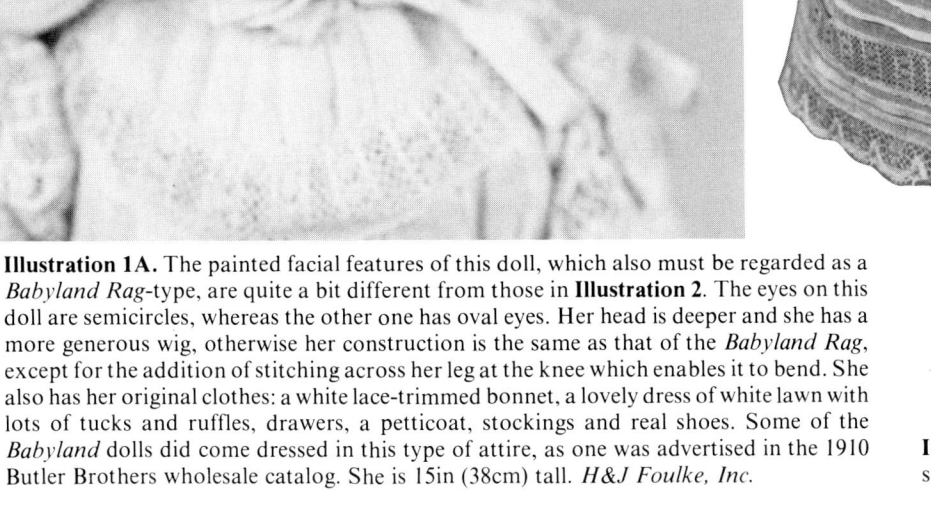

Illustration 1A. The painted facial features of this doll, which also must be regarded as a *Babyland Rag*-type, are quite a bit different from those in **Illustration 2**. The eyes on this doll are semicircles, whereas the other one has oval eyes. Her head is deeper and she has a more generous wig, otherwise her construction is the same as that of the *Babyland Rag*, except for the addition of stitching across her leg at the knee which enables it to bend. She also has her original clothes: a white lace-trimmed bonnet, a lovely dress of white lawn with lots of tucks and ruffles, drawers, a petticoat, stockings and real shoes. Some of the *Babyland* dolls did come dressed in this type of attire, as one was advertised in the 1910 Butler Brothers wholesale catalog. She is 15in (38cm) tall. *H&J Foulke, Inc.*

Illustration 1B. Full-length view of the doll shown in **Illustration 1A**.

Some doll lovers collect only the cute dolls; some want all of their dolls to look pretty; others want dolls which are pouty or wistful; but I personally am drawn to the dolls which most collectors, for want of a better word, refer to as "charming," not as in "smiling and cute," but as in "this doll is kind of a mess, but we have to describe it so that it sounds acceptable." These "charming" dolls may be papier-mâchés that have been much loved (another euphemism for "beat-up"), waxes that have wide cracks, woodens with not much of the paint left, or, as in my favorite case, cloth dolls with printed faces, partially obscured by wear and dirt.

I am not exactly sure just what the appeal of these dolls really is to me. At first, I thought that I just liked dolls which were printed on cloth, so I started to accumulate the printed "cut-out-and-sew" dolls, until one day I found a different type of cloth doll which really excited me. She is the doll which is shown in **Illustration 2**, and I was so excited when I discovered her that I could not believe that she had been sitting for two days on the sales table at a regional convention and no one had bought her! Where had these dolls been for all of my collecting days? What were they? And why didn't the whole doll sorority collect them? I discovered that I was really and truly hooked on these dolls when I was getting ready for my next show a few weeks after I had bought her and found

April/May 1981 Doll Reader

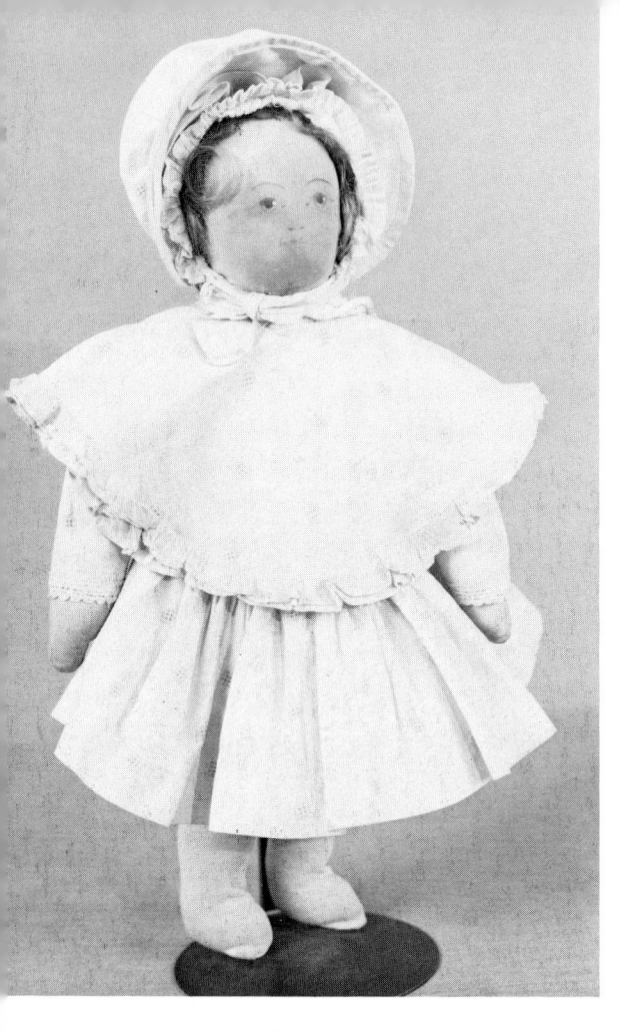

LEFT: Illustration 2. This is the doll that won my heart of the type marketed as a *Babyland Rag Doll*. She has her original clothes: lace-trimmed drawers and petticoat, pink cotton stockings and a white cotton dress with a very wide bertha trimmed with pink cotton ruffles. Her white cotton cap is topped by a lovely poke bonnet which matches her dress. A bit of mohair is tacked to her head just around the edges of her under cap. Her eyes are painted a light blue with a white highlight, a red dot at the inner corner of her eye and widely spaced eyelashes. Her mouth is curved up in just the beginning of a smile. Her face is dirty and her features have faded, but her "charm" shines through all! She is 14in (36cm). *Jan Foulke Collection.*

RIGHT: Illustration 3. Made from at least 1909 to 1911 is this 14in (36cm) *Golf Boy*. He has the printed "Lifelike" face, with a lovely pouty look, so popular on the German bisque character dolls. His matching cap and knickers are of a plaid cotton; he is wearing black cotton hose and real shoes. His original costume also included a hand-knit sweater, which is missing on this fellow. A good guess is that it was thrown away because the moths got to it. *H&J Foulke, Inc.*

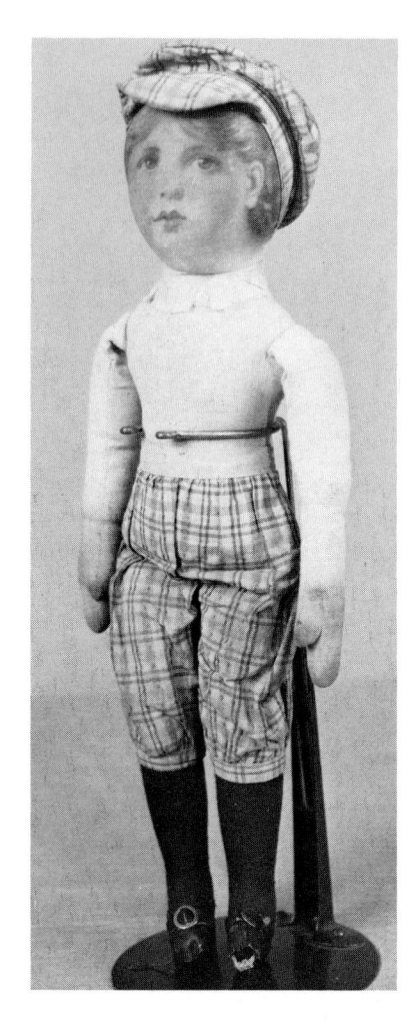

myself putting price tags on all of my "cut-out-and-sew" cloth dolls, even my sweet *Dolly Dear*! (That is always the acid test for me: if I can part with it, then it really was not meant for me. Every time I have broken this rule, I have been sorry afterwards.) After five years I still have accumulated only a few of these "charming" dolls as they are very difficult to find. Apparently, the "throwaway" rate on them after they became dirty was rather high. I have passed up only a few on which I thought the prices were quite steep.

I soon found out from research in *Playthings*, catalog reprints, and *The Collector's Encyclopedia of Dolls* that my "charming" doll was of the type made by the E. I. Horsman Company and marketed under the trademark *Babyland Rag Dolls*. The line was introduced in 1904 and apparently was fairly successful, as it was continued with modifications until 1920. The construction of the dolls was quite simple. The bodies were made of strong cotton; the arms and legs were separate pieces stitched very securely to the one-piece head and torso. This is shown in the line drawing. A piece of flesh-colored muslin was placed over the face, and this was covered by a piece of

Illustration 4. The *Topsy-Turvy* dolls, with one end having a white face and the other end having a black face, were apparently very popular during the period of the manufacture of the *Babyland* dolls since a large number of this type have survived. This doll is showing the black face of a *Topsy-Turvy*. She has a very appealing painted face with lovely amber eyes and white highlights; her cheeks are still rosy. She has a wisp of black hair tacked just under her white lace bonnet. Two tiny red ribbon hair bows are tacked at the side of each eye. Her red cotton dress with a white apron is typical of this type of doll. The white part of the doll is not shown as her face is completely gone, which is surprising because the black face is in such fine condition, but possibly the child who played with this doll preferred the white face and just wore it off! She is 14in (36cm) tall, and may be the doll which Horsman advertised in 1910 and 1911 as a *Topsy-Turvy* with *Topsy* (the black doll) at one end and *Betty* (the white doll) at the other. Horsman also said at this time that faces could be washed with soap and water, but I would not try it! *H&J Foulke, Inc.*

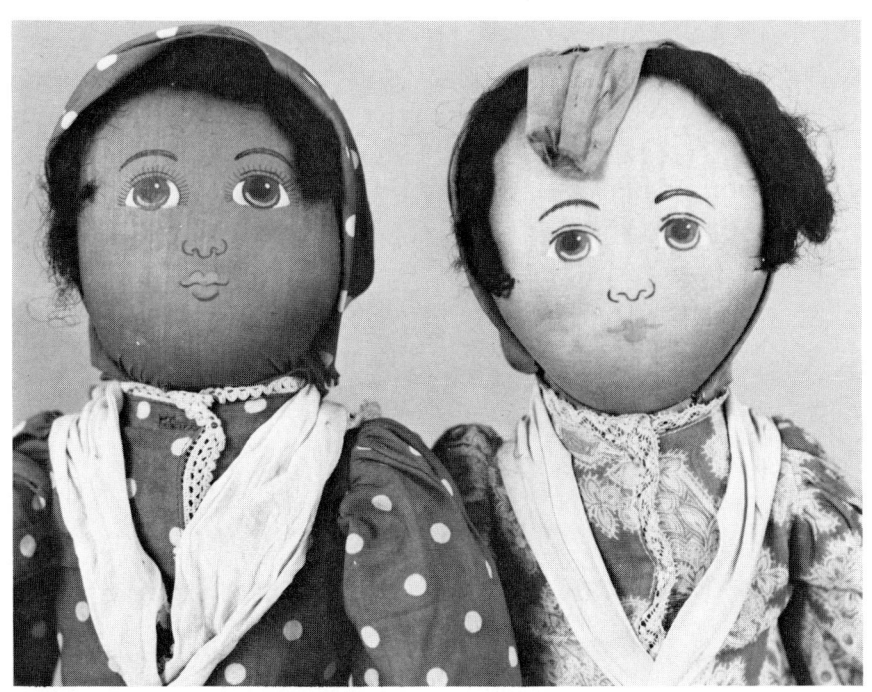

Illustration 5. These 20in (51cm) dolls are probably *Babyland Dinah* dolls which were advertised in 1910 and 1911 for $2.50 each. They are all original and in excellent condition for this type of doll. The faces are painted with some variation in the eye and lip treatment. On the darker black doll, the artist has not only added eyelashes, but has also shaded the underside of each lip. Both of these features are missing on the lighter mulatto doll. The fabric of the costumes of the two dolls is of a different red print, but the design is identical, including the white scarves and the bandana. The construction of the dolls is the same as that of the typical *Babyland* doll except that the black doll is stitched across the knee to make a bendable joint. Both dolls have underwear and black stockings, but the mulatto has lost her shoes; the black doll has leather shoes which appear to be original. *Jan Foulke Collection.*

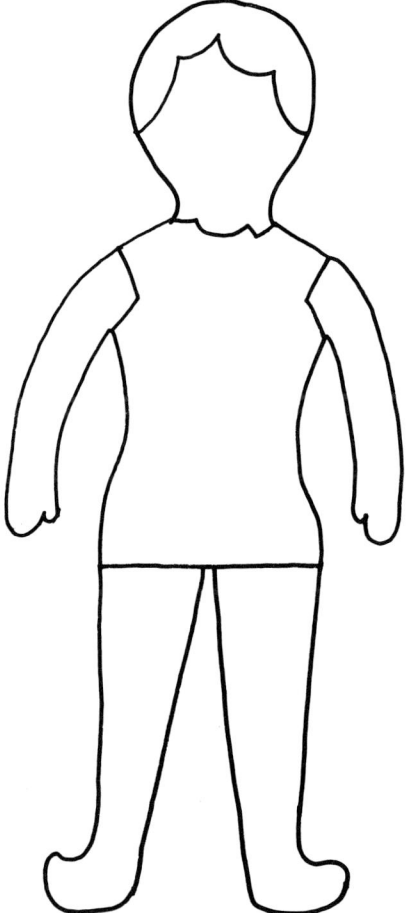

Illustration 6. Babyland Rag referred to as *Topsy*. She has a red bandana under her poke bonnet which matches her red plaid dress. Her shoes are replacements. Her underwear consists of lace-trimmed drawers and a half-slip. *H&J Foulke, Inc.*

fine silk-like cotton on which was drawn (or later printed) the facial features. The dolls had painted faces until 1907 when the new "Lifelike" faces, which were printed in color, were introduced. For a few years both the painted and printed faces were available. In 1909 some of the line were shown with celluloid faces and with so-called "patent" faces, which appear to be the ubiquitous Bruckner face with the 1901 patent date. Recently I found one with a celluloid face. She is interesting, but the charm is missing. The dolls ranged in size from 13in (33cm) to 30in (76cm).

In the 1908 *Playthings*, Horsman advertised "34 different styles made of the very best materials" ranging in price from $2.00 to $39.00 per dozen

Illustration 7. Body construction of the Horsman *Babyland Rag* dolls.

wholesale; retail prices ran 25¢ each for the patent and celluloid faces; $1.00 to $1.25 for the "Lifelike" faces in the 14in (36cm) to 15in (38cm) size up to $5.00 for the 30in (76cm) size. Styles included babies, children, Topsy-Turvies, black dolls, storybook characters and geographical dolls.

Since the *Babyland* dolls are unmarked, I have referred to them as *Babyland*-type in the illustrations, if I felt there was any possible doubt about the manufacturer.

Apparently other companies manufactured dolls which were similar to the *Babyland* dolls. One such was the Fairyland Doll Company of Plainfield, New Jersey. In a 1908 *Playthings* advertisement, several of their dolls are shown with a round paper label on the clothes. The construction and clothing styles look much like those of the *Babyland* dolls.

129

Focusing On...

Steiff Dolls

LEFT: Illustration 1. This 17in (43.2cm) *Irish Footman* has a Steiff button in his ear. A caricature, he exhibits one of Steiff's exaggerated profiles. His clothing is an integral part of his torso with the addition of coattails and lapels; his sleeve is separate from his arm, but attached at the shoulder joint so that it cannot be removed. His boots have leather bottoms and felt gaiters.

BELOW: Illustration 2. In this close-up of the 17in (43.2cm) *Irish Footman*, seen in *Illustration 1*, construction details of the mouth and ears can be seen. The mouth is particularly clever with inset lips. His hair is formed with inset mohair as are his sideburns. His eyes are black buttons.

While people are generally familiar with the Margarete Steiff company of Giengen, West Germany, as the originator of the Teddy Bear and premier maker today of teddies and other soft animals, few realize what fanciers of cloth dolls also know: Margarete Steiff manufactured a series of unique and interesting felt character and comic dolls with exaggerated features, which present a pleasant contrast to the plethora of "pretty" cloth dolls available to the collector. To some people they are whimsical, to some grotesque, but to all the Steiff dolls are very distinctive. While most doll ideas were widely imitated, few, if any, companies were successful copiers of the Steiff dolls.

Just a glance at the illustrations accompanying this article will serve to help outline the characteristics which make the Steiff cloth dolls so unique. The Steiff catalog referred to them as "Comic" dolls, but perhaps caricatures is a better term, as they do have ludicrously exaggerated features. Some have great protruding stomachs, others are pencil thin; some have an overwhelming proboscis, others a slight bump of a nose; some have large eyes, others just a bead. In 1911, Steiff advertised that the dolls could stand on their own because of their large feet and shoes and because of the way the bodies were balanced.

The Steiff dolls were constructed predominantly of felt with meticulous care and attention to small details. The most widely recognized characteristic is a seam down the center of the face which allows for shaping the profile, particularly the forehead, nose and chin. The ears are separate pieces of felt which are gathered on the inside edge and sewed onto the head. Sometimes the mouths were simply painted on, but often they were separately formed with pieces of felt indicating lips sewn into a slit in the felt, which certainly involved quite a bit of extra skill and effort. Some of the dolls have natural glass eyes, and some have shoe buttons or beads. Some dolls were constructed to have completely removable clothing. Others were made with some of the clothing being an integral part of the body, usually arms, legs or torso. A man might have a jacket torso, but an arm covered by a sleeve, pants which formed his legs, but wear knee boots. Many dolls have large hands; fingers were defined only by stitching in most cases, but a few have separately formed fingers. The heads swivel, and the shoulders and hips are jointed with a metal disk. Some dolls also have a knee joint, also with a metal disk. Sometimes the dolls have hair painted on; others have pieces of mohair used as the scalp to create their hair. Mohair was also inserted to indicate sideburns, mustaches and beards. All of the dolls were stuffed with excelsior.

As with Steiff products even today, the dolls were not cheaply priced. They were quality products and the cost was commensurate. A 28cm (11-1/16in) to 35cm (12¾in) comic doll cost $2.00 to $2.50. However, more elaborate dolls with accessories, such as soldiers, could cost $4.00 or $5.00. Many Steiff caricatures came with accessories, such as guns, rakes, musical instruments, bags, caps, canteens and other equipment. Also adding to the price could be some of the elaborate footwear. Many had shoes or boots handmade of leather and showing exquisite workmanship.

There are two main classes into which Steiff divides the cloth dolls in the 1913 catalog and those terms will be used here: The *comic* or *caricature* dolls, already discussed, and the *character* dolls. (The 1913 Steiff Catalog has been reproduced by Flora Gill Jacobs of The Washington Dolls' House & Toy Museum. This is an indispensable document for studying early Steiff dolls.) To Steiff the character dolls were simply the child dolls. These did not have funny or comic faces or exaggerated features. They looked like little children. The character dolls were very well constructed and advertised as "Unbreakable." They were completely of felt with disk-jointed shoulders and hips. They also had a seam down the center of their faces and a seam from the eye to the ear to aid modeling. The children have tiny glass eyes and painted mouths. Both noses

ABOVE LEFT: Illustration 3. In 1911, Steiff made a variety of soldiers — American, German, English, French, Italian, Austrian, Belgian and Dutch. This 16in (40.6cm) fellow has yet to be positively identified, but perhaps because of the short trousers he is an Australian. He is in mint condition and appears never to have been played with, and retains excellent cheek and lip color. His reddish brown hair is painted on. His jacket is part of his torso, but his pants are separate; his knee socks are knitted and his shoes are leather. **ABOVE RIGHT: Illustration 4.** The *Fire Brigade Commander* is 17in (43.2cm) tall without his helmet. He appears in one of the 1913 catalogs. His costume is marvelous with brass buttons, insignia and double leather belt; his brass helmet has a red tassel and leather strap. His boots are sturdily constructed with Steiff buttons used as studs on the soles. His knees are jointed.

Illustration 5. The profile view of the 17in (43.2cm) *Fire Brigade Commander*, seen in *Illustrations 5* and *6*, shows to advantage his prominent proboscis and his hair and sideburns which are inset mohair. His ears are also very intricately formed.

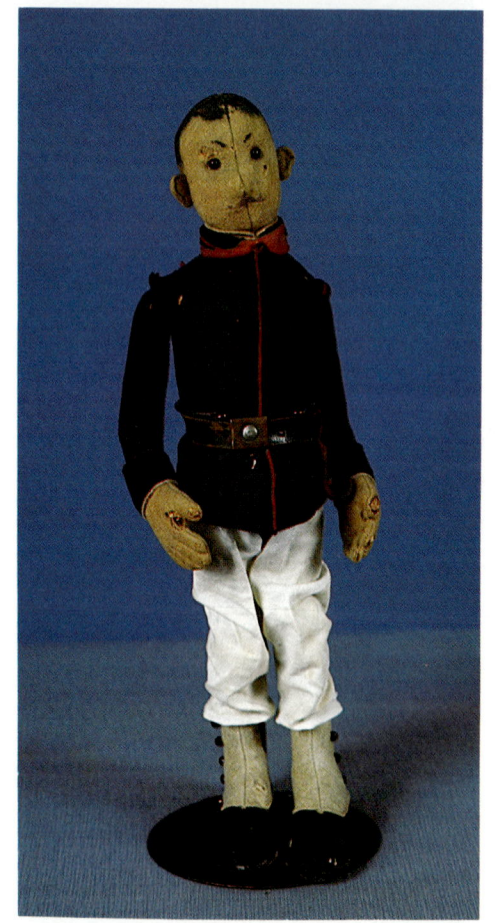

ABOVE LEFT: Illustration 6. From the 1913 catalog, this 14in (35.6cm) fellow appears to be *Schneid the Tailor*. Also part of this artisan series were a butcher and shoemaker. His clothing is all removable and appears to be original with a striped cotton shirt, wool pants, leather suspenders and leather shoes.

ABOVE RIGHT: Illustration 7. The *Sailor* is 20in (50.8cm) tall, with his Steiff button in his left ear. His hair is painted, and there is a circular seam around his head to facilitate shaping. The center facial seam allows for forming his profile; his mouth is painted on; his eyes are black buttons. He has metal disk-jointed shoulders, hips and knees. His clothing, which appears original, is removable. A *Sailor* is shown in a 1913 catalog, but with a different cap.

LEFT: Illustration 8. The identity of this 14in (35.6cm) gentleman has not been ascertained, but he is perhaps a policeman, maybe an Italian. His torso and arms are an integral part of his body with attached collar, cuffs and jacket skirt. His leather belt carries the Steiff insignia. Undoubtedly, he originally had some type of headgear. His hands are very large with fingers indicated by stitching.

LEFT: Illustration 9. This is the *Golliwog*, Teddy Bear's best friend. He appears in a 1913 catalog in 35cm (13¾in) and 43cm (16-15/16in) sizes, although this one is only 10in (25.4cm). He still has his Steiff button in his left ear. His face seaming is different from the other caricatures in that the seam runs horizontal instead of vertical and his ears are formed from the same piece of fabric as his face. His hair is inset of black shaggy mohair. His black bead eyes are on top of white felt. His wide smiling mouth is stitched on. He wears the golliwog's traditional red, white and blue costume. **RIGHT: Illustration 10.** The 22cm (8-11/16in) Gnome is *Snik* in the 1913 catalog. He also had a partner Gnome named *Snak*. In spite of his small size, he was a fairly expensive $2.75 wholesale, probably $5.00 retail. *Snik* has inset glass eyes, which makes him quite unusual. His hair, eyebrows and beard are of inset mohair. His mouth is also inset, so altogether he represents quite a bit of work for a small fellow. He is fully jointed with removable clothes, which appear original, as are his leather belt and pouch. His feet are particularly large with stitching to indicate shoes. Originally, he had a peaked cap and slip-on shoes. The Gnomes also came in a 30cm (11-7/16in) size, and *Snak* also came in a big 43cm (16-15/16in) size.

and mouths were shaped slightly by tiny stitches. Their legs were naturally shaped with a seam front and back as well as seams to shape knees and calves. Usually the hands were shaped with stitched fingers, although some children have stubby hands. The elbows, knees and tops of hands were rose tinted, as were the cheeks. The dolls are firmly stuffed and the clothing is removable. Most of the wigs are of mohair, but are constructed as integral parts of the dolls. In 1910, Steiff patented a special kind of hair. This was "hair threaded through the skin of cloth and fastened on its back side" so that it could not be pulled out. Dolls with this type of hair were offered in the 1913 catalog.

A paragraph at the front of the 1913 catalog is significant as it gives Steiff's comments on their dolls: "Our unbreakable Character Dolls of felt have brought about a complete reform on the doll-market. We are the originators of the name 'Character Dolls' the dolls which, on account of their individual features fascinate the mind of children. The costumes are true to the originals. The clothes take off. The brilliant hair can be combed even if wet and will not come out." Of course, it is quite debatable whether or not they originated the term "Character Dolls," which became widely used in the doll trade to describe the new type of doll introduced after 1908 which more closely resembled a real child than the stereotypical dolly faces. Actually "Character Doll" was a registered trademark of Kämmer & Reinhardt.

The costumes on the Steiff dolls were those of schoolchildren, or charming regional outfits, and dolls could be dressed and undressed. These simple costumes came into style with the German character doll movement. The dolls were listed in sizes from 28cm (11-1/16in) to 43cm (16-15/16in), although *Red* [Riding] *Hood* and *Walter* are listed at 50cm (19⅝in) and *Hubertus Hunter* at 50cm (19⅝in) and 60cm (25⅝in).

It is interesting that Steiff calls the dolls unbreakable. The fact that the heads would not break (like the more widely produced bisque or china dolls) and the bodies would not come apart (like the elastic strung composition bodies of the bisque head dolls) would be important selling points to parents buying dolls for children to play with. Of course, arms or legs could possibly be pulled off, but the Steiff dolls were extremely well jointed and seldom is one found limbless today.

The original price of the Steiff child doll is also worth noting. They were not inexpensive toys as a 14in (35.6cm) doll would cost about $5.00. It is interesting to compare with other contemporary dolls: a 14in (35.6cm) Schoenhut (no dress) was about $4.00, a bisque head character baby about $3.00, a composition head doll with cloth body 48¢, a cloth doll (like a Bruckner) 25¢.

A few paragraphs about the history of the Steiff company seem in order here. According to a recently published Steiff company bulletin, Margarete Steiff, born in 1847, was struck with polio at the age of two. This left her with weakened right hand and legs. Wanting to be independent, she learned sewing and in 1877 opened her workshop where she made women's and children's clothing from wool felt. In 1880 she made an elephant from felt scraps as a pincushion, but the popularity of the item with her nieces and nephews, who of course saw the play potential of such an object, actually got her starting producing small animals commercially. (The Steiff company issued a replica of this item in 1984 to 1985 as a part of their "Museum Collection" Limited Edition program.)

The *German Doll Encyclopedia* by Jürgen and Marianne Cieslik gives some background information about early Steiff production, as does *Steiff Teddy Bears, Dolls and Toys* by Jean Wilson and Shirley Conway. The latter source is also important for showing parts of Steiff catalogs for the early years. In 1893, the first felt dolls were produced. Illustrations in an 1897 catalog show some dolls which might have porcelain heads with clothing and/or bodies made by Steiff. Dolls of this period seem fairly mundane. In 1904 Steiff advertised that they produced 1,000 models of "cloth felt, plush, velvet, silk, satin, astrakhan, fur, wool, cotton, [and] leather." All of these were designed by Paul, Richard and Franz Steiff, nephews of Fraulein Steiff. Their greatest novelty was "funny, jointed caricature dolls." In 1904 they won a Grand Prize for their display at the St. Louis, Missouri, Exposition.

In 1905, Steiff registered the now-famous "Button in Ear" (Knopf im Ohr) trademark, with a notice to customers in 1904 stating that from November 1 of that year, each product would have a small nickel button in the left ear. The 1905 catalog shows a good sampling of felt caricature dolls, a clown doll, quite a few policeman or soldier-type dolls in different uniforms, *Captain* and *Missis*. Although Margarete Steiff died in 1909, the business continued to thrive with 2,000 em-

LEFT: Illustration 11. Steiff made a wide variety of clown dolls, several are shown as early as 1905. The 1913 catalog shows three clowns, but all are different from this one. This clown is 13½in (34.3cm) tall. He has clown makeup on his face, but most of it has been worn off. His costume is completely of felt as is his neck ruffle with bell trim. **RIGHT: Illustration 12.** These 28cm (11-1/16in) Character Dolls appear to be the Tyrolean boy and girl, *Anthony* and *Lizzie* which also came in 35cm (13¾in) and 43cm (16-15/16in) sizes. The construction of the dolls is given in detail in the text of the article; however, the hands on these particular dolls are very stubby when compared to other Steiff dolls of this type. *Anthony's* outfit shows the careful detail that Steiff used in creating the dolls. His jacket is topstitched with contrasting lapels and leather circle buttons, his pants are embroidered, and he has knitted socks with ties to hold them up at the knee. Real leather was used to make his shoes.

Illustration 13. Here are the 28cm (11-1/16in) *School Boy* and *School Girl*. These are the dolls which Steiff referred to as the Character Dolls. They both have glass eyes and hair of inset mohair. They are fully-jointed play dolls with removable clothing. The little girl originally had a school bag and slate as accessories, but now she has an early tiny jointed Steiff teddy. Both dolls are all original except for the boy's replaced shoes. The children came in a variety of play clothes and were also available in 35cm (13¾in) and 43cm (16-15/16in) sizes, but the 25cm (9-13/16in) ones are the most commonly found. Some of them had jointed knees.

Illustration 14. This 15½in (39.4cm) Elf has no button in his ear but he does appear to be a Steiff creation. He is fully mohair except for his felt face and hands, even the black decoration on his costume is inset mohair.

ployees in the factory. Apparently the soldiers had become very popular as Steiff advertised that for Christmas they had a request from the eldest son of the Crown Prince for a barracks square of Steiff Soldiers, further stating "Each soldier has a different feature, and each...is so droll that the children have much fun."

In 1911, the caricature dolls were even more expanded with designs introduced by Arthur Schlopsnies, a Munich artist. Added were American Indians, blacks, cowboys, sailors, Salvation Army people, Eskimos, Gibson girls, an Irish footman, a German, a Pole and other clowns.

In 1913, a large selection was offered in a 30-page catalog. This is available in reprinted form. (See information above.) The catalog is particularly informative as it not only shows the dolls, but gives their names, lists sizes in which they were available, material and price. (I have assumed throughout this article in referring to the prices given in the catalog that they are the wholesale cost to dealers, and that the retail price would be approximately double.) Seven pages of dolls were offered. Comic or caricature dolls included farmer, *Scoutboy*, jester, *Max* and *Moritz*, baseball player, circus acrobat and clowns, jockey, gnomes, "Golliwog," butcher, tailor, shoemaker, barkeeper, hunter, messenger boy, soldiers and policemen, American Indian, Mexican and Chinaman. Character Dolls included a variety of boys and girls, farmer and fisher folk, *Red [Riding] Hood*, Eskimo on skis and baby dolls.

1914 saw the demise of production of the Steiff Caricature Dolls because of the outbreak of World War I. By 1920 Steiff was back in production, but the large variety of dolls was not offered as before the war. From then on only a few caricature and Character Dolls were made.

There is a group of avid collectors who actively seek out Steiff dolls, which are quite difficult to find, especially in very good condition, so prices of old Steiff dolls are escalating and prime examples are bringing $3000. The highest prices are reserved for dolls with very good faces, unusual outfits, all of their accessories, and, of course, those which have been well preserved.

With the continuing collector interest in Steiff designs of the past as shown by the enormous success of the reintroduction of Teddy Bear models from their archives, for 1986 the Steiff company is reintroducing two if its original doll models, an 18in (45.7cm) *Gentleman in Morning Coat* and 16in (40.6cm) *Tennis Lady, Betty*.

The *Gentleman in Morning Coat* is a caricature with great presence. He has black bead eyes, and inset mohair mustache and hair; his mouth is painted, his nose upturned. Outfitted as a German gentleman of the early 1900s, he was originally produced in 1914 and designed by Albert Schlopsnies. He is attired in a black felt coat and trousers with white tuxedo shirt, black cardboard top hat with black leather shoes on his elongated feet; his hands are white felt with stitch-outlined fingers to indicate gloves. He is a handsome man indeed!

Tennis Lady, Betty is fashionably dressed as a lady in a sporting costume, which was first made in 1914. Whether or not she could play tennis in this outfit is debatable, as there is no way to move fast in the hobble skirt. Her outfit is of cream felt trimmed with gold lapels and cuffs which match her gloves. Her hat is coordinated with her suit. Her face is of felt with the typical center seam construction with small nose and painted mouth. She has blue glass eyes and a mohair wig and is certainly a worthy companion for the gentleman.

These dolls are actually a reissue as they are made in exactly the same way with exactly the same types of materials as the old dolls. The fabrics, stuffing and finishing details, even the facial painting are all authentic and faithful to the original models. The dolls will also have a Steiff button in the left ear; a white label affixed with the button will indicate that the doll is a Steiff Limited Edition and will differentiate the antique model from the re-creation. Steiff originally intended an edition of 2,000 each with 1500 for United States distribution, but the April 1986 **Doll Reader**® announced that Steiff would make 3000 sets worldwide with the extra production being offered primarily to European collectors. Dealers and collectors both anticipate that the demand for the Steiff dolls will be strong and that the prices will rise rapidly on the secondary market above the issue prices of $275 for the *Gentleman* and $300 for *Betty*. □

LEFT: Illustration 15. The soldier boy, seen in *Illustration 3*, has some interesting original accessories. Collectors are very excited to find dolls with their original gadgets as these little items were so easily lost. He has a haversack, canteen and hatchet. His belt, hatband and strap, handle on haversack and hatchet holder are all real leather, showing Steiff's attention to quality detail work. In the 1913 wholesale catalog, the price of a soldier with equipment was $1.10 more than one without. **Illustration 16.** The accessories of the 17in (43.2cm) *Fire Brigade Commander*, seen in *Illustration 5*, include a rope and hatchet which are hooked to rings sewn onto the back of his coat.

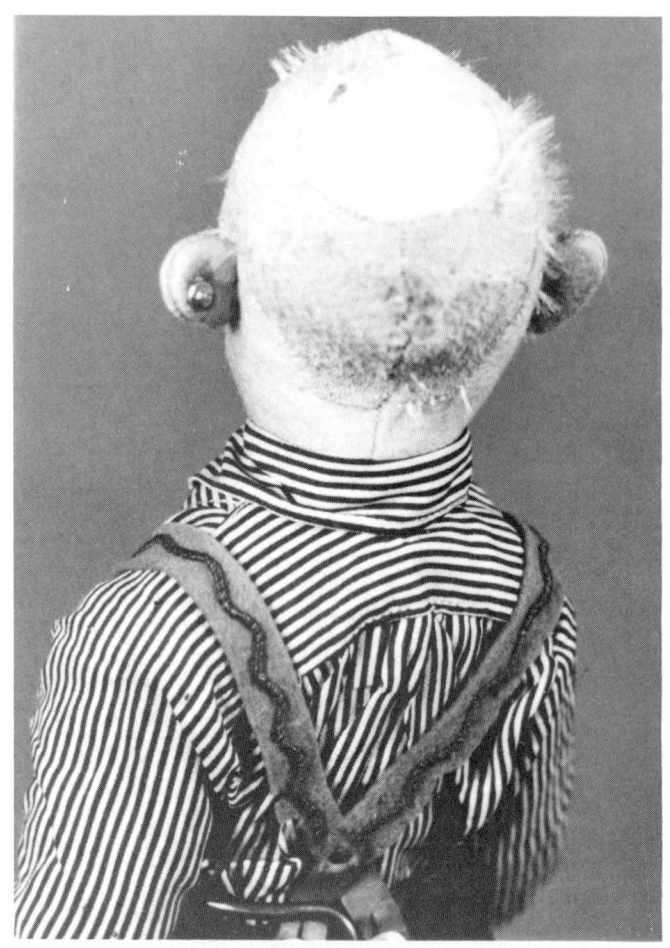

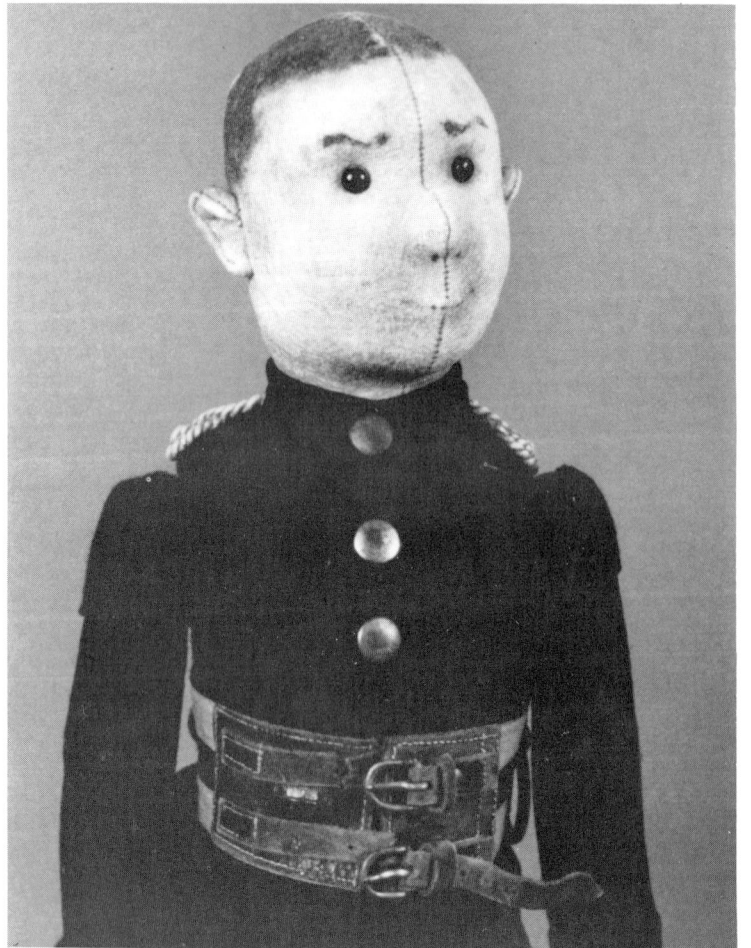

ABOVE LEFT: Illustration 17. *Schneid the Tailor* still has his Steiff button in his left ear. This back view shows how the mohair is inserted around his felt bald spot. He also has a mohair mustache.

LEFT: Illustration 18. This is another *Fireman*, but his face is not quite so distinctive as that of the *Fire Brigade Commander*, although his wavy eyebrows are somewhat roguish. This face turns up with some regularity, for of course every caricature could not have a different face. Like the other *Fireman*, this doll also has jointed knees.

ABOVE RIGHT: Illustration 19. This profile view of the clown, seen in *Illustration 16*, shows his upturned nose, specially painted eyebrows and his inset hair of real mohair.

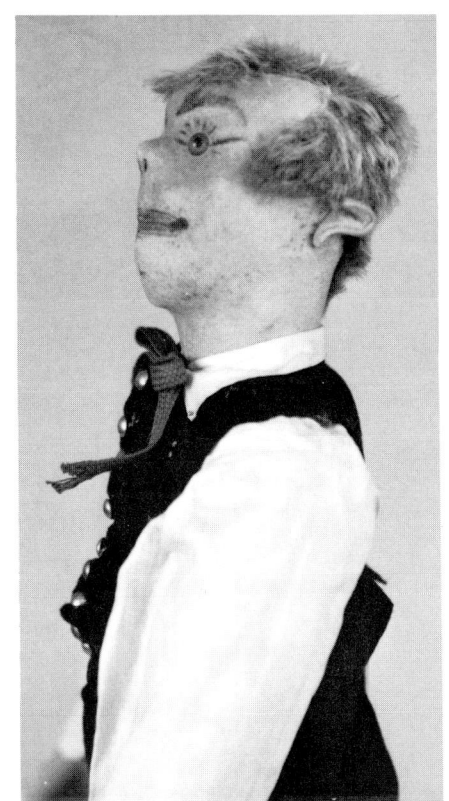

ABOVE RIGHT: Illustration 20. 1986 reissues of the 1914 *Gentleman in Morning Coat* and the 1913 *Tennis Lady, Betty* are re-creations of the original antique models. They are each a limited edition of 3000 and demand for these dolls is expected to be very heavy.

ABOVE LEFT: Illustration 21. 20in (50.8cm) Steiff man caricature, apparently *Mich* from a 1913 catalog, all original except incorrect hat. This was a fairly expensive doll selling for $4.75 wholesale or about $9.00 retail. *H&J Foulke, Inc.*

LEFT: Illustration 22. A closer view of 20in (50.8cm) *Mich*, seen in *Illustration 21*, showing wonderful construction detail of ears, inset mohair hair, unusual glass eyes with painted eyelashes and emphasis line, and inset lips. *H&J Foulke, Inc.*

139

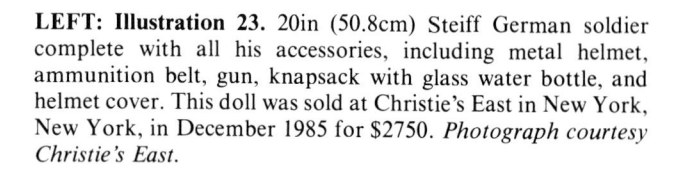

LEFT: Illustration 23. 20in (50.8cm) Steiff German soldier complete with all his accessories, including metal helmet, ammunition belt, gun, knapsack with glass water bottle, and helmet cover. This doll was sold at Christie's East in New York, New York, in December 1985 for $2750. *Photograph courtesy Christie's East.*

RIGHT: Illustration 24. 26in (66cm) Steiff German soldier in full uniform with ammunition belt and knapsack and metal helmet. This doll was sold at Robert W. Skinner's auction in December 1985 for $1900. *Photograph courtesy Robert W. Skinner, Inc.*

Illustration 25. Knee joint of the *Sailor* from *Illustration 7* showing that the lower leg rotates on a metal rivet.

Illustration 26. Back view of the *Soldier* from *Illustration 3* showing his accessories: backpack, axe and canteen.

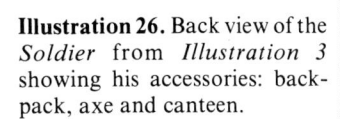

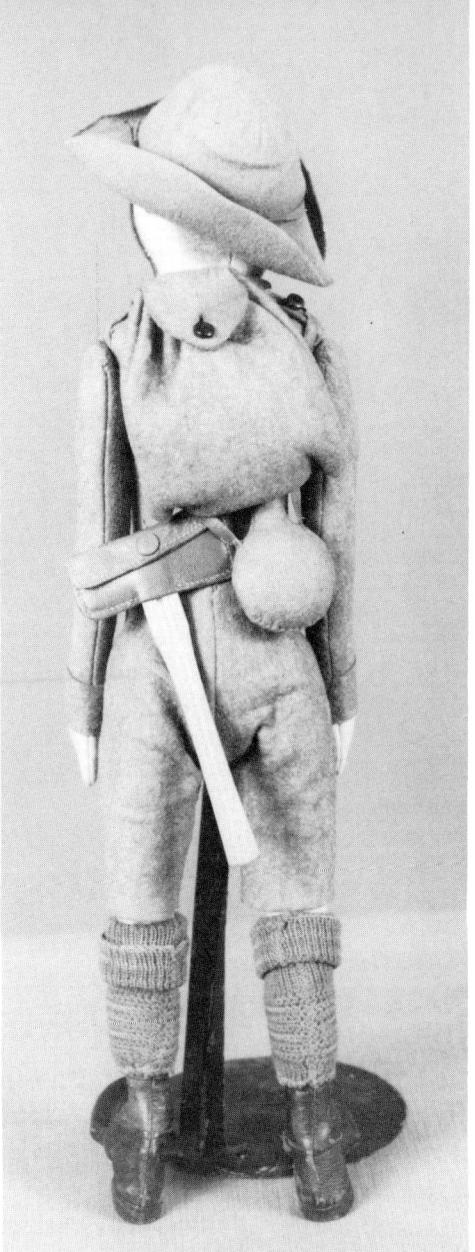

Illustration 28. Back view of the *Fire Brigade Commander* from *Illustration 4* showing his accessories and how they are clipped on his belt by metal rings and hooks.

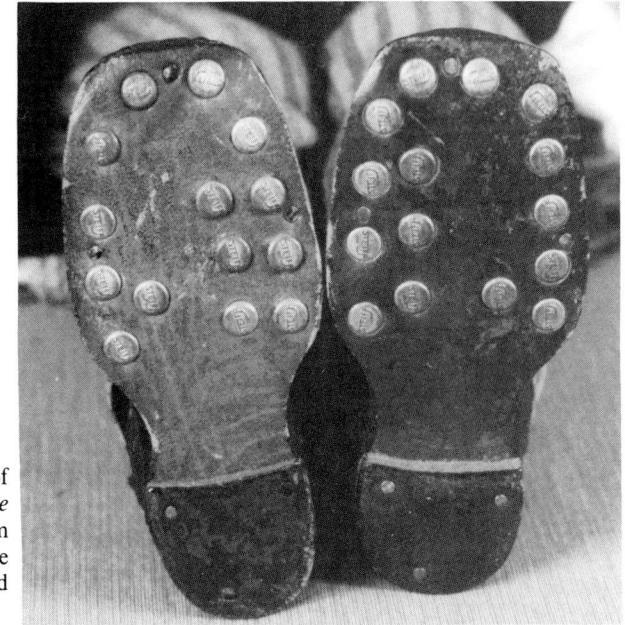

Illustration 27. Soles of the boots of the *Fire Brigade Compander* from *Illustration 4* showing the metal Steiff buttons used as studs.

Focusing On...

— A Photographic Essay on the Lenci —

The lovely Lenci dolls date from 1920 until the present. Originally created and designed by Madame di E. Scavini of Turin, Italy, the older Lenci dolls are characterized by collectors as some of the finest cloth dolls ever made. We know that you will enjoy this varied selection of Lencis from the Beth Foulke Collection. All Lencis in original clothing.

RIGHT: Illustration 1. Circa 1930 pair of schoolboy and schoolgirl. Unmarked; 17in (43cm). Unusual face mold with puffy cheeks and round protruding chin. Girl has blonde mohair with braids coiled at ears; wearing blue felt dress with white collar and cuffs; yellow ducks for trim. Boy has blonde mohair inset all over head; wearing white felt shirt, brown tie with aqua stripes, rust felt pants, leather belt and leather shoes. Both with side-glancing eyes.

BOTTOM: Illustration 3. Circa 1940 unmarked 17in (43cm) Lenci girl with blue eyes to side. Blonde mohair wig styled in braids with band of felt flowers around head. Pink organdy dress with ruffles, bouquet of felt flowers at waist.

ABOVE: Illustration 2. Circa late 1920s child's pocketbook with cloth Lenci label; 6in (15cm) tall. Pink felt with decorative felt trim; carrying handle also of pink felt. Mask face as used on the Mascottes; blue eyes looking to side.

Illustration 4. Circa late 1930s *Little Orphant Annie* in original box. Lenci cloth label; 8in (20cm). White felt dress with stripes of red felt; white apron with red felt rickrack.

LEFT: Illustration 5. Circa 1922 Oriental, the same doll pictured on the early Lenci trademark. Unmarked; 13in (33cm) tall including headdress. Eyes are closed, eyebrows very high and circular; hole in mouth for opium pipe which is missing; black yarn hair with queue in back. Jacket is yellow felt with aqua trim; pants are black felt with gold trim; aqua and yellow shoes.

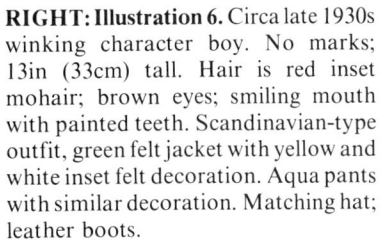

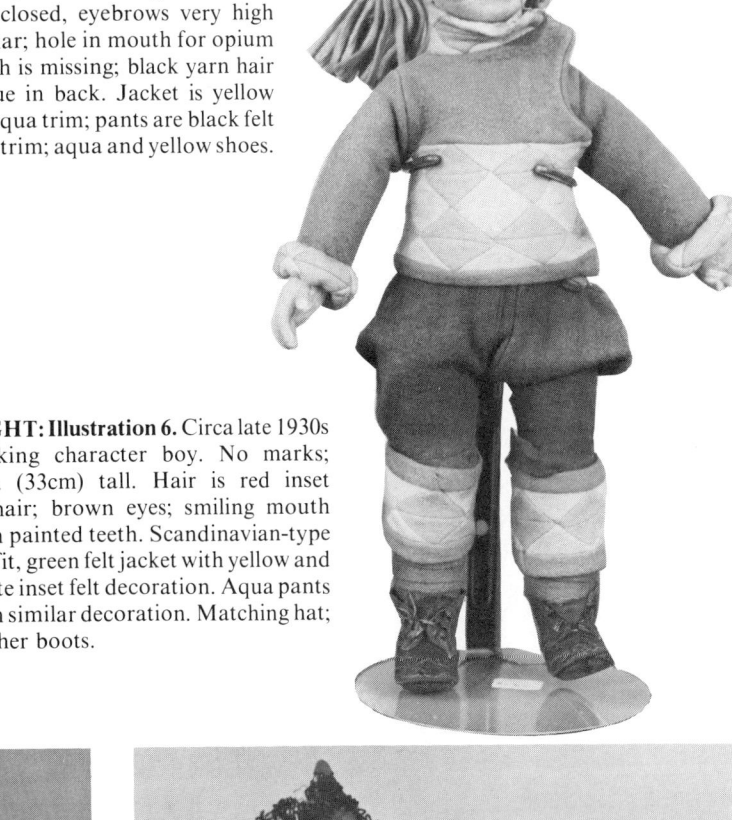

RIGHT: Illustration 6. Circa late 1930s winking character boy. No marks; 13in (33cm) tall. Hair is red inset mohair; brown eyes; smiling mouth with painted teeth. Scandinavian-type outfit, green felt jacket with yellow and white inset felt decoration. Aqua pants with similar decoration. Matching hat; leather boots.

Illustration 7. Circa 1930 pouty face, number 1500. Unmarked; 18in (46cm) tall. Strawberry blonde mohair inset all over head; deep-set brown eyes. Yellow felt dress with white collar and sleeves with overall flower trim, blue felt bolero.

Illustration 8. Circa 1936 Señorita with Lenci cloth and paper labels. 6in (15cm) including headdress. Unusual wooden head with painted black hair and features. Red felt dress, black lace mantilla with felt flowers, bead necklace.

143

Illustration 9. Circa 1930 boy (number 300/11) and girl (number 300/V); both with cloth label; both 17½in (44cm). Boy has light brown mohair; brown eyes; he wears a black fuzzy cap, red felt shirt, black jacket, green and blue patchwork pants. Girl has blonde mohair wig, blue eyes; she wears brown felt dress with white sleeves and pink and blue felt stripes, blue apron, white lace cap, topped by pink felt cap with felt flower decoration.

Illustration 10. Circa 1940 *Lucia*, the Lenci factory name for this particular face mold. Unmarked; 14in (36cm). Blonde mohair inset at hairline; pearl earrings, blue eyes to side. Pink organdy gown with bows and ruffles; pink felt flowers trim down front of dress and interspersed around back of skirt.

Illustration 11. Circa late 1920s long-limbed lady doll of unusually small size. Unmarked; 14in (36cm) to 15in (38cm). Side-glancing sultry half-closed eyes and light brown curly mohair wig. Two-tiered light green organdy dress with white "fur" trim and white organdy bodice. Felt flowers at waist; matching bonnet also has felt flowers.

LEFT: Illustration 12. Circa 1929 Lenci of the *Sport Series* using number 300 face. Unmarked; 17½in (44cm). Light brown mohair, brown eyes to side. White felt boxing shorts, red felt shirt, black felt cap, brown leather boxing gloves and shoes.

RIGHT: Illustration 13. Circa 1940(?) *The Widow Allegra* with Lenci cloth label; 20in (51cm). Rare glass flirty eyes. Black taffeta dress with bustle in back; black felt hat with felt flowers; blonde mohair pulled back in long curls.

Focusing On...

Lenci Children

Some time ago when my daughter Beth and I were visiting a doll shop, she latched onto a doll and carried it all around with her. "Oh, Mom," she pleaded, "buy this doll for me. I just love it."

So, I looked it over. It was a very appealing 16in (41cm) to 18in (46cm) child doll with a felt face, body and clothes in very nice condition — and I figured Beth had been good and that the doll would be $30.00 to $40.00, so I would get it for her. Imagine my surprise when I asked the proprietor the price and discovered the cost to be well over $100. "Wow," I responded. "What makes him so expensive?"

"Well, it's a Lenci doll, all original and in perfect condition."

And so, we made our acquaintance with Lenci dolls! With their expressive faces, side-glancing eyes and lovely clothes, Beth loved them from the first, but it took me longer to adjust to them because I love bisque dolls, and I kept thinking I could be getting a nice bisque doll for the same price as these "rag" dolls were costing. But gradually I, too, became convinced (but not until after I let two fantastic Lencis slip through my hands).

The paper label found on some Lencis (mostly they were removed by original owners) says that the doll was patented by E. di Scavini in Turin, Italy, in 1921. Supposedly Lenci was a pet name for Elena Konig di Scavini, and when the first dolls were made they were called Lenci's dolls and the name stuck. Rumor gives two reasons for Mme. Lenci's going into the doll business — both connected to World War I. Some say Mme. Lenci's work grew out of loneliness after the tragedy of losing her husband in the war — making dolls offered not only financial support but also a satisfying, meaningful way to occupy her time. Others say that wives of artists whose husbands served in the war needed means to supplement allowances and started to make fabric dolls. As their artist husbands came home wounded and unable to pursue their artist careers, they, too, joined in the doll making business. Whatever is true really does not matter, for it is certain that the doll world would be poorer without the artistic fabric dolls of Mme. Lenci and the hundreds of workers she employed.

Lenci dolls are renowned for the skillful way they are fashioned entirely from flesh-colored felt (later ones have cloth torsos). Bodies are stuffed hard, however, we have two which seem to have hollow torsos. The dolls are jointed at the neck, shoulders and hips; limbs are shaped and fingers are separated except two and three which usually seem to be together. The faces are of pressed and shaped felt — artistically painted with appealing pouty or winsome expressions. The eyes are nearly always looking to the side; the ears are applied; and the wigs are of soft, natural-looking mohair.

One old Lenci advertisement claims: "Every Lenci is Made in Italy by Italian Artists and is an individual work of Art." In 1920, Lenci advertised 50 original designs; in 1921, 100 models of character dolls; in 1923, they advertised dolls from 5in (13cm) to 45in (114cm). (These larger ones were often flapper-type lady bed dolls.) A 1928 catalog shows Lenci dolls retailing in the United States for $1.95 for a 15in (38cm) size and $1.19 for an 11in (28cm) size. This seems a comparatively high price for a cloth doll at the time.

Mme. Lenci's dolls are marked with exquisite taste for she was an artist before she became a doll maker. She claimed her trade secret was: "You must always use supremely good taste." And this taste is shown not only in the construction of the doll itself, but also in the costuming which was fanciful, charming and elaborate. The clothes were usually of felt, sometimes combined with organdy.

Illustration 1. A fantastic 18in (46cm) girl; her turned head is permanently attached; blonde mohair wig in long curls; lovely brown eyes with painted upper eyelashes and blue shadow beneath; mouth has two highlights on the lower lip; cheeks are pleasingly rouged; dress is of fuchsia organdy and felt with turquoise trim, turquoise hat with intricately made felt flowers. The original paper label is 1½in (4cm) square, buff with brown lettering and reads: "Prodvizone//Originale//Lenci." *Beth Foulke Collection.*

Illustration 2. This 16in (41cm) boy looks very Victorian. He has a wig of soft brown mohair; his eyes are lovely with extremely long eyelashes; he has fuller cheeks and a more wistful rather than pouty expression and his cheeks are highly colored; his entire costume including the spats is of felt in shades of brown and his shoes are black leather. His thumb and forefinger are curled as though he perhaps held a walking stick or a valise. *Beth Foulke Collection.*

Illustration 3. A pair of 17in (43cm) Dutch children. Their costumes are quaint and colorful, are beautifully made and can be removed. The girl's cap is of pink felt with applied felt flowers and white lace; her dress and apron are entirely of felt with much detail of applique and embroidery; she has a felt tulip in her pot. The boy's clothes are entirely of felt with a red shirt, a black jacket and green and blue trousers; his hat is black and fuzzy; he wears a water yoke. Both are wearing wooden shoes. There is a tag on the girl's skirt which reads: "Lenci//Made in Italy." Both have heart-shaped paper labels which read: "Dutch." *Beth Foulke Collection. Collection.*

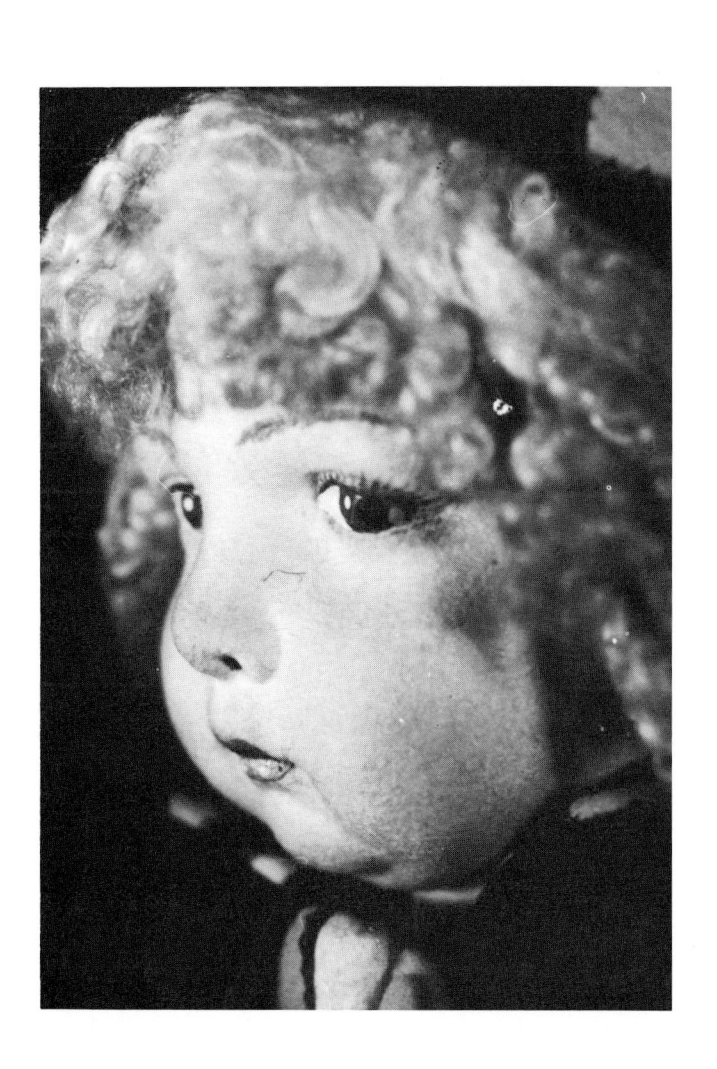

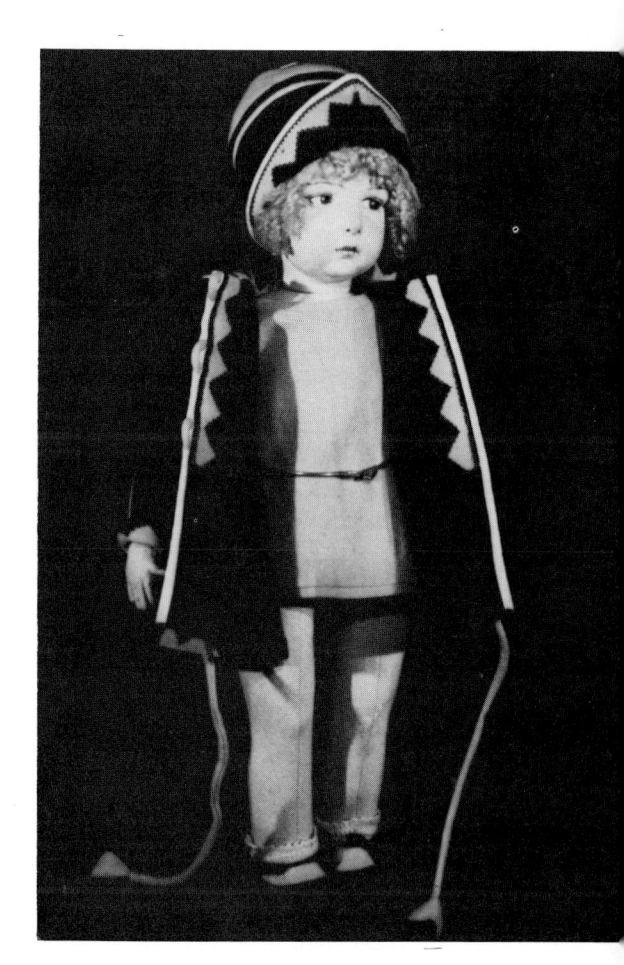

Illustration 4. 23in (58cm) child; tightly curled blonde mohair wig; brown eyes with blue shadow and white highlights; lower lip has two highlights; costume is completely of felt in turquoise, fuchsia and white. On the back of her hat is a very intricate flower decoration. She is wearing typical felt Lenci shoes to match her turquoise coat. Her dress and belt are also fuchsia. *Beth Foulke Collection.*

Illustration 5. Close-up of the 23in (58cm) child shown in **Illustration 4**. *Beth Foulke Collection.*

Focusing On...

Lenci Dolls, Part II

What particular qualities of Lenci dolls cause collectors and even casual observers to respond overwhelmingly to these dolls? Foremost it is perhaps the expression on the doll's face — the manner in which the artist has created the features to show the child as pouty, winsome, friendly, coy, serene, startled, mischievous, shy, flirtations, sad, forlorn and surprised. A collection showing a variety of Lenci faces can run almost the whole gamut of emotions. Some of the tiny ones have scrunched-up funny faces, and some are even grinning, while others appear ready to cry. And then one must consider the fact that a winsome child evokes an emotional response that is nearly universal in all human beings.

Secondly, the detail and attractiveness of the costuming, in itself an artistic feat on most Lenci dolls, is appealing. Although some of these are garbed in a rather plain fashion, most of them are outfitted in bright costumes obviously designed by artists and executed in workmanship of the highest order. Dresses, coats and hats have piping and trimming of contrasting color with felt flowers or ornaments of very intricate design. Squares of stripes of fabric of varying colors are sewn together in pleasing designs. Felt and organdy are favorite fabrics, the organdy being very adaptable to rows and rows of ruffles on dresses and puffy sleeves on bodices. Many costumes are completed with some sort of an accessory, such as a parasol, flowerpot, walking stick or other item.

Shown here are a variety of Lenci types — several child dolls, geographic dolls, bed dolls and a baby.

Illustration 1. A pair of 17in (43cm) Oriental Lenci dolls constructed of pale yellow felt. Both have wigs of black mohair inset into the felt in tiny clumps and the girl has clusters of felt flowers on each side of her head for adornment. Their eyes, outlined in black with thick lower eyelashes, are delicately molded to slant upward. The girl's costume is apparently Japanese. Her kimono is turquoise and violet felt with overall embroidery in various colors. She is wearing felt sandals. Her hand is positioned to hold an accessory, perhaps a parasol, which has been lost. The boy's costume appears to be Chinese and consists of yellow-gold trousers and coat with a black vest. He is wearing wooden clog-type shoes and possibly at one time had a hat. *Beth Foulke Collection.*

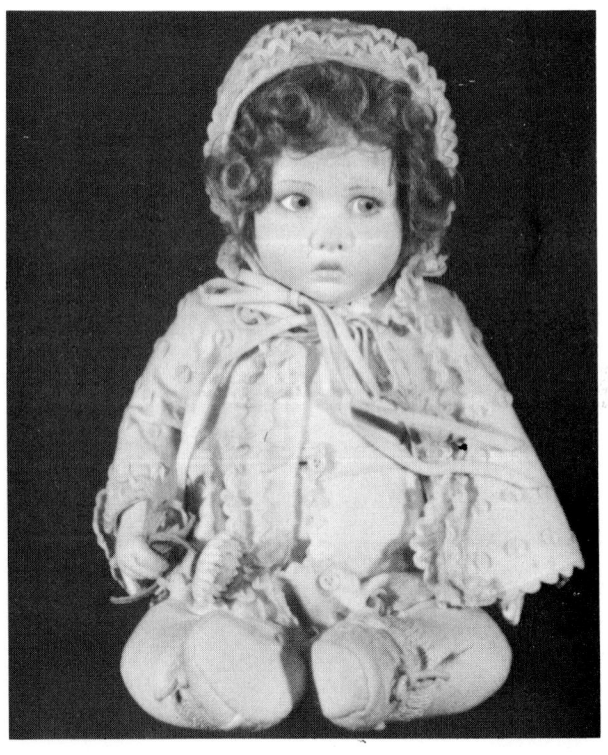

Illustration 2. A rare Lenci baby with curved arms and legs. She has a soft brown curly mohair wig. Her mouth is tiny and pink with a lighter shade and two even lighter highlights on the lower lip. Her eyes are light brown with lovely painted eyelashes and pale shadow on the lower eyelid. Her outfit consists of a two-toned pink felt coat and hat with white organdy ruffles covering a white felt romper suit. The whole costume is exquisitely made. In her hand she holds a felt flower. The fingers of her left hand are all separate, very unusual in a Lenci. She has a portion of her large Lenci paper tag remaining. *Beth Foulke Collection.*

Illustration 3. This 13in (33cm) fellow with an impish expression has no label, but appears to be a Lenci. He has a curly red mohair wig, large roguish eyes, and a smiling mouth — altogether a real character. *Mrs. Ronald Bell Collection. Photograph courtesy Mrs. Ronald Bell.*

Illustration 4. A large 34in (86cm) Lenci girl. Her blonde mohair is in corkscrew curls. Her dress is very plain orange felt with brown trim, but her cape is constructed of squares of orange, yellow, tan and pale yellow felt between strips of brown. The cloche hat has a bouquet of felt flowers on the crown. She is a darling flapper girl. As characteristic of most Lencis which we have examined, she has two white highlights painted on each eye, and two pink highlights on her lower lip. *Beth Foulke Collection.*

Illustration 5. This Lenci girl is number 149/T from the 1925 to 1926 Lenci catalog. Her very large dark eyes and tiny bow mouth make this 16in (41cm) girl look quite mischievous. She is wearing a fuchsia dress and hat with blue trim. She has a mitten-type hand, unusual on a Lenci. She is in such perfect condition that the rogue has not faded from her cheeks, knees and elbows. She is wearing typical Lenci shoes and socks. *Beth Foulke Collection.*

Illustration 6. This Lenci lady bed doll is 28in (70cm) tall with extremely long limbs. She has a mature-looking face. Her dark eyes are shadowed with blue. Her wig is of auburn mohair in long curl style. The costume is exquisite, the skirt being made of tiers of white organdy ruffles with black and pale yellow felt trim. Her picture hat is of pale yellow felt trimmed with pink felt roses, which also adorn her dress. She is wearing lace gloves, lace stockings and high-heeled shoes. Her parasol is also of white organdy. She is identified as Raquel Meller, the famous dancer, in the 1925 to 1926 Lenci catalog. *H&J Foulke Inc.*

149

Illustration 7. This Lenci bed doll has a young lady face with blue eyes, raised eyebrows and tinted cheeks. Her blonde hair is covered by a white lace headdress. She is wearing a long green felt dress, white lace apron and fringed shawl with felt flower decoration. She carries a basket of felt flowers. She has a cloth Lenci label. *Mrs. J. Franke Collection. Photograph courtesy of Mrs. J. Franke.*

Illustration 8. Lenci produced a large variety of dolls in provincial or geographic costumes of which this 17in (43cm) doll is an excellent example. Her facial expression makes her look almost mad. She is wearing gold wooden earrings, and her black mohair wig is arranged in a very elaborate style — a circular braid held in place by a circle of gold wooden pins. Her felt costume has lovely embroidery work on the green apron, rust bodice and white head scarf. Her skirt is blue with stripes of tan and brown. Her shoes have wooden soles. Her accessory appears to be flax stick. She has a square "Produzione Oraginale//Lenci" paper label on her apron, and a large paper label on her back giving her style number as "282." *P. J. Lembo Collection. Photograph courtesy of P. J. Lembo.*

Illustration 9. This beautiful 22½in (57cm) pouty child has strawberry blonde mohair styled with center part and braids coiled over each ear and expressive brown eyes. Her dress is of felt pieces sewn together in a plaid design of fuchsia, gray, white and turquoise, typical of the painstaking construction of most Lenci costumes. She has her large Lenci paper label which identifies her as number "109/48." She is shown with her original Lenci box which has the same paper label on its end. *Norma Rodenbaugh Collection. Photograph courtesy of Norma Rodenbaugh.*

```
Lenci                    TURIN
DI E. SCAVINI            (Italy)

        MADE IN ITALY
           109/48

Pat. Sept. 8, 1921    Pat. N. 142433
STE, SGDGX 87395   BREVETTO 501-178
```

Illustration 10. A typical Lenci paper label, approximately 1⅛in (3cm) by 2in (5cm).

```
Lenci
MADE IN ITALY
```

Illustration 11. A typical Lenci cloth label 5/8in (1.6cm) by 2in (5cm).

Focusing On...

A Collection of Norah Wellings Creations Circa 1926 to 1957

All dolls from the *Kimberly Parada Collection*

Souvenir Boys

It is not hard to get hooked on Norah Wellings' dolls. Norah Wellings has created such impish and appealing dolls that gathering a shelf full of them has got to be fun!

The general construction of the dolls is superior. Strong fabrics of good quality are used. Construction is sturdy. Attention is given to details in outfits including accessories and trims. Faces are carefully hand-painted. The most commonly found Wellings face mold is the one with the toothy grin used for the 8in (20cm) to 11in (28cm) souvenir characters. Fabric for the face is of felt, velvet or stockinette, apparently as available. Some dolls have applied ears; most do not. Eyes are molded and painted looking to the side, accented by dark upper eyelashes and topped by arched eyebrows. Face modeling features a hump of a nose, round pinchable cheeks and a wide grinning mouth with painted teeth.

Illustration 1. Most ubiquitous of all Wellings dolls are the sailors. Millions were sold aboard ship and from sailing spots. Each carried the name of the ship or port on the sailor's cap. This 8in (20cm) one is from "Victoria, B.C." His blue velvet sailor suit is an integral part of his body. His tie, whistle and hat are removable and his face, hands and feet are of flesh-colored felt.

Illustration 2. This 9in (23cm) fellow, representing the Royal Canadian Mounted Police, has a face of felt and also sports applied ears. His outfit is blue and red velvet, even the riding pants are an integral part of his body. His separate hat is tan felt. His belt, buttons, epaulets, collar and whistle complete his uniform. He also has a label up under his back collar.

LEFT: Illustration 3. A less commonly found doll is this 10in (25cm) one dressed in light blue velvet with a black fuzzy hat. He probably represents one of the English Ceremonial Regiments. The uniform is decorated with a belt, buttons and braid. His hat has a chin strap and a felt ornament.

RIGHT: Illustration 4. The last dolls shown in this souvenir group are two 10in (25cm) Scots boys in traditional costumes. The one on the left has the same smiling face as others without the toothy look. His face is of stockinette with felt ears. The top of his outfit is red velvet and yellow felt, an integral part of him. His kilt is a separate article of dark plaid cotton. The facial mold of the boy on the right is entirely different, a more serious expression, done in stockinette with painted hair, eyes looking straight ahead and a small mouth. His costume is fairly elaborate with a black velvet top, white stock, red plaid kilt, shawl and stockings.

December 1977 Doll Reader

Character

Illustration 5. A truly outstanding doll is this 9in (23cm) American Indian. His brown character face is of an entirely different mold, apparently done especially for this doll, with a large nose, age and frown lines, somber expression with tightly closed mouth and small eyes. He has black yarn hair which does not show. His costume is of light green felt with colorful contrasting felt fringe, headdress and other trim.

Large Souvenir Dolls

Illustration 6. This face is different from that of the smaller dolls. It is a happy smiling face, with smaller eyes having crinkled smile lines under them. The mouth is painted open and happy, but not showing so much tooth for its size as the smaller dolls. The wig is of soft black mohair. Her face and body are of very dark velvet. The 14in (36cm) native island girl on the left has the very desirable glass eyes. She is wearing a green, blue and yellow grass dress and is adorned with colorful earrings, necklace, arm and ankle bracelets. Her companion on the right is, I think, a native island policeman (British Colony) with red sash. Rank stripes are painted on his sleeve.

Girls

Illustration 7. Two 8in (20cm) souvenir girls in ethnic costume. They both have sweet stockinette faces, nicely painted eyes to the side and small rosebud mouths. They are sweet "dolly" faces, not as winning as the character ones. The girl on the left has lost her paper label, so we are not sure what country she represents, perhaps an eastern European one with her black mohair, peasant costume of red velvet and gold earrings. The girl on the left has "Dutch" stamped on the reverse of her original paper tag. Her outfit is blue velvet and her hair is blonde in pigtails.

Illustration 8. These two girls are identified as *Miss Smith* in 8in (20cm) and 11in (28cm) sizes. They both have stockinette faces and mohair pigtails. The bodies are cloth, the dresses are velvet and the bonnets are felt. They are also sometimes called *Old-Fashioned Girls*.

Illustration 9. This 15in (38cm) Dutch girl's face is a larger version of *Miss Smith* but it has quite a bit more detail and is executed in felt. There is more modeling around the nose and mouth, which makes her look like she is about ready to break into a wide smile. Her wig is of soft blonde mohair and her eyes are painted brown. She is different from the smaller dolls in that all her clothes are removable. Her body is of velvet, her dress, hat and shoes are of felt, and she is holding a felt flower.

MADE IN ENGLAND
BY
NORAH WELLINGS

Illustration 10. All of the Wellings dolls have a black, green or white woven cloth label sewn on the foot or arm. They also had a round paper wrist tag as shown with the small Dutch girl, but this was mostly always removed. The identity of the doll is stamped on the back of the paper tag.

Focusing On...

Alexander Cloth Dolls

All dolls from the *Ann Tardie Collection*

Everyone in "doll land" is acquainted with the magic name Madame Alexander. It conjures up the image of a cute little girl dressed in a straw hat and ruffled cotton dress or a soft cuddly baby in pink organdy or a fashionably dressed Gainsborough lady.

Alexander dolls have always been popular with both children and collectors and are without a doubt the number one modern doll today.

Few collectors, and even some who collect only Alexander dolls, however, do not realize that the first dolls which Madame Alexander made when she opened the Alexander Doll Company in 1923 were entirely of cloth.

Always intrigued by characters from fiction, Madame Alexander chose *Alice in Wonderland* for her first cloth doll. At first her face was flat; then a mask face with raised features was used.

Madame Alexander herself painted the features. *Alice* was soon followed by *Little Women* and many characters from the books of Charles Dickens.

The construction of the Alexander rag dolls is very simple. First, a turning head with a mask face of suede cloth, a felt-like fabric; lovely hand-painted brown or blue eyes, usually looking to the right, with iris, pupil and several highlights, red dot at corner, painted upper and side eyelashes; one stroke eyebrows; and a bow-shaped mouth. This is topped by a mohair wig on a cloth cap, glued or pinned to the head. The body torso is rectangular, unshaped; legs and arms are sewn on; the thumb is separate on each hand. The bodies are of pink cotton and are unmarked.

Clothes are all carefully made mostly of cottons. They have an Alexander tag which identifies the character (if it has not been clipped off down through the years). The undies are all of cotton or organdy constructed in one piece with long legs, a ruffle bottom and a slip attached at the waist.

Illustration 1. 16in (41cm) *Little Women* doll; reddish mohair styled with braids around her head; brown eyes; dress of white organdy with red figures, original undies, replaced shoes and socks; tagged: " 'Meg'//'Little Women'//Copyright//Madame Alexander N.Y."

Illustration 2. 16in (41cm) *Little Women* doll; blonde mohair styled in bangs; brown eyes; face is the same as the doll shown in **Illustration 1**; wearing a blue cotton dress with red print apron, original undies, replaced shoes and socks; tagged: " 'Little Women'//Jo//Copyright Pending//Madame Alexander N.Y."

Illustration 3. 16in (41cm) *Little Women* doll; light brown hair styled with a side part; brown eyes; same face as the dolls shown in **Illustrations 1** and **2**; wearing white dress with printed flowers, pink organdy hat, original undies, replaced shoes and socks; tagged: " 'Little Women'//Beth//Copyright Pending//Madame Alexander N.Y."

October 1976 Doll Reader

Illustration 4. Completely original *Little Em'ly*, a character from Dickens; blonde side-parted mohair wig; blue eyes; red print dress and matching bonnet; tagged: " 'Little Em'ly'//Madame Alexander//New York."

Illustration 5. *Little Dorritt*, a character from Dickens; lovely hand-painted eyes; face the same as the doll shown in **Illustration 4**; original dress and hat are in a green print with white trim; tagged: " 'Little Dorritt'//Madame Alexander//New York."

Illustration 6. *Little Nell*, a character from Dickens; same face as the dolls shown in **Illustrations 4** and **5** but with a slightly different expression; pink print cotton dress; tagged: " 'Little Nell'//Madame Alexander//New York."

Illustration 7. *Babbie*; brown mohair styled with bangs; brown eyes; peasant style dress with red skirt and yellow print blouse, replacement shoes and socks; dress tag reads: " 'Babbie'//Adapted from 'Little Minister'//Madame Alexander//New York;" wrist tag reads: "BABBIE//Inspired by//Katherine Hepburn//In//R.K.O. Radio Pictures//'The Little Minister.' " The reverse of the tag reads: "Created//by//Madame//Alexander//New York."

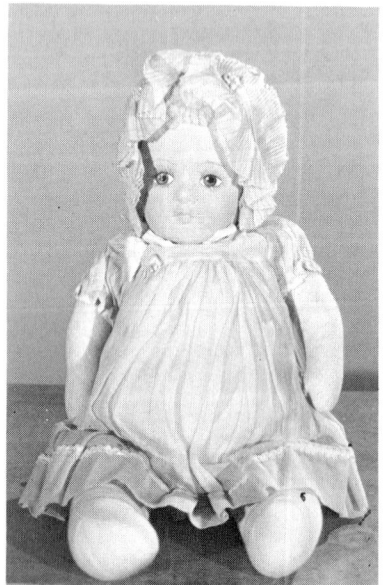

Illustration 8. A rare find is this plump cuddly baby with a body of pink stockinette; yellow yarn hair which is covered by her hat; large brown eyes done in exquisite detail with painted lower and upper eyelashes; dress and bonnet are of pink organdy, wearing cotton petticoat and diaper; dress tagged: "Madame Alexander//New York."

Illustration 9. 24in (61cm) leggy bed doll; mature looking face, long and thin with extremely long applied eyelashes; all original clothing tagged: "Madame//Alexander//New York."

Focusing On...
—Selected Effanbee Composition Dolls—

Effanbee Doll Corporation was one of the first American manufacturers of dolls and one of the few still in operation today. The company was founded in 1910 by Bernard E. Fleischaker and Hugo Baum. In the first few years they distributed toys, then in about 1912 to 1913 they started to manufacture their own dolls. Since the 1920s, Effanbee dolls have been known for their high quality construction, well-designed models and beautifully made clothes.

In surveying the composition dolls produced by Effanbee through the 1940s, I have found the Historical Dolls of 1939 to be the most interesting and ambitious series created in composition. The original Historical Dolls, of which three sets of 30 different dolls were made, were display models which were shown in department stores around the country. They were 20in (51cm) to 21in (53cm) tall and dressed elaborately in costumes of silk, brocade, velvet and satin, which presented the history of American fashion. The replicas, 14in (36cm) to 15in (38cm) tall dressed in cotton copies of the costumes, were offered as one of Effanbee's 1939 lines.

Illustration 1. One of the 30 Historical Dolls, 1607. The doll for this date represents the Indian squaw after the white man's arrival. The missionaries taught the Indians to dress more modestly. (The primitive Indian wore a more brief outfit.) Her tunic and leggings are of white buckskin with fringe and beads for decoration. The doll herself is reddish brown with black hair. Her body is marked: "EFFANBEE// ANNE-SHIRLEY." Her head is unmarked. *H&J Foulke, Inc.*

Illustration 2. One of the 30 Historical Dolls, 1658. The ladies of this date in the Carolina settlement followed the current English court fashions. The dress is deep forest green with much gold braid trim and gold fabric lining the train. A touch of white lace accents the neckline and the lower sleeves are of white ruffles. Her black hair is arranged in a bun and her eyes are brown. *Rosemary Dent Collection.*

Illustration 3. One of the 30 Historical Dolls, 1682. The doll for this date represents the Philadelphia Quaker women. The dress of the Quaker ladies reflects their outlook on life — styles are simple; colors are muted. Her frock is gold with a black lace weskit and white collar and cuffs. Her green apron indicates that she is of the Quaker persuasion. Her wig is gray and is pulled back in a simple bun. *Rosemary Dent Collection.*

February 1978 Doll Reader

Illustration 4. One of the 30 Historical Dolls, 1896. The ladies of this period wore dresses with interest primarily at the top. Shirts were gored with lace insets. Sleeves were very full. Jackets were short with peplums. Lace jabots were popular. The doll's red hair is arranged in the Gibson style. *Rosemary Dent Collection.*

Illustration 5. *Bubbles.* Effanbee's first big success was *Bubbles*, introduced in 1924 to 1925. She was a happy baby, smiling with joy. Her head, arms and legs are of composition; torso is of cloth. Her eyes open and close and her mouth is open with teeth. The doll shown is completely original in her white organdy outfit with leather moccasins. She has unusual cloth legs. Her dress has a "Bubbles" label. *Maxine Salaman Collection.*

Illustration 6. *Patsy.* Judging by the millions sold, *Patsy* was one of Effanbee's greatest successes. Since these dolls were so played with and loved, it is difficult for a collector today to find one in mint condition with original clothes. She is 14in (36cm) tall, all of composition with molded hair, painted eyes to the side and a tiny closed mouth. Her arms are distinctive as one is bent at the elbow and one is straight at the elbow swinging away from her body. *Patsy* was so popular that Effanbee created a whole family of *Patsy* dolls ranging in size from 5½in (14cm) *Wee Patsy* to 30in (76cm) *Patsy Mae.* The doll shown is wearing her original yellow chiffon dress and hat with blue trim. Shoes, socks and undies are also original. Her body is marked: "EFfanBEE//PATSY//DOLL." Head may or may not be marked. *Maxine Salaman Collection.*

Illustration 7. *Patsy Babyette.* This *Patsy* family baby came out in 1927. These twins are wearing original white batiste outfits trimmed in eyelet. They are completely of composition with molded hair, sleep eyes and closed mouths. *Maxine Salaman Collection.*

Illustration 8. *American Children.* The most realistic and lifelike composition dolls ever manufactured were those designed by Dewees Cochran. They were variously called *American Children, Portrait Dolls, Portraits of America's Children* and *Portrait Children.* Several different faces were produced. All were of extremely fine quality. The doll shown is 19in (48cm) to 20in (51cm) tall. Her brown wig is of human hair. Her brown eyes are painted with extraordinary detail. She is marked: "AMERICAN CHILDREN" on the head and "EFFANBEE//ANNE SHIRLEY" on the body. *Rosemary Dent Collection.*

Illustration 9. *Anne Shirley.* This doll, based on the movie star, was another of Effanbee's popular dolls. She has a typical full-cheeked dolly face, which is reminiscent of the earlier bisque-headed dolls. The body was of high quality sturdy composition and is distinctive because of its lovely modeled hands with individual fingers. She has soft natural human hair, a closed mouth usually with full pink lips and sleep eyes with lashes. The doll shown is 19in (48cm) tall and is wearing her original black velvet dress. *H&J Foulke, Inc.*

Focusing On...

Incomparable Compos

There is something about the American-made composition dolls of the 1930s and 1940s which instinctively draws me to them. I am sure a large part of this appeal is nostalgic: these are the types of dolls that I played with as a child. I have fond memories of playing with my dolls for hours and hours. Every Christmas my special gift was always a new doll to add to my growing family. Most of them have long disappeared to I know not where, as my mother was very conscientious about giving no longer needed items away. Somehow I managed to end up with two of my original dolls, an unmarked composition baby and a Kewpie. I have bought two others which I know I had but which did not survive: an Alexander *Jeannie Walker* and an Ideal *Magic Skin Baby*. I think it is this reminder of childhood which draws many collectors to the composition dolls. Many start by collecting what they had as a child or collecting what they wanted as a child, but were never given.

Then there is, too, the appeal of the medium. Composition has a warm look about it, a softness which is appropriate to a child, and the natural tint of the complexion, the rosy cheeks, the shining sleep eyes, the real hair which can be combed, the beautifully designed and made clothes, all combine to present an object which is most appealing to look at as well as to play with.

Some say there is a sadness about a doll which has never been played with, but I do not see it that way. For me it is remarkable to find a composition doll which has been preserved for 40 or 50 years in excellent condition with its original clothes, tags, buttons, labels and box. I can hardly resist these, and although I cannot collect them, I personally adore them, and buy as many as I can for resale.

Unfortunately, I did not have this fantastic *Wendy Ann*, seen in **Illustrations 7, 8** and **10**, when I wrote my book *Treasury of Mme. Alexander Dolls* to include in the chapter on the "Wendy Ann" face. The *Wendy Ann* doll was announced in the September 1938 *Playthings* and was discontinued in about 1940, so she was only made for a few years, although her face was used for other dolls. She has a very appealing face with a distinctive pointed chin and closed rosebud mouth, but it is her body construction which was her selling point. In an October 1938 news release she was described as being

Illustration 1. Unfortunately, my daughter, Beth, did not have this doll when I wrote my book *EFFanBEE Composition Dolls*. It would have been a marvelous addition to have been able to put her on page 23 after her 21in (53cm) sister, *Barbara Lou*. Dewees Cochran designed this open-mouth smiling child with the body of a five-year-old in 1938 for Effanbee. In her book, *As If They Might Speak*, on pages 27 and 28, she describes the design problems she encountered because of the machines which set the teeth and eyes in these dolls. Since this design is not marked on the head, collectors have questioned whether or not this doll is an American Child. The original label and box indicate that certainly Effanbee considered this doll one of that series. Miss Cochran also says that Effanbee called this smiling doll *The Skating Queen*, as some were dressed in fur-trimmed skating outfits. Also Miss Cochran does not mention that the doll was manufactured in the 17in (43cm) and 21in (53cm) sizes; she mentions only the 15in (38cm) doll. The original wrist tags are also interesting because they document the names given to these smiling dolls. Every tagged 21in (53cm) one has been *Barbara Lou*; every 17in (43cm) one, *Barbara Ann*; every 15in (38cm) one, *Barbara Joan*.

Barbara Ann has a light brown human hair wig in a pageboy style with bangs; her blue sleep eyes have real lashes; she has four tiny upper teeth. Her skirt and tam are of maroon wool which matches the buttons and piping on her jacket. Her composition is of excellent quality, having retained its beautiful rosy color. The composition of the Effanbee dolls of this period is of the finest quality, unsurpassed by those of any other maker. They are certainly top-of-the-line, the Brus of the compo world. *Beth Foulke Collection.*

August/September 1981 Doll Reader and April/May 1982 Doll Reader

Illustration 2. The end of the original box for the 17in (43cm) *Barbara Ann*, seen in **Illustration 1**. *Beth Foulke Collection.*

Illustration 3. Original tag for 17in (43cm) *Barbara Ann*, seen in **Illustration 1**. *Beth Foulke Collection.*

Illustration 4. This is a marvelous series of dolls which I would loved to have included in my book, *EFFanBEE Composition Dolls*, but they were not available to me at that time. The problem with identifying this series is that they are unmarked and not shown in doll literature except for a small photograph in Kelly Ellenburg's *EFFanBEE — The Dolls with the Golden Hearts*, which gives the dolls' size as 12in (31cm), but all of these which I have had were 11in (28cm).

The ballerina is shown in her original box with a metallic golden heart label identifying her as "Another in the Portrait Series of Effanbee Durable Dolls." The box itself is very interesting of heavy wood-grained cardboard with a silver colored background. A clear sheet of heavy cellophane covers the box. The doll is tied securely inside. Her blonde mohair wig is styled with bangs and braids tied to the top of her head with flowers and a bow. Her white tutu is trimmed with gold braid and a pink flower; her shoes are gold with pink ribbons, which also are tied around her wrists. The small heart-shaped faces on these dolls are very appealing and reminiscent of the *Anne Shirley* dolls. *H & J Foulke.*

modeled like any little girl of seven or eight years old with a slender body and long thin arms and legs. She had a swivel waist which allowed her to touch her toes and bend backwards and forwards. She was supposed to be able to assume 12 different positions. Her arm molding is interesting in that one arm is bent in at the elbow, while the other swings gracefully out. This poseable *Wendy Ann* came in only a 13in (33cm) to 14in (36cm) size.

This lovely pictured *Wendy Ann* has the usual dark blonde human hair wig styled with tiny curls across her forehead, then in princess style with turned up and curled ends just above her shoulders. Her brown sleep eyes have real lashes across the top. She is wearing a white dotted swiss dress with picot edging on her sleeves and red ribbon and lace insertion on her bodice. Her hat is of red felt. The label on her box which describes her as "graceful" and "adorable" shows four versions of her, including one with molded hair.

Her original octagonal wrist tag is gold. The original postcard also attached to her wrist is shown on both front and back sides, and gives her date right on the postmark. She certainly is a choice example.

Another doll by Madame Alexander which I would have loved to include in my chapter on the *Scarlett O'Hara* dolls is the one shown in **Illustration 11**. The *Scarlett* doll has the same sweet heart-shaped face as the *Wendy Ann* doll, and usually has a black human hair wig and green sleep eyes with real upper lashes, but there are some variations. She was not advertised in *Playthings* until January 1940, but she was probably on the market sooner as Mme. Alexander's trademark for her was issued in April 1937. The *Scarlett* doll was tremendously popular, judging from the numbers still seen, and came in sizes from 10in (25cm) or 11in (28cm) up to 21in (53cm). Madame Alexander designed a wide variety of dresses for *Scarlett* made in a broad range of cotton print, organdy, taffeta and velvet fabrics, usually in greens.

The pictured *Scarlett*, however, is wearing a quite rare costume consisting of a white organdy underskirt and overdress of red and white cotton with white lace and organdy trim as well as red satin bows. Her shoes and straw hat are red. She is a very striking doll with her black hair, green eyes and still bright complexion. On her skirt is the original gold paper label, also shown is the label from her original box. She is 11in (28cm) tall.

Here is another 11in (28cm) *Scarlett*, seen in **Illustration 15**, shown because she has her original wrist tag. This is the same type of scene which was used in the Alexander January 1940 ad in *Playthings*. The *Scarlett* pictured is wearing a green taffeta dress, which apparently was a popular choice. She has a black human hair wig with a white magnolia. This outfit did not come with a straw hat.

Illustration 5. The Gibson Girl is shown along with the ballerina, seen in **Illustration 4**. She has a light brown mohair wig with braids coiled above her ears. Her dress is a pink and white striped cotton with a lace jabot and rows of dark rickrack and matching ribbon trim. Her hat is white felt with ribbon trim, and her parasol matches her dress. *H & J Foulke.*

ABOVE RIGHT: Illustration 6. A dancing couple is shown here. Their original wood-grained cardboard box is falling apart, but it was originally designed as a frame. There are two metal loops on the back along with a printed message: "This beautiful Portrait has been framed for you to hang on your wall as you would your favorite picture." The girl has auburn mohair styled like that of the ballerina with a red flower and ribbon on top. Her dress is white organdy with ruffles at the sleeves and hem; red rickrack and ribbon are used for trim. Her shoes gold. The boy is dressed in a black suit with long pants and a short bolero jacket trimmed in gold; his shirt is white; his cummerbund is gold also. His hair is the same auburn color as his partner's.

Kelly Ellenburg also shows a Bo-Peep and a bride and groom pair a part of this seris. I hope someday to be able to add photographs of these to my file. *H & J Foulke.*

Illustration 7. *Wendy Ann* by Madame Alexander.

Illustration 9. Original octagonal gold wrist tag on *Wendy Ann*.

Illustration 8. Close-up of *Wendy Ann* by Madame Alexander.

Illustration 10. Original postcard attached to *Wendy Ann's* wrist.

Illustration 11. 11in (28cm) *Scarlett* by Madame Alexander.

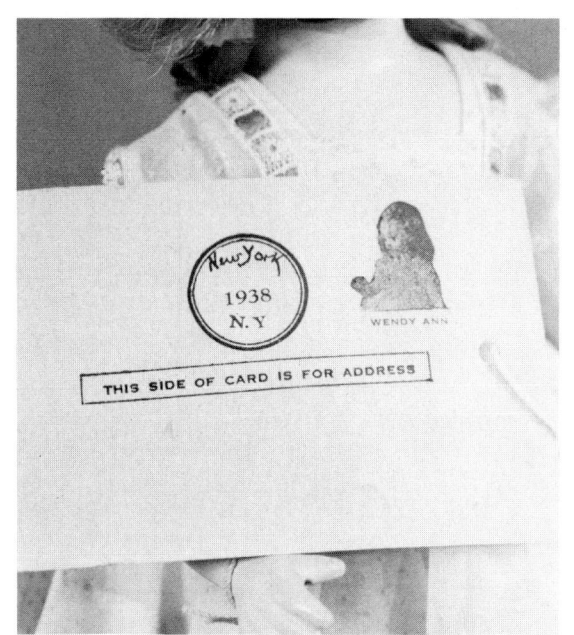

Illustration 13. The original box for the 11in (28cm) *Scarlett* shown in **Illustration 11**.

Illustration 12. Detail of the other side of the postcard attached to *Wendy Ann's* wrist.

ABOVE: Illustration 14. Detail of the original gold paper label on the 11in (28cm) *Scarlett* shown in **Illustration 11**.

LEFT: Illustration 15. 11in (28cm) *Scarlett* by Madame Alexander.

Illustration 16. Detail of the original wrist tag on the 11in (28cm) *Scarlett* shown in **Illustration 15**.

Focusing On...

"Hi! I'm Ginny"

All dolls from the Beth Foulke Collection

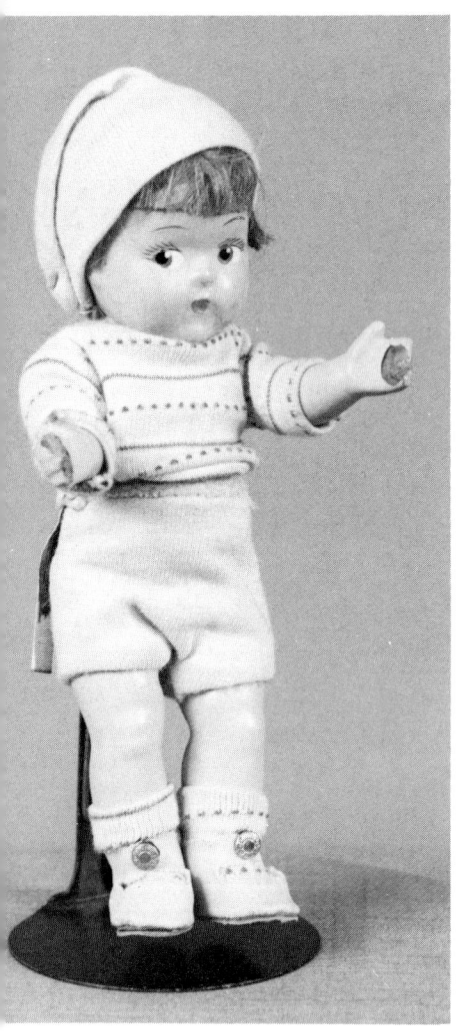

Illustration 1. This sweet little girl, obviously *Alice in Wonderland*, dates from the early 1940s when Vogue produced a series of *Nursery Rhyme* and storybook characters. Her composition is of excellent quality, smooth and colorful. Her cobalt blue eyes look to the left; she has faintly molded hair under a blonde mohair wig; her arms are molded alike. She is marked "VOGUE" on both the back of her head and torso. Her outfit is all original, tagged with the blue and white Vogue label. Her blue cotton dress has two rows of white piping around the bottom and is topped with a white organdy apron with lace and rickrack trim. Her stockings go up over her knee, and she is wearing black snap shoes.

Vogue Dolls, Inc. MEDFORD, MASS.

Illustration 2. This *Toddles* composition boy has the same body as the girl in the first illustration. Even his eyes with the widespread lashes and white highlight are painted the same. His outfit is of pink cotton knit; his shirt with blue, white and maroon stripes matches his socks; his snap shoes are pink. He is from the same early 1940s period and has a sister in a matching costume with a skirt instead of shorts. I have also seen this outfit in white and blue cotton knit. He also has the blue and white Vogue label on his clothes.

I am not really sure how my daughter, Beth, became interested in the *Ginny* dolls made by Vogue, but there are now 35 of these little imps occupying a treasured place in her doll collection. I think she is just particularly drawn to their sweet faces; there is no underplaying the appeal of these charming little dolls. With all of her accessories, *Ginny* just makes a fun collectible. There is always some goodie to look for at a doll show or flea market: in addition to her furniture (bed, chairs, table, chest, wardrobe), there are trunks, suitcases, hair bands, hangers, hats, shoes, glasses, parasols, skis, skates, purses, jewelry and even her own Steiff dog! Not to mention her extensive and fashionable wardrobe. In 1953 alone, she had more than 40 outfits!

After beginning her collecting with all *Ginny* dolls, Beth has traded off and narrowed her interests down to only those dolls made in 1953 and before. These are the composition *Toddles* and the hard-plastic dolls with painted eyes or moving eyes with painted lashes which do not have a walking mechanism. As for accessories and clothes, she has allowed herself to go beyond this date, feeling that a little girl with a *Ginny* doll would have continued to add items over a period of years.

Since the *Ginny* dolls have become so popular in the past few years (prices are up over 600% in five years), Beth has agreed to share some of the dolls from her collection in this article. Just a little background material is given on the manufacturer, Vogue Dolls, Inc. For more detailed information in an indispensable guide for the *Ginny* doll collector refer to *That Doll, Ginny*, by Jeanne Niswonger.

Up to 1937 — Jennie Graves started her Vogue Doll Shoppe business by dressing German bisque dolls and selling them to department stores. One of the little dolls which she used extensively was the *Just Me* doll made by Armand Marseille. The first time I saw one of these dolls with a tagged Vogue outfit, I just assumed that someone had been clever enough to put a cute ready-made outfit on the doll, but after several of these turned up, I realized that it was certainly no coincidence, and that Mrs. Graves did indeed use the *Just Me* as one of her

Illustration 3. This girl *Toddles* is made of a different type of composition from the previous two; her finishing is not as fine, and her coloring is darker, not so peachy as the first two. She has one arm bent and one arm outstretched like the *Patsy* doll. She is marked "VOGUE" on her head and "DOLL CO." down near her back waist. Her eyes are more turquoise than blue, but they still look to the left. Over slightly molded hair her blonde mohair wig is built on just a small piece of gauze running under her machine-stitched side part. Her outfit is all original, a blue organdy dress and matching hat with pink, white and blue lace trim. She is also from the 1940s.

Illustration 4. The composition girl on the left is the same type as the doll in **Illustration 3**. She is clearly identified by the stamp "JILL" on the sole of her shoe, where many of the *Toddles* are stamped. She dates from 1943 and is part of the *Character* and *Nursery Rhyme* series. Beth is now looking for her companion doll *Jack*. Jill is wearing a dress with blue and white checked skirt with attached panties and a yellow bodice with blue trim. Her hat matches her skirt, and her shoes are yellow. The composition dolls came with either slip ons, snap or tie shoes of a leather-like material. As with many of the early dolls, her outfit is not tagged. Probably less than half of these early dolls had tagged clothes, but one soon learns to recognize the Vogue clothes because of their fine styling and finishing detail. (Also they nearly all have a metal hook and thread eye as a back fastener.)

The hard-plastic doll on the right is *Tina* of 1953. She has brown eyes and auburn braids. Her school dress is of brown check with green, yellow and white trim. Vogue often gave individual dolls girls' names and the doll in the center is the original *Ginny* of 1951 with the new hair which could be wet, curled and combed; in 1952 she was one of the *Ginny* series. Her dress is pink and white check with white eyelet trim. Both *Tina* and *Ginny* have the narrow white label with the blue script "Vogue."

The dolls are marked "VOGUE" on the heads and "VOGUE DOLL" on the torso. The use of "Ginny" to apply to the doll in general apparently did not come about until 1953, when she was finally named for Mrs. Graves' daughter, Virginia, who designed all the lovely little clothes.

LEFT: Illustration 5. This 8in (20cm) hard-plastic boy with painted eyes is the *Prince* from the *Cinderella* set of 1949 and 1950, which also included *Cinderella* and her *Fairy Godmother*. His blonde mohair wig is over faintly molded hair. His tights are of blue cotton knit with an attached white organdy top with lace trim. His plumed hat and cushion holding Cinderella's slipper are blue satin. He is missing his blue satin jacket. His costume has the white Vogue label with blue letters.

RIGHT: Illustration 6. This 8in (20cm) girl is another of the storybook characters from the 1948 to 1950 period, but we are not exactly sure which one, perhaps *Bo-Peep*. She matches the *Prince* in construction, and also wears her original tagged clothes. Her dress is of pink cotton with an attached pinafore of white nylon with pink flowers and white trim. Her hat matches. Her blonde wig is very full, held together with a gauze strip sewn to her side part. She has the same clothes label as the *Prince*. Both dolls are marked "VOGUE" on the head and "VOGUE DOLLS" on the back torso.

Illustration 7. The curved-limb babies with the same face as the toddler doll seem to have always been a part of the Vogue line. Beth does not have any of the composition babies in her collection (a gap which must be filled!), but she does have several of the hard plastic ones. This line was advertised as the *Crib Crowd* and featured "special ringlet wigs of real lambskin." The baby on the left is probably *Sally* from 1950; although she has a tagged Vogue dress, it is of later vintage than she is. The baby on the right is *Betsy* also from 1950; she has never been played with. Her pink dimity romper with eyelet ruffles has the same clothing tag shown with **Illustration 6**. She also has her original silver cardboard wrist tag.

The doll in the middle is a hard-plastic toddler with the lambswool wig, which was made in 1952 only, so is rather difficult to locate. He is *Wee Willie* from the *Frolicking Fables* series, and has his silver wrist tag, which says "Willie" on the reverse side. He is wearing a pink printed one-piece pajama and white nightcap. Blue pompons decorate his pajama, cap and slippers. His original pink box with blue and white pasted-on label is not shown. All of these dolls are marked "VOGUE" on the head and "VOGUE DOLL" on the back torso.

early dolls. One of these dolls in a storybook-type outfit is pictured on page 157 of the *2nd Blue Book of Dolls and Values*.

1937 to 1947 — With the turmoil in Europe prior to the outbreak of World War II, Mrs. Graves could no longer obtain German dolls, so she was forced to find a domestic supplier. During this period she apparently purchased some 8in (20cm) composition dolls from Arranbee, so it is not necessarily incorrect for a marked R & B doll to have tagged Vogue clothes. At this time also she commissioned an 8in (20cm) composition toddler doll to be designed. The company referred to these dolls as *Toddles*, but today collectors refer to them as the composition *Ginny* although at this period Vogue was not using the name "Ginny." Beth has ten of these small composition dolls in her collection, four of which are shown in **Illustrations 1 through 4**.

1948 to 1950 — During this period most of the doll manufacturers turned to the use of hard plastic which turned out to be one of the most satisfactory mediums used to make dolls, and Vogue was no exception. Their dolls of this period were made entirely of hard plastic with painted turquoise-blue eyes looking to the left, still having wide-spaced upper eyelashes and white highlights. The plastic allowed for a more shapely arm and for fingers with greater detail than those on the composition dolls. Dolls from this period are shown in **Illustrations 5** and **6**.

1950 to 1953 — During this period, the *Ginny* dolls were made of hard plastic with the added feature of sleep eyes. These dolls did not walk, as that mechanism was not added until 1954. Now the dolls had both blue and brown eyes with painted upper lashes. They also had both mohair and synthetic wigs in a wide variety of shades and colors from champagne blonde to bright red. This was also the period of the silver wrist tag with blue lettering: "A Vogue Doll."

Some tags had the name of the doll on the back. These dolls are shown in **Illustrations 4** and **7 through 11**.

Illustration 8. A prized doll in Beth's collection is this baby which was issued as a special promotion doll for the 1950 Easter holiday. She has a blonde lambskin wig with attached bunny ears of light green poodle cloth and pink felt. Her costume is also of the light green poodle cloth with pink satin bows and white net trim.

Illustration 9. Pairs of dolls were always a popular feature with Vogue. In 1952 this pair in Alpine outfits was offered along with a *Holland* pair, a *Rodeo* pair, a *Brother and Sister* series and a square dancing pair. The dolls pictured both have blonde wigs; his is mohair and hers is synthetic. They are wearing matching outfits wiht blue felt caps, pants and skirt, white organdy blouses and yellow felt vests. Their cheeks are soft pink.

Illustration 10. Skating dolls on both ice and roller skates were offered almost every year by Vogue. This little girl from the 1953 *Gadabout Series* is especially attractive as she has beautiful red hair, dark blue eyes, and a skating outfit of purple velvet with gold trim. Like the pair in **Illustration 9**, she is marked "VOGUE" on the head and "VOGUE DOLL" on the back torso. Her dress tag is slightly different, as is her silver wrist tag which says "Vogue Dolls, Inc."

Illustration 11. The doll on the left is *Ginger* of 1953. (Remember that Vogue often gave their dolls names of little girls; this is not to be confused with the Cosmopolitan *Ginger* doll.) She is a beautiful blue-eyed blonde dressed in a red velvet outfit. Her hat is trimmed with white fur and red cherries; she is carrying a red purse and some cherries; her shoes are red suede with red bows. Many Vogue dolls from this period wore tie rather than snap shoes. (The plastic "Ginny" shoes were not used extensively until 1955.) The doll on the right is from the 1952 *Kindergarten Series;* although she looks a little fancy for attending school; perhaps she is dressed for a party. She is very striking with her champagne blonde hair and dark brown eyes. Her dress is white satin with a green print, overhung with green velvet. A very large light green bow adorns her hair. Both dolls are marked "VOGUE" on the head and "VOGUE DOLL" on the back torso. They have the same label as *Tina* in **Illustration 4**.

Focusing On...
100 Years of Christmas Wishes

Part of the magic of Christmas for most little girls is finding a doll under the Christmas tree. Dolls just seem to go naturally with little girls and Christmas. I am sure that as far back as the custom of giving gifts at Yuletide time goes, little girls often received some sort of doll. I remember with fondness my own childhood Christmases when I received a succession of dolls: *Betsy Wetsy, Jeannie Walker, Kewpie, Magic Skin Baby* just to mention a few among many which did not have specific names and included a selection of mama dolls, baby dolls and bride dolls. There is something right about a beautiful doll sitting under the Christmas tree; it just seems to belong there. Following is a selection of Christmas dolls which could have thrilled little girls of long ago as well as make some big girls of today quite happy.

Illustration 1. A little girl of the 1850s could have received this large doll with china head for a Christmas gift. This truly would have been an exciting doll since it had a very rare feature: inset glass eyes, when the vast majority of china head dolls had only painted eyes. Also of note are the finely painted upper and lower eyelashes. The doll's hair is painted black with molded curls which even show comb marks. Her ears are partially exposed and her mouth is turned up, almost as though she is smiling. Her face is plump with a double chin and a sturdy neck. The graceful slope of the shoulders is characteristic of the earlier china heads of this period. Her body is cloth with leather arms. Her tan cotton print dress appears original. *Richard Wright.*

Illustration 2. For Christmas 1877, an indulgent mother or father could have ordered a beautiful French lady doll through *Ehrichs' Fashion Quarterly*. An elegantly costumed Parisienne of fine quality with jointed kid body, bisque turning head, glass eyes, natural hair, earrings and necklace in an 18in (46cm) size would have cost at least $10. The doll pictured here of about the same period is in her original light brown silk taffeta costume with a Paris toy store label in her jacket. She is completely original except perhaps for her accessories. Obviously, she was a very treasured possession to have been preserved for so many years in such marvelous condition. *H & J Foulke.*

Illustration 3. For Christmas 1899, parents could choose a pretty German-made child doll with a bisque head from a very wide selection of both dressed and undressed models ranging in price from about $1 up, but the very finest dressed dolls from companies such as J. D. Kestner and Kämmer & Reinhardt could cost $15 or more for a particularly elegant model. The doll pictured is a 21in (53cm) tall Kämmer & Reinhardt model in original outfit. She has blue sleep eyes, pierced ears with pearl earrings and a luxurious blonde mohair wig styled with tiny little curls. Her natural straw hat has satin ribbon and flower trim; her white lawn dress in Kate Greenaway style has a generous amount of lace trim, tucks and lace insertion. Her excellent quality ball-jointed body would also have added to her desirability. She probably would have cost about $7. *H & J Foulke.*

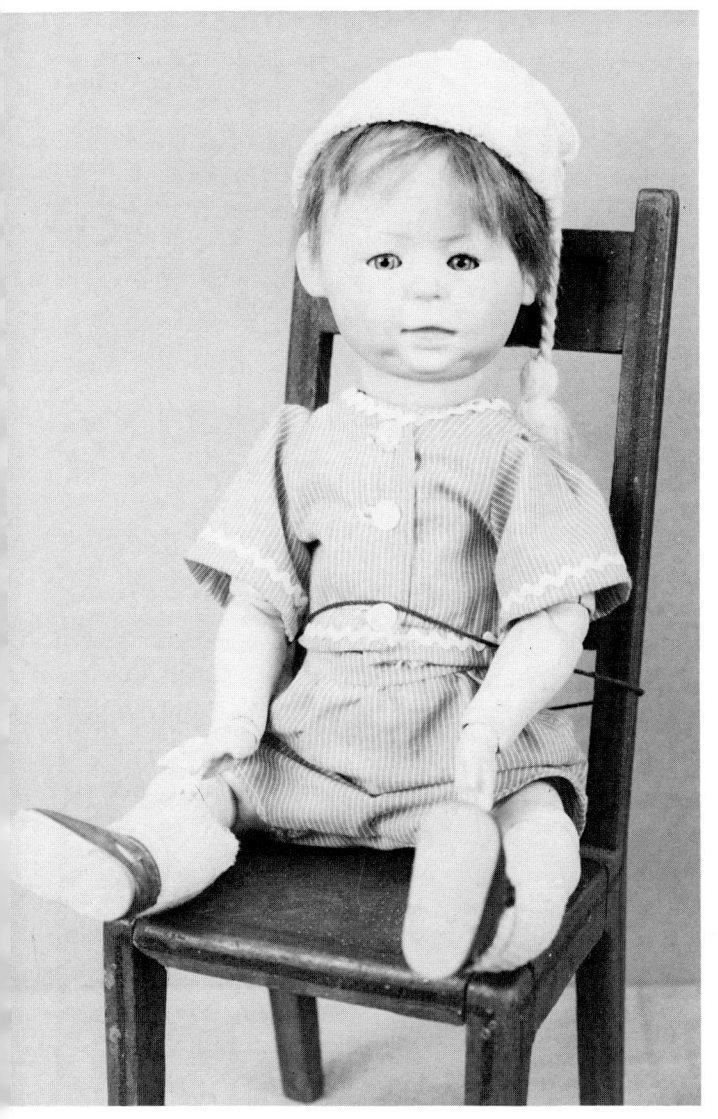

Illustration 4. By Christmas 1914, the German bisque-head character dolls designed with natural expressions to look like real children were in abundant supply in the toy stores. Models were offered as babies as well as boy and girl children. This boy character incised only 1428, but usually attributed to Simon & Halbig, could have been a Christmas doll of 1914. He has a wonderfully expressive face with tiny blue sleep eyes, light eyebrows of one wedge-shaped stroke, a cute pug nose, protruding ears, a double chin and an open/closed mouth with no teeth. His wispy mohair wig is light brown. Just 15in (38cm) tall on an excellent quality jointed composition body, he was most likely just wearing a chemise when he was originally purchased and probably cost about $6. His current clothes are replacements. *Ruth Noden Collection.*

Illustration 5. One of the possibilities for Christmas dolls of the late 1920s was an Italian art doll from the workshops of Madame Lenci. In the larger sizes, these were truly luxury items. The Lenci doll pictured is 18in (46cm) tall, and one of similar size was offered in a 1925 catalog for $20. She certainly would have pleased a little girl who enjoyed beautiful things. Her blonde mohair is pulled back at the sides in a braided bun, but she has two long curls at each side to frame her face. Her large side-glancing eyes are brown with gray eyeshadow underneath. Her original costume is of fuchsia felt and ruffled organdy with turquoise felt collar, cuffs and bow to match her felt picture hat which has a nosegay of pink and white felt flowers trimming one side. Her shoes match the skirt of her dress, and she retains her Lenci cardboard label. *Beth Foulke Collection.*

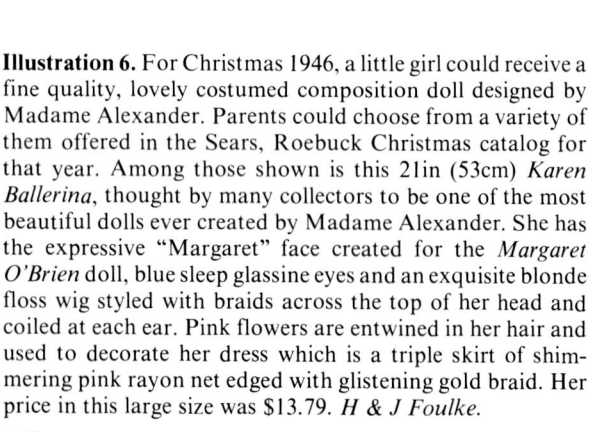

Illustration 6. For Christmas 1946, a little girl could receive a fine quality, lovely costumed composition doll designed by Madame Alexander. Parents could choose from a variety of them offered in the Sears, Roebuck Christmas catalog for that year. Among those shown is this 21in (53cm) *Karen Ballerina*, thought by many collectors to be one of the most beautiful dolls ever created by Madame Alexander. She has the expressive "Margaret" face created for the *Margaret O'Brien* doll, blue sleep glassine eyes and an exquisite blonde floss wig styled with braids across the top of her head and coiled at each ear. Pink flowers are entwined in her hair and used to decorate her dress which is a triple skirt of shimmering pink rayon net edged with glistening gold braid. Her price in this large size was $13.79. *H & J Foulke.*

Focusing On...

Romantic Dolls from *Gone With The Wind*

Dolls from the collections of Virginia Ann Heyerdahl and Virginia M. Slade

The romantic feeling of the *Gone With the Wind* period has been captured by Madame Alexander in the designs she has created for her *Scarlett* and *Melanie* dolls. *Scarlett* has played a prominent part in the Alexander doll line ever since the late 1930s and *Melanie* has been included since about 1956. The costume variations from the film which appear most frequently on Alexander dolls are the white dress with many-flounced skirt which "Scarlett" wore in the opening scenes, the sprigged muslin dress with straw hat and parasol which she wore to the barbecue, and the green velvet gown which she made from her mother's draperies so that she could go to Atlanta to borrow money from Rhett. Of course, Madame Alexander designed dozens of other romantic costumes for her *Scarlett* dolls. In the novel, "Scarlett" did wear a lot of green, and Madame Alexander has used this color in many of her designs in different fabrics: cotton prints, satin, taffeta and velvet. Not only that, but the green costumes complement *Scarlett's* green eyes. There is always a lot of excitement among collectors when Madame Alexander announces a new *Scarlett* doll.

Drawing from the original souvenir program of the movie premiere. *Dorothy Radcliff Collection.*

Illustration 1. These three *Scarlett* dolls wear versions of the same white organdy dress which was first designed for the 14in (36cm) doll in 1968, the largest doll in this photograph. Although her dress is labeled "Gone With the Wind," she was listed in the Alexander Company catalog as *Scarlett O'Hara*. The dress has a full skirt with rows of white lace to give the appearance of tiers. Lace trims her bodice and elbow-length puff sleeves. Her green velvet sash with a rhinestone ornament complements her vivid green eyes. Her long wavy dark hair is softly rolled up at the ends; two tiny rolled curls across the top of her head are held in place with green satin bows. Her catalog number was 1490, then 1590. The middle-sized doll is the 11in (28cm) *Southern Belle* made as part of the Portrette Series from 1971 to 1973 using the adult-bodied *Cissette* doll. Her eyes are glamorized with blue shadow on the lids and accented with a heavy eye line. Her dress is of the same style as that of the larger doll; her sash is of green satin ribbon and she wears a gold-colored metal heart necklace. Her white straw hat has net and flower trim with a green satin bow at back. Her dark hair is center-parted and pulled to clusters on each side behind her ears; her eyes are brown. Her catalog numbers were 1184 and 1185. The small 8in (20cm) doll is one of the favorites in the Alexander line was first made in 1973, catalog number 725, then 425. She wears the same style white organdy dress as the other dolls; a green satin sash with tiny ornament trim circles her waist. The bangs of her dark center-parted hair are brushed to each side into tiny green satin ribbons to match her green eyes. She is a straight-legged non-walker. Her dress is tagged "Scarlett."

Illustration 2. This 21in (53cm) *Scarlett* Portrait, catalog number 2240, was first made in 1979. A lovely doll, she wears an emerald green velvet gown and matching bustle-length jacket, both of which are trimmed with green braid. Her matching poke bonnet with stiff brim and gathered crown has decoration of green ribbons and feathers as well as a flower corsage. Her dark brown hair is styled with bangs combed to each side and elegant shoulder-length curls.

Illustration 3. Two 8in (20cm) *Scarletts* from the 1966 to 1972 period wearing flower print dresses and straw bonnets. They are hard plastic with bending knees, but do not walk. Their clothes are labeled "Scarlett O'Hara" or simply "Scarlett." All have dark hair softly curled at the ends and bangs usually center-parted and swept to the sides.

170

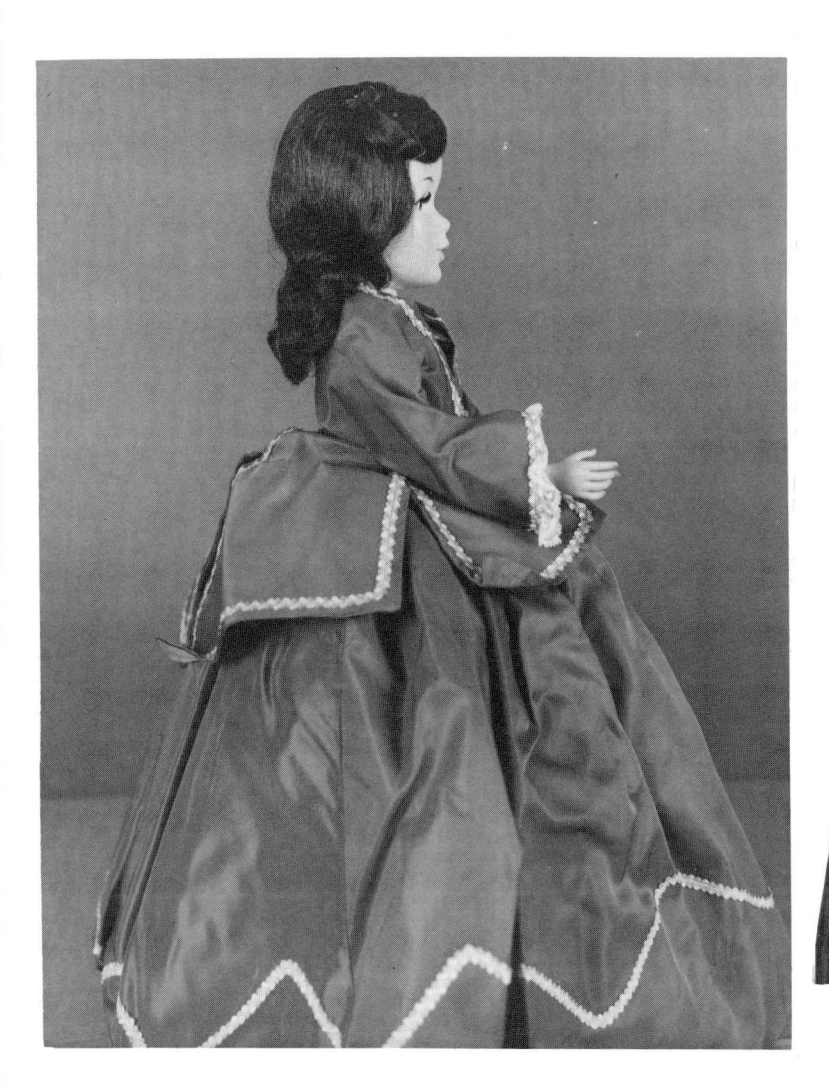

Illustration 4. These four 8in (20cm) *Scarletts* were made from 1965 until 1972. Some of the later ones will have straight legs because of overlapping production. They are hard plastic with bending knees, but do not walk. Their clothes are labeled "Scarlett O'Hara" or simply "Scarlett." All have dark hair softly curled at the ends and bangs usually center-parted and swept to the sides. Their eyes are usually green, but a few blue- or gray-eyed ones do turn up. The doll third from the left is the 1965 model wearing a white taffeta full-skirted dress with a ruffle around the hem trimmed with green rickrack and two tiny pink roses. Her elbow-length sleeves are also trimmed with green rickrack which matches her satin ribbon sash. Her natural straw hat is trimmed with the same pink rosebuds which decorate her dress. From 1966 to 1972 *Scarlett* wore a cotton print dress with skirt the same as the 1965 doll, but with a lace-trimmed scoop neckline and puffed sleeves. Three dolls from this period are shown in this illustration. The dress was made in a variety of print fabrics, nearly always in green. The accessories included a green satin sash and a natural straw hat, which came in different styles as shown.

Illustrations 5 & 6. Since Alexander began the 21in (53cm) Portrait Series in 1965 using a vinyl and hard plastic adult-bodied doll with the *Jacqueline* face, at least seven different versions of *Scarlett* have been designed. This doll, the 1969 version, is catalog number 2190. She is wearing the popular green taffeta gown with a voluminous gathered skirt, very full at the back. Her matching jacket is long, cut to points in both the front and back. A faint green and white braid trims both the jacket and skirt; the full sleeves are edged in white lace. Her matching poke bonnet with stiff brim and gathered crown is decorated with a flower corsage and ties under her chin. Her jewelry consists of a gold heart necklace and a sparkling ring. As shown in the profile illustration, her long wavy dark hair is curled softly under at the ends and pulled up at the sides with two rolled curls across the top of her head. Her green eyes are accented with blue eye shadow.

ABOVE, ABOVE RIGHT: Illustrations 7 & 8. A 21in (53cm) doll representing *Melanie* has appeared in at least seven versions. One of the most striking is this doll from 1970, catalog number 2196. Her white dotted swiss dress has a skirt of ruffled tiers inset with white lace and red satin ribbon; the bodice has a plunging V neckline and elbow-length sleeves both trimmed with self ruffles and white lace with red satin ribbon insertion. Her wide dotted swiss sash is tied in a large bow with long streamers hanging down the back. A white straw hat trimmed with white net and red roses sits on the back of her head. She carries a red organdy parasol trimmed with white lace and wears a cameo necklace and a diamond ring. Green eye shadow and very long natural eyelashes with heavily painted lashes at the outer corners accent her luminous brown eyes. As shown in the profile view, her brown hair is parted in the center and pulled to the sides in two clusters of four curls each.

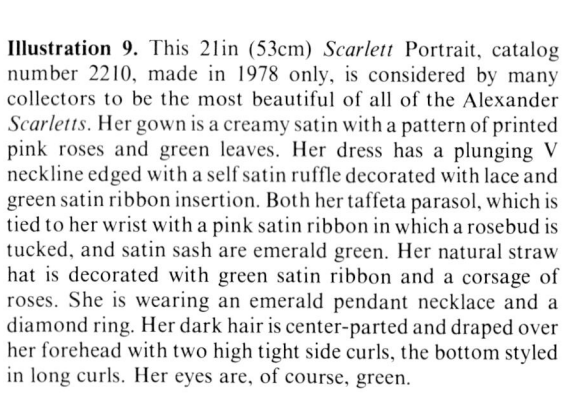

Illustration 9. This 21in (53cm) *Scarlett* Portrait, catalog number 2210, made in 1978 only, is considered by many collectors to be the most beautiful of all of the Alexander *Scarletts*. Her gown is a creamy satin with a pattern of printed pink roses and green leaves. Her dress has a plunging V neckline edged with a self satin ruffle decorated with lace and green satin ribbon insertion. Both her taffeta parasol, which is tied to her wrist with a pink satin ribbon in which a rosebud is tucked, and satin sash are emerald green. Her natural straw hat is decorated with green satin ribbon and a corsage of roses. She is wearing an emerald pendant necklace and a diamond ring. Her dark hair is center-parted and draped over her forehead with two high tight side curls, the bottom styled in long curls. Her eyes are, of course, green.

173

PREVIOUS PAGE: Illustration 10. This very rare 14in (36cm) *Scarlett* was made for only one year, 1968 catalog number 1495, wearing a sprigged muslin gown hence she is one of the hardest to find of the discontinued *Scarlett* models. Her bodice has a deep V neckline with self ruffle trim, white lace and green satin ribbon insertion; her very full gathered skirt is held out by a petticoat with hoop. Her natural straw hat has a green velvet band around the crown as well as a green velvet tie. Her eyes are the most vivid bright green of any of the *Scarletts* and her long dark hair is styled in loose waves.

Illustration 11. This 11in (28cm) *Melanie* is one of the Portrait Miniature Series from 1970, catalog number 1182, using the adult-bodied *Cissette* doll. She has glamorized eyes with blue eye shadow and long painted lashes, as well as red fingernail polish. Her lovely blonde hair is center-parted, her bangs are brushed back and caught up in two yellow bows at the top; the sides and back are arranged in two rows of curls. Her lovely gown is made of yellow organdy with eight rows of yellow lace on her skirt. Lace also trims her neckline and serves as a cap sleeve. A yellow satin sash with a pink rosebud trim circles her waist. Gold high-heeled sandals complete her costume.

Illustration 12. New to the Alexander line in 1981 were the 12in (31cm) *Scarlett* and her companion, *Rhett*, catalog numbers 1385 and 1380. *Scarlett* wears a green taffeta skirt and matching separate jacket; her bodice is white with a double row of lace at the front. Lace also trims her long sleeves. Green and gold rickrack trims both the skirt and bodice. Her matching brimmed bonnet is decorated with green satin ribbon and two pink rosebuds; white lace frames her face. She is wearing a cameo pendant necklace. She has green eyes and long painted lashes; her dark hair is in a long wavy style. *Rhett* has short dark hair, dark eyes and painted mustache. His stylish outfit consists of gray flannel trousers, black felt jacket, jacquard vest and red cravat. A white felt planter's hat sits atop his head.

Index

A
"Alaska Tot:" 123
Alexander: 153, 154, 157, 158, 169-174
Alexander Doll Company: 153
Alexander, Madame: 154, 158-161, 168, 169
Alice in Wonderland: 153, 162
Alma: 114
Alt, Beck & Gottschalk: 58, 94, 99
Amberg: 117
Amberg, Louis & Son: 116
American Child: 157
American Children: 156
Anne Shirley: 156, 158
Anthony: 134
Arranbee: 116, 117, 164
Au Nain Bleu: 43
Averill, Georgene: 58
AW Special: 114

B
Babbie: 154
Baby: 92
Baby Gloria: 118
Babykins: 118
Babyland Dinah: 129
Babyland Rag: 127-129
Baby Phyllis: 118
Baby Steiner: 7
Baby Stuart: 34
Bähr & Proschild: 94, 99, 101, 103, 115
Barbara Ann: 157, 158
Barbara Joan: 157
Barbara Lou: 157
Baum, Hugo: 155
Bébé Mascotte: 21
Bébé Schmitt: 22
Bébé Teteur: 116
Bergmann: 114
Bergmann, C. M.: 99, 107
Beth: 153
Betsy: 163
Betsy Wetsy: 166
Betty: 128
Black: 33, 74, 78, 79, 111
Bonnie Babe: 24, 34, 58
Bo-Peep: 159, 163
Borgfeldt, George: 35, 58, 116
Borgfeldt, George & Co.: 102
Bourgoin, J.: 9
Bourgoin Steiner: 6-9, 18, 20
Brother and Sister: 165
Bru: 19, 116, 157
Bruckner: 129, 134
Bru Jne: 19, 23
Bru Jne & Cie: 19
Bubbles: 156
Bye-Lo Baby: 99, 102, 116, 117

C
"Campbell Kid:" 102
Captain: 134
Character: 163
"Character Dolls:" 133-135, 137
Chase, Martha: 116, 125
Chinaman: 137
Chin Chin Baby: 72-74
Cinderella: 163
Cissette: 169, 174
Cochran, Dewees: 156, 157
Coquette: 34, 37, 47, 57
Cosmopolitan: 165
Crib Crowd: 164

D
Dainty Dorothy: 66
Danel & Cie: 20
Daspres, E.: 107
Dietrich, Johannes: 38
Dolly Dear: 128
Dolly Dimple: 33, 34, 51, 52
Dressel, Cuno & Otto: 38, 39, 90, 101, 107, 112
Dutch: 147, 152

E
Effanbee: 114, 155-157
Effanbee Doll Corporation: 155
Eisenmann & Company: 38, 63
E. J. Jumeau: 14-16, 18, 22
Elf: 136
Elizabeth: 65
English Ceremonial Regiments: 151

F
Fairy Godmother: 163
Fairyland Doll Company: 129
Fany: 95
F.G.: 23
Fire Brigade Commander: 131, 137, 138, 141
Fireman: 138
Fleischaker, Bernard E.: 155
Fréres, May, Cie: 21
Frolicking Fables: 164
Frozen Charlottes: 116
F.S & Co.: 118

G
Gadabout Series: 165
Gaultier: 23
Gentleman in Morning Coat: 137, 139
Gerling, Arthur A.: 118
Gibson Girl: 91, 159
Ginger: 165
Ginny: 162-165
Gnome: 133
Goebel, Wm.: 105
Golf Boy: 128
Golliwog: 133, 137
Googly: 25, 32, 34, 63-66, 101, 102, 103, 105, 106, 120
Graves, Jennie: 162, 164
Gretchen: 111

H
Hamburger: 90
Handwerck: 114, 115
Handwerck, Heinrich: 90, 107
Hertel, August: 101
Hertel, Schwab & Co.: 99, 101-103, 105, 106
Heubach: 24-86
Heubach, Ernst: 101
Heubach, Gebrüder: 31, 32, 35-37, 66, 68, 78, 92, 95, 96
Heubach Köppelsdorf: 114, 118
Historical Dolls: 155, 156
Holland: 165
Horsman: 116-118, 128, 129
Horsman, E. I. Company: 128
Hubertus Hunter: 133
Hulss, Adolf: 107

I
Ideal: 157
Igodi: 38
Indian (American): 28, 31, 34, 137, 152

J
Jack: 163
Jacqueline: 171
J.D.K.: 87, 92-94
Jeannie Walker: 157, 166
Jill: 163
Jo: 153
"Jubilee:" 103
"Jubilee Doll:" 106
Jumeau: 2, 10-17, 20, 22, 90, 107
Jumeau, Emile: 14, 22
Jumeau, Maison: 13
Just Me: 162
Juszko, Jeno: 116

K
Kämmer & Reinhardt: 35, 46, 90, 92, 93, 95, 98, 99, 107, 111, 114, 115, 118, 133, 167
Karen Ballerina: 168
Kaulitz, Marion: 35, 92
Kellerman, Annette: 118
Kestner: 46, 87-89, 92, 97, 102, 103, 105, 114
Kestner & Co.: 99, 101
Kestner, J. D.: 87, 93, 94, 97, 99, 116, 120, 167
Kewpie: 73, 157, 166
Kiddiejoy: 117
Kindergarten Series: 165
Kley & Hahn: 94, 95, 98, 99, 102-105, 106, 114, 115
Kling & Co.: 99
Koenig & Wernicke: 99, 100, 102, 106
Kruse, Käthe: 92

L
Lenci: 142-150, 168
Lenci, Madame: 168
Le Parisien: 9
Le Petit Parisien: 20
Lindner, Louis, & Sons: 35

Lipfert, Bernard: 117
Little Dorritt: 154
Little Em'ly: 154
Little Nell: 154
Little Orphant Annie: 142
Little Women: 153
Lizzie: 134
London Rag Baby: 116
Long Face Jumeau: 13, 16
Louis Wolf & Co.: 106
Lucia: 145

M

Magic Skin Baby: 157, 166
Margaret: 168
Margaret O'Brien: 168
Marseille, Armand: 93, 95, 96, 101, 112, 116, 117, 162
Mascottes: 142
Max: 137
Meg: 153
Melanie: 169, 172, 174
Meller, Raquel: 149
Mexican: 137
Mich: 139
"Million Dollar Baby:" 116
Missis: 134
Miss Smith: 152
Miss Viola: 115
Morimora Brothers: 73
Moritz: 137
Munich Art Dolls: 35, 92
My Dream Baby: 117

N

New Born Babe: 116, 117
Nursery Rhyme: 162, 163

O

Ohlhaver, Gebrüder: 38
OIC: 118
Old-Fashioned Girls: 152
O'Neill, Rose: 73
Oriental: 107, 143, 148
Our Baby: 102, 106
Our Fairy: 105

P

Paris Bébé: 20
Parisienne: 15, 166
Pat-a-Cake Baby: 61
Patsy: 114, 156, 163
Patsy Babyette: 156
Patsy Mae: 156
Peg-wooden: 116
Philadelphia Baby: 116
Portrait: 158, 159, 170, 172
Portrait Children: 156
Portrait Dolls: 156
Portrait Jumeau: 16
Portraits of America's Children: 156
Portrette Series: 169, 171, 174
Porzellanfabrik Mergersgereuth (P.M.): 101

Poupards: 116
Pouty Baby: 118
Prince: 163
Putnam, Grace S.: 116, 118

Q

Queen Anne: 116
Queue San Babies: 73

R

R & B: 163
Recknagel: 116
Red [Riding] Hood: 133, 137
Rhett: 174
Rodeo: 165
Rosenbusch, Hogo: 101
Roullet and Decamps: 107
Royal Canadian Mounted Police: 151

S

Sailor: 132, 141
Sally: 164
Samstag & Hilder Bros.: 51
Santa: 52, 90
S&C: 107
Scarlett: 158, 160, 161, 169-173
Scarlett O'Hara: 158, 169-171
Scavini, Elena Konig di: 146
Scavini, Madame di E.: 142, 146
Schachne, Albert: 102, 106
Schilling, F. M.: 101
Schlopsnies, Arthur: 137
Schmidt, Bruno: 99
Schmidt, Franz: 99, 107
Schmitt & Fils: 22
Schneid the Tailor: 132, 138
Schoenau, Arthur: 101
Schoenau & Hoffmeister: 101, 114, 115, 118
Schoenau Hoffmeister Porzellanfabrik Burggrub: 118
Schoenhut: 134
School Boy: 135
School Girl: 135
Schwab, Heinrich: 101
Schwarz, G. A.: 97
Scoutboy: 137
Sears, Roebuck & Co.: 66
Selchow & Righter: 35
Señorita: 143
S.F.B.J.: 6
Siegfried: 118
Simon & Halbig: 90, 91, 96-99, 107-111, 112, 114, 115, 117, 120, 121, 167
The Skating Queen: 157
Smiling Doll: 35
The Smiling "Jubilee" Babies: 30, 35
Snak: 133
Snik: 133
Société Steiner: 6
Southern Belle: 169
Sport Series: 145
Steiff: 92, 130-141, 162

Steiff, Franz: 134
Steiff, Margarete: 130, 134
Steiff, Paul: 134
Steiff, Richard: 134
Steiner: 6-9
Steiner, Herm: 116, 118
Steiner, J.: 9
Steiner, Jules Nicholas: 6, 20
Stier, Heinrich: 101
Strobel & Wilkin: 30, 35, 99, 102, 103, 106
Stuart Baby: 49, 50
Stuthauser Porzellanfabrik: 99, 106

T

Taufling: 116
Tennis Lady, Betty: 137, 139
Tête Jumeau: 14-16, 18, 19, 22, 23
Tina: 163, 165
Toddles: 162-164
Tommy Tucker: 102
Topsy: 128, 129
Topsy-Turvy: 128, 129
Tynie Baby: 117, 118

V

Vogue: 162-165
Vogue Doll Co.: 163
Vogue Doll Shoppe: 162
Vogue Dolls, Inc.: 162, 165

W

Wagner & Zetzsche: 38, 67
Walch, Rudolph: 102, 106
Walker, Izannah: 125, 126
Walkure: 114
Walter: 133
Wee Patsy: 156
Wee Willie: 164
"Weinde:" 106
Wellings, Norah: 151, 152
Wendy Ann: 157-161
Whistling Jim: 24, 34, 62
Whistling Tom: 62
The Widow Allegra: 145
Wiesenthal, Schindel & Kallenberg: 102, 107
Wolf, Louis & Co.: 102, 105